Locative Tourism Applications

Travel through time. Walk the streets as they were. See through floors. Hunt for ghosts (with drink in hand). Hear the walls speak. These are just a few of the ways that locative tourism applications seek to augment the urban experience. This book explores the universe of locative tourism applications. It uses multi-sited sensory ethnography with diverse apps in 12 cities around the world to interrogate how these applications layer (often branded) maps of meaning over the urban environment, and exposes what their use – at the embodied intersection of physical and digital space – can tell us about the production of cityscapes for touristic consumption. *Locative Tourism Applications* takes a journey in three parts to evaluate how these "extensions of the senses" mediate users' experience of urban locales. The first offers the reader some theoretical and methodological orientation, the second takes them on a whirlwind tour of locative apps, and the third settles in for an extended exploration of two destinations: Montreal and Christchurch. With broad cross-disciplinary appeal, this volume will be of interest to scholars from tourism studies, cultural geography, urban studies, new media studies, and sensory studies and will be particularly valuable for sensory ethnographers examining mobile and location-aware media.

Erin E. Lynch is Senior Fellow in the Centre for Sensory Studies at Concordia University, Canada.

Sensory Studies
Series editor: David Howes

This series comprises cutting-edge case studies and syntheses in the emergent field of sensory studies. It provides an invaluable resource for those involved in research or teaching on the senses as object of study and/or means of inquiry. Embracing the insights of a wide array of humanities and social science disciplines, the field of sensory studies has emerged as the most comprehensive and dynamic framework yet for making sense of human experience. This series offers something for every disciplinary taste and sensory inclination.

Heritage Formation and the Senses in Post-Apartheid South Africa
Aesthetics of Power
Duane Jethro

Race and the Senses
The Felt Politics of Racial Embodiment
Sachi Sekimoto, Christopher Brown

A Sensory Education
Anna Harris

Sounding Out Japan
A Sensory Ethnographic Tour
Richard Chenhall, Tamara Kohn and Carolyn S. Stevens

Doing Ethnography in the Wake of the Displacement of Transnational Sex Workers in Yokohama
Sensuous Remembering
Ayaka Yoshimizu

Locative Tourism Applications
A Sensory Ethnography of the Augmented City
Erin E. Lynch

https://www.routledge.com/Sensory-Studies/book-series/BLANTSS

Locative Tourism Applications

A Sensory Ethnography of the Augmented City

Erin E. Lynch

Routledge
Taylor & Francis Group
LONDON AND NEW YORK

First published 2023
by Routledge
4 Park Square, Milton Park, Abingdon, Oxon OX14 4RN

and by Routledge
605 Third Avenue, New York, NY 10158

Routledge is an imprint of the Taylor & Francis Group, an informa business

British Library Cataloguing-in-Publication Data
A catalogue record for this book is available from the British Library

Library of Congress Cataloging-in-Publication Data
A catalog record has been requested for this book

ISBN: 978-0-367-69484-5 (hbk)
ISBN: 978-0-367-69582-8 (pbk)
ISBN: 978-1-003-14238-6 (ebk)

DOI: 10.4324/9781003142386

Typeset in Sabon
by SPi Technologies India Pvt Ltd (Straive)

For my parents, Clare and Robert MacKenzie, for their endless love and support, and in fond memory of my father, Michael F. Lynch.

Contents

List of figures viii
Acknowledgements x

Introduction 1

PART I
Departure points and orientations 5

1 Departure points 7
2 Orientations 20

PART II
A tour of locative tourism apps: between gaze and performance 33

3 Gaze 35
4 Performance 68

PART III
A tale of two cities (case studies) 91

5 A city of gaps – mediating the ruin in Christchurch 93
6 A city of screens – augmenting the branded cityscape in Montreal 125

Conclusion 156
Appendix: Twelve-city tour of applications 162
Bibliography 165
Index 186

Figures

3.1	Taking the archive to the streets in *Streetmuseum.*	37
3.2	Gamifying the tourist gaze in Edinburgh.	39
3.3	The Arsenal, askew (overlay of archival image with street view, created using *Historic NOLA).*	41
3.4	Positioning the user in Montreal – a navigation overlay helps users line up the augmented reality feature with the world around them.	42
3.5	An iconic sign just below Derry's history city walls (in the Bogside neighbourhood, a historically Catholic/Nationalist stronghold) reads "Welcome to Free Derry."	46
3.6	A sign visible from the city walls (in the traditionally protestant/Unionist west bank of the city) declares the area "still under siege."	47
3.7	Derry's symbolic Peace Bridge, which is integrated into the Derry tourism logo.	48
3.8	Derry's remaining border wall, visible from the route of *Walk the Walls.*	49
3.9	An augmented panorama, with an animated Space Needle front and centre.	52
3.10	Extending the tourist gaze with the *Space Needle* app: the augmented "view below" through a "space spot."	53
3.11	"Digging" for the past with *Streetmuseum Londinium.*	54
3.12	An artefact is (virtually) revealed on the site as the user sweeps away the digital dirt with their fingers.	55
3.13	Traces of others on Hume's (lucky) toe, Edinburgh.	57
3.14	Feeling for ghosts at Muriel's séance lounge in New Orleans.	61
3.15	Small fish hang in water-filled plastic bags along the stalls of the Hong Kong fish market.	64
3.16	Parrots in the Hong Kong bird market – for looking and listening to, but not for touching.	65
3.17	Incense hangs in the air at Man Mo Temple.	66

4.1 From market to museum – neon signage points tourists towards the main attractions in Seattle's Pike Place Market. 73
4.2 Melbourne's stately Shrine of Remembrance in a moment of quiet between tours. The Shrine is a common stop on tours of the city – locative and otherwise. 74
4.3 Heritage haunts the streetscape in *Melbourne's Lost! 100.* 78
4.4 Nature as a canvas for other urban inscriptions in Melbourne's Botanical Gardens. 82
5.1 The ruins of the city's once-iconic Christchurch Cathedral, as they remained in late 2016. 94
5.2 Evidence of life and porous boundaries at Christchurch's SOL Square. 104
5.3 Disorientation on High Street – an app user attempts to navigate the rapidly changing streetscape of the Transitional City. 108
5.4 Phil Price's sculpture *Nucleus* (2006) on post-earthquake High Street. 112
5.5 A street print of Tony Fomison's (1971) *No!* in the context of High Street's urban inscription. 114
5.6 A wall of resilient plant life conceals a building site on High Street. 117
5.7 Mark Catley's (2016) installation *Sign o' the Times.* 118
5.8 A temporary inscription comments on the politics of the rebuild. (On a bench outside High Street's C1 Café). 119
6.1 Gazing between screens at *Cité Mémoire*'s "Babylon of the North." 129
6.2 Spectacular intimacy at *Cité Mémoire*'s "The First Executioner." 130
6.3 Seams in the tour – a wild cursor appears at *Cité Mémoire*'s "The Creation of the World." 131
6.4 The various projections of *Cité Mémoire* are collected into one narrative at the "Grand Tableau." 134
6.5 "Faces of Montreal" personalise the Old Port's carnivalesque atmosphere. 142
6.6 Ghosts of Montreal past by day. 144
6.7 Ghosts of Montreal past by night, in *Cité Mémoire*'s "From Marie-Josephe to Jackie Robinson." 145
6.8 Intimate gaze in an AR tableau at Dalhousie station. 146
6.9 Enabling the city to sense you in *Cité Mémoire.* 147
6.10 Co-producing the projection with others in *Cité Mémoire*'s "The Creation of the World." 150

Acknowledgements

I am deeply indebted to my doctoral supervisor, Dr. David Howes, for his expert guidance, unfailing encouragement, and immeasurable support over the course of the research that would eventually become this book. Thank you, David, for seeing the potential in this project and for pushing me to get it out in the world. Similarly, I must thank the other members of my doctoral thesis committee – Dr. Katja Neves and Dr. Bart Simon – and my external examiners – Dr. Jill Didur and Dr. Zoe Tew-Thompson – for their careful reflection and insightful feedback on the earlier iteration of this work. I would also like to acknowledge the very helpful feedback of the anonymous reviewers who previewed an earlier version of this book. I count myself lucky to have had such a remarkable, diverse group of academics weigh in on this text. My research trajectory has also been shaped for the better by my involvement with Concordia University's Centre for Sensory Studies, which has exposed me to so many thoroughly rewarding new ways of making sense.

In addition to the support I received from the Social Sciences and Humanities Research Council of Canada (SSHRC) in the form of a doctoral fellowship (no. 767-2014-1093) to carry out the research on which this book is based, the final stages of the writing were made possible by my tenure as a research associate on the "Explorations in Sensory Design" research project, directed by David Howes, which was also supported by the SSHRC (no. 435-2020-1279).

I want to thank my doctoral cohort for being wonderful sounding boards, first readers, and companions on this journey. I am a better academic for having done this alongside you. To my friends, near and far, for their cheerleading, humour, and perspective, and to my family, for providing a centre, a home, and a constant source of support through it all. I love you. Thank you.

My sincere thanks to all the participants – tourists, locals, and creators – who took the time to share their experiences with me, whether that meant walking a tour route or sharing a story. Your contributions to this work have been invaluable. As I worked to finish this book, Christchurch marked the tenth anniversary of the earthquakes that devastated that city. I would like to especially acknowledge the 185 lives lost in those quakes, as well as the people of Christchurch, whose resilience and creativity in the face of immense adversity inspires me to this day.

Introduction

Travel through time. Walk the streets as they were. See through floors. Hunt for ghosts (with drink in hand). Hear the walls speak. Re-make the map. These are just a few of the experiences purportedly on offer in the domain of "locative tourism."

Cities around the world have begun offering augmented reality tourism applications for mobile users. By doing so, they seek to differentiate themselves from a parade of standardised cities – so uniformly spectacular that they become banal (Debord, 1970) – and enliven their streets as cultural destinations. Marketed as a form of self-directed urban exploration, these apps layer audio, text, and visuals over the built environment and are a type of "locative media" – a genre of site-specific platforms that use location-aware mobile technologies to enable interplay between digital content and "real" geographies (Farman, 2012; Frith, 2015; Hemment, 2006; Reiser, 2009; Tuters & Varnelis, 2006). In their earliest and simplest forms (like London's *Streetmuseum*), these apps attempted to take the museum to the street, turning the dynamic stage of the city into one big open-air exhibit of its cultural attractions.

At first glance, these apps might seem like a boldfaced attempt to impose a digital script on what many have lauded as the last "free" way of encountering the city – walking. From the *flaneur* of Benjamin and Baudelaire, to the *derivé* of the psychogeographers, to de Certeau's walkers (who write a story they cannot read), walking has been idolised as a way to break free from the smooth mobility, plotted courses, and accelerated pace of the mechanised city. Walking supposedly "allows the individual to experience the world at a rhythm which digital technology denies" (Lavery, 2009; see also Highmore, 2005).

However, framing the cultural life of the city through the locative tour is far from a uniform process. As these apps at once animate and are animated by the streetscape they attempt to frame, gaps and seams between the urban environment and the digital layer come into focus. Locative media's cartographies are not only overlaid but "entangled" with locations and their existing representations (Pink & Hjorth, 2012), weaving a narrative of the city that is set on a shifting stage.

DOI: 10.4324/9781003142386-1

This study draws from sensory ethnographic research with diverse apps in 12 cities – including comparative case studies in Montreal and Christchurch – to interrogate how these applications layer maps of meaning over the urban environment, and consider what their use – at the embodied intersection of physical and digital space – can tell us about the production of cityscapes for touristic consumption. To do so, *Locative Tourism Applications* takes a journey in three parts. The first offers the reader some theoretical and methodological orientation, the second takes them on a whirlwind tour of locative apps, and the third settles in for an extended stay in two destinations (the case studies).

In Part I ("Departure Points and Orientations"), I offer the reader some theoretical background regarding the emergence of locative tourism, positioning it as a culturally situated practice of sensing the city. Chapter 1, "Departure Points," situates my study of locative tourism in the relevant (and very interdisciplinary) topical literature, drawing from the sociology of tourism, cultural geography and urban studies, the anthropology of the senses, and new media studies. I begin with a brief tour of tourism studies – particularly noting the tension between concepts of gaze and performance – before examining how the construction and perception of cities is value laden (drawing insights from cultural geography and the anthropology of the senses). This chapter then situates my exploratory study of locative tourism apps within the broader locative media literature, which offers key insights regarding the potential for locative tourism to thicken the urban informational layer and engage users in co-authoring the city. Primed with this interdisciplinary array of literature, Chapter 1 concludes by laying out some general directions for the analysis to come.

Chapter 2, "Orientations," introduces the notion of sensing the city as both theory and method in the context of a sensory ethnography of locative tourism apps. This chapters situates locative tourism practices within a history of sensing the city, and it reflects on the value of a sensory ethnographic approach for studying locative tourism apps (in particular) and urban rhythms, sensations, and mediations (more broadly). Finally, I reflect on how the precarious nature of locative tourism, along with the contingent experience of co-creating routes with others, has shaped the contributions of this book.

Part II of this study, "A Tour of Locative Tourism Apps," uses sensory ethnographic encounters with a variety of locative apps in 10 different cities to survey the locative tourism landscape, think through the experience of touring with app in hand, and tease out relevant lines of inquiry. In line with the dual trains of thought in tourism studies laid out in Part I, this tour offers two interrelated themes – "Gaze" and "Performance."

In Chapter 3, "Gaze," I examine the role of locative apps in extending and framing the tourist gaze before taking a turn towards the "more-than-visual" (Edensor, 2018b) elements of locative tourism. The chapter begins with a section on "Framing the City," which first considers how locative media's move to "take the museum to the street" shapes the experience of the urban through these apps. Here, we also examine how locative "time travel" apps gamify the tourist gaze and position users in space in particular ways, and we reflect on the implications of this positioning for what is "in place" or "out of place" within the frame of the tour. The second section of this chapter ("Constructing [and Contesting] the Urban Brand") introduces the concept of urban branding via locative tour and considers what gets excluded from the brand image in a locative tourism app. Finally, in "Sensing the City (with App in Hand)," we explore how locative apps extend the tourist gaze by augmenting the panorama, before turning our attention to the activation of other(ed) senses in locative tours.

In Chapter 4, "Performance," I turn my attention particularly towards the "stage" of the tour, examining how the locative tour encounters rhythms, change, and "others" in the urban environment and how the city streets "act back." This chapter explores what it means for users to perform the map. The first section of this chapter, "In Place, Out of Sync," traces the embodied rhythm(s) of locative tourism, including the glitches and discordances that tend to occur when the app confronts other rhythms circulating in the cityscape (be they touristic or more mundane). The next section, "Ruin and Mastery," examines how locative apps can layer conflicting narratives about urban change and development, even across a single city. Finally, "Encountering the Other in Layered Space" describes how performing the locative tour can reveal othered histories (and othered people) within the city, effectively multiplying the readings of the map.

Part III, "A Tale of Two Cities," continues the story of locative tourism apps through two comparative case studies. The first, "A City of Gaps," takes us to Christchurch to consider the role of locative tourism in disaster recovery. The second, "A City of Screens," explores how embedding part of the interface of an app in the urban environment shifts the experience of locative tourism in Montreal. These chapters situate each app in relation to its city's tourism brand, investigates the design behind its proffered experiences, tours its unique rhythms and sensescapes, and walks along with users as they co-create the space of the tour.

In Chapter 5, we examine how Christchurch's *High Street Stories* aims to restore a sense of place to a neighbourhood levelled by devastating earthquakes in 2010–2011 (and by subsequent redevelopment). Initially envisioned as a site for locals to collectively mourn their (nearly un-recognisable) downtown, the app was later advertised as offering locals and tourists alike a way to "walk the streets as they were" (*High Street Stories*). This chapter offers readers a glimpse into the precarity of doing locative tourism in "ruined" and transitional cityscapes. It also suggests that engaging with locative narratives in the context of this rapidly changing streetscape provokes powerful encounters with the past, present, and future of the city (both real and imagined).

Chapter 6 takes us to Montreal, where the once modestly scaled locative tourism app *Montréal en Histoires* was expanded into a full-scale urban spectacle with the addition of *Cité Mémoire*. Unveiled in 2017 as part of the city's 375th anniversary celebrations, *Cité Mémoire* mounted towering night-time projections (designed to work with the app) onto the sides of buildings throughout Old Montreal. This chapter offers us an opportunity to further analyse locative tourism as an extension of urban branding, particularly in the context of the experience economy. Given its introduction of night-time projections into the sensory melange of locative tourism, *Montréal en Histoires/Cité Mémoire* also gives us the unique opportunity to consider what happens to the urban sensory experience when city walls become the locative screen. Not all of the projections are designed to be viewed from a distance, however, and *Cité Mémoire*'s multimedia spectacle offers us a chance to consider how the body of the user – moving through a city that senses back – becomes central to the locative re-enchantment of the streetscape. Tour guides, tourists, and locals all play a part in the co-creation of these sensational worlds.

In the concluding chapter, I reflect on the variety of sensory experiences enabled by these applications, as well as some meanings and experiences of the space which they obscure. I argue that exploring the practice of locative tourism through sensory ethnography offers valuable perspective on the patterns, traces, and entanglements of urban meaning making in the digital age.

Part I

Departure points and orientations

Departing as this study does from an interdisciplinary perspective, the "map" I have sketched here for my exploration of locative tourism apps is, itself, a layered one. Chapter 1, "Departure Points," situates *Locative Tourism Applications* at the intersection of several schools of thought – tourism studies, cultural geography, urban sociology, the anthropology of the senses, and new media scholarship. Each of these disciplines contributes valuable context as we move to explore how the tourist's experience of the city is mediated by the locative app, and *Locative Tourism Applications* aims to contribute to each field in return. Chapter 2, "Orientations," frames the locative tour with the broader history of sensing the city and identifies the need for (and value of) a sensory ethnographic approach to locative tourism practices. The structure of *Locative Tourism Applications* reflects my desire to map the contours of a gap in the literature surrounding locative tourism (as identified in Chapter 1), but also to think between the levels of design and experience in these apps – between the "Concept City" (de Certeau, 1984) of the locative tour and the encounter with the city that it engenders at the street level.

DOI: 10.4324/9781003142386-2

1 Departure points

A brief tour of tourism studies

Between gaze and performance

To fully situate our discussion of locative tourism apps, it is worthwhile to begin this chapter with a brief review of the state of tourism studies as a discipline. John Urry, in his influential 1990 book *The Tourist Gaze*, suggests that tourists are guided to and through the spaces that they visit by a socially constructed gaze. Led by this gaze, the tourist navigates sites by looking for "signposts" – must-see vistas and attractions that mark out what is exceptional about these sites (Urry, 1990). However, *The Tourist Gaze* has been criticised in recent years for downplaying the dynamic nature of sites/sights (Franklin & Crang, 2001) and for discounting the embodied nature of touring (in which more than just the gaze is at play) (Edensor, 2001; Franklin & Crang, 2001; Germann Molz, 2012).

As such, some tourism researchers have turned their focus to acts and actors, suggesting that the embodied interactions of tourists with both tour sites and technologies might better be understood through the lens of tourism as performance (Edensor, 1998, 2001, 2007; Haldrup & Larsen, 2010; Larsen, 2008). This attention to the embodied act of tour*ing* also allows the performative turn in tourism studies to better accommodate counter-normative and emerging practices in the field (Franklin & Crang, 2001) – including urban exploration and augmented reality technologies – than an approach that takes tour*ism* as a more monolithic institution. Taking into account the dynamic character of spaces, performative tourism theory also gives us a lens through which to apprehend how the material and social conditions of everyday life intersect –and sometimes destabilise – tourism practices (Baerenholdt et al., 2004; Coleman & Crang, 2002; Edensor, 2001). In other words, we can consider how living and lived-in tour sites *act back*.

However, numerous scholars have argued that tourism sites – and particularly urban tourism sites – are increasingly subject to control as "themed" or "branded" spaces (Dinnie, 2011; Lukas, 2007a; MacCannell, 2001; Manovich, 2006; Urry & Larsen, 2011). Urry and Larsen (2011) argue that theming reflects the broader "Disneyfication" of the city as

DOI: 10.4324/9781003142386-3

observed by Zukin (1995) and Sorkin (1992), wherein landscapes are increasingly composed in a style of inauthentic pastiche designed for consumption by the tourist gaze (Urry & Larsen, 2011: 120; see also van Hoven, 2011). These bubbles of themed space (MacCannell, 2001: 26) are also frequently typified by privatisation and surveillance (Urry & Larsen, 2011: 125), since it is easier to police the meaning of a space that is not strictly public. Since theming is in many respects a stereotype – a limited "approximation of place, time, event, culture or person" (Lukas, 2007b: 272) – it is a sociopolitically charged exercise in inclusion and exclusion (Little, 1991; Lukas, 2007b). Performative approaches to the study of tourism, while injecting a much-needed dynamism and nuance to the field, must take care not to disregard the "big picture" being offered up on a silver platter; namely, what is included or excluded in the thematic vision of the city being marketed to tourists.

Part of the apparent power of locative media applications lies in their function as mobile representations; they are ostensibly drivers of both tourist mobility and interpretation. Running on a parallel and at times intersecting track with the performance turn, the mobilities turn in tourism research has also been gaining traction in recent years (Cohen & Cohen, 2012), with research focused on flows of movement through an increasingly globalised world (Sheller & Urry, 2004). The mobilities turn argues that that which moves us through space has a fundamental impact on the way we experience that space (Schivelbusch, 1986; Sheller & Urry, 2004). Technological advancements extend our range of motion (McLuhan, 1964; Parrinello, 2001), but they also condition how we move and shape the experiential affordances of the geographies which they make available (Germann Molz, 2012; Schivelbusch, 1986; Sheller & Urry, 2004). In addition, new media formats precipitate a reorientation of the sense ratios involved in perception (McLuhan, 1964), acting as "extensions of the senses" that enable certain realms of sensual experience while downplaying others (McLuhan, 1964; Germann Molz, 2012). Given that mobile tourism applications offer both a new representational medium and a locative interface (one that not only guides users' movement through space but often requires that movement to unlock content), mobile tourism applications have fundamental implications for the perception and performance of tourist spaces. With this context in mind, let us establish the literature – or lack thereof – on mobile tourism applications.

Tourism research's digital blind spot

It has been rightly observed that mobile devices and ubiquitous computing affect how we move through and interact with the world around us (Kenyon, 2006; Larsen et al., 2007; Urry, 2011) and are reshaping our relations to and within public space (Castells et al., 2007; Crawford & Goggin, 2009; Hjorth, 2009; Ito et al., 2010; Ling, 2004). Furthermore, recent literature certainly suggests that mobile devices have the potential to shape the touristic experience of users (Foster, 2009; Germann Molz, 2012; Larsen, 2008; Larsen et al., 2007; Tussyadiah & Zach, 2012; Wang et al., 2012). However, as other authors have noted, tourism theory has been slow to account for emergent technologies and is thus in urgent need of re-evaluation in light of new techno-centric tourism practices (Germann Molz, 2012; Larsen, 2008). Haldrup and Larsen (2010) also contend that tourism studies has often been "disembodied and dematerialized," largely neglecting the role both tourists and nonhuman actors play in shaping tourism (277). *Locative Tourism Applications* represents an attempt to partially correct for this technological and performative blind spot in tourism research. Similarly, while mobile technologies are increasingly vital to city life, urban studies has been slow to incorporate discussions of technology into its purview (Sheller & Urry, 2006). The study of urban tourism can thus doubly benefit from placing emergent technologies front and centre.

The construction and perception of urban space

Cultural geography and the construction of space

Both performative and gaze-centred approaches to tourism sites often build on theories regarding the construction and representation of space developed by cultural geographers, many of which are fundamental to the current study. Itself heavily influenced by the cultural turn in social theory, cultural geography acknowledges the importance of cultural artefacts and the value of interdisciplinary analysis (Anderson, 2010; Foote, 1994). Cultural geographers understand landscapes as symbolic (Cosgrove, 1984; Meinig, 1979), an approach that enables them to interpret geography as text (Cosgrove & Jackson, 1987: 96), and they further propose that this kind of interpretation is embedded in everyday life. (It is worth noting here that sensuous geographers have resisted this notion of geography as a text to be read, preferring to explore the practices of mediation that shape the multisensory experience of place [Howes, 2018a], an argument that we will revisit in Chapter 2).

Cultural geographers argue that culture gives form to space by shaping our shared "maps of meaning," thereby shaping how we interpret the world around us (Jackson, 1989). Spaces are "social locations" that are given form through everyday practices (Anderson, 2010) and are constantly being reinterpreted and reimagined (Soja, 1996: 61). They are, as Cresswell puts it, "combinations of the material and the mental, and cannot be reduced to either" (1996: 13). The physical geography of a location is always entangled with our cultural and personal imaginings of that space. As such, attending to processes of representation is a key concern for cultural geographers. As Cosgrove (2008) notes:

> Geographical representations – in the form of maps, texts and pictorial images of various kinds – and the look of landscapes themselves are not merely traces or sources, of greater or lesser value for disinterested investigation by geographical science. They are active, constitutive elements in shaping social and spatial practices and the environments we occupy. (15)

Representations of space thus not only reflect but actively shape the spaces – and spatial practices – of our everyday lives (Anderson, 2010; Cosgrove, 2008; Cresswell, 1996; Jackson, 1989; Lynch, 2013).

There is also a distinct critical vein in cultural geography, notably in its focus on how the sociopolitical mores and cultural meanings of space are contested (Cresswell, 1996; Jackson, 1989). Much of this work builds on Henri Lefebvre's (1991) *The Production of Space* (see Cresswell, 1996: 27; Soja, 1996), particularly Lefebvre's foregrounding of the spatial in social relationships. Lefebvre rejected the notion of space as simply a neutral container in which the social happens, writing, "To speak of 'producing space' sounds bizarre, so great is the sway still held by the idea that empty space is prior to whatever ends up filling it" (1991: 15). In line with the broader spatial turn in social theory, cultural geographers have been at the forefront of our reconceptualisation of space as "political, social, cultural, and anything but neutral" (Lynch, 2013: 12; see also Cresswell, 1996; Jackson, 1989).

Other authors have taken up Lefebvre's work, particularly his concept of representational space (the lived space that our imagination seizes upon and attempts to change) (1991: 38–39; see also Donald, 1999: 13), in an attempt to consider how sociopolitical meanings are layered over the experience of space, and how they are then contested (Donald, 1999; Soja, 1996). Several have also drawn from Lefebvre in developing the concept of "thirdspace," which locates the construction of our cultural maps of meaning "somewhere between the imagined and the real" (Lynch, 2013: 13–14; see also Lagerkvist, 2008; Soja, 1996).

Acknowledging, as Lefebvre does, that fragmenting the study of space along disciplinary lines only serves to further conceal its embedded and emergent sociopolitics (1991: 11), this study embraces interdisciplinarity in its attempt to think between multiple levels of space and interrogate the "real-imagined" (Lagerkvist, 2008) qualities of its mediation. As cultural geographers have noted, media representations both reflect and actively construct the meanings of the street (Burgess & Gold, 1985; Cresswell, 1996). When people consume and then perform the mediated meanings of the streetscape, these meanings are further entrenched, and this recycled "reality" feeds back into media representation of the space (Muzzio & Halper, 2002). This feedback loop contributes to the spell of "disenchantment" or "re-enchantment" that gets cast over certain locales (Jaguaribe, 2005), helping to script spatial performances and further defining the boundaries of who and what is included or excluded from a particular space (Lagerkvist, 2008; Penglase, 2007). This concept has particular bearing on the heavily mediated sites – or sights – of major tourist destinations. Tourists carry popular representations of these spaces into the sites with them – representations that both shape and are reinforced by normative performances of touring (Lagerkvist, 2008; Urry, 1990). By layering multisensory information over these sites as they are experienced, mobile tourism applications may contribute to the strategic re-enchantment of particular types of urban spaces at the expense of other possible spatial configurations.

Representations and perceptions of the city

While our tendency is to think of cities as imbued with meaning over time, city spaces are designed and built with particular interpretations already in mind (Hayward, 2004; Zukin, 1995). The architecture of the city is engaged in the ongoing re-presentation of its past and present (Sorkin, 1992; Zukin, 1989, 1995). Historical preservation societies have been a key force in the contested redevelopment and gentrification of urban space, given their power to decide what of the city's material history remains constant throughout processes of deconstruction and revitalisation (Zukin, 1995). These organisations have the power to designate landmarks and historic buildings, and often exert considerable pressure on building owners to maintain a neighbourhood's "character" through visual homogeneity (Zukin, 1995: 122). The effect of this selective preservation of history is that city streets tell a cleaned-up version of their own stories – a single, smooth, and aesthetically pleasing past stands in for the many messy histories and fragmented forms of urban life (Boyer, 1992; Sorkin, 1992; Zukin, 1995).

Representations of space can have homogenising qualities, reinforcing normative aesthetics and narratives around urban space through repetition. The concept of "imageability" – or "legibility" – has informed both the construction of the material environment of the city and its branding as an object for consumption (Donald & Gammack, 2007: 8). A space is considered imageable when it is arranged in a manner that "facilitates the making of vividly identified, powerfully structured, highly useful mental images of the city" (Lynch, 1960: 9). The legible city tells a particular story; it is organised in such a way as to make sense even without a map (Lynch, 1960). The idea that urban space can weave a cohesive narrative is strongly tied to tourism practices and the consumption of space (Donald & Gammack, 2007). Spring (2006) notes how the city guidebook was both a map key and a blueprint of the streets of Vienna, which in the late 19th century were reshaped according to a tourist-friendly imagining of urbanity: the linear city, a space associated with clear lines of sight, privileged paths, and consumable spatial narratives (21). However, creating a consistent, branded image of the city that works at street level is actually easier said than done; the experience of the city is contextual and "soaked in memories and meanings" (Lynch, 1960: 1) derived from a lifetime of potentially contradictory interactions with city spaces and urban representations (Donald & Gammack, 2007: 61). One way to manage the perception of the city as a consistent narrative is through the creation of landmarks, which serve as points of reference around which a traveller in the city can orient herself (Lynch, 1960). Consequently, tourism is both shaped by and shapes the social production of urban spaces.

Locative media adds another layer of complexity to this process of making the city legible. Given that our cognitive maps are frequently now offloaded to smartphones (Ozkul, 2015), it follows that the markers designed to orient people and enable them to make sense of the city – the landmarks in Lynch's (1960) conceptualisation of the legible city – have similarly migrated into the information layer (Ozkul, 2015: 14). In most cases, both physical landmarks and digital signposts exist at once, and, as such, the city viewed through the locative app might be interpreted as hyper-legible – or, at least, hyper-landmarked. Harkening back to Urry's (1990) description of the signposted destination space, the concern is a familiar one: at what point does all of this information begin to occlude alternate possibilities for experiencing urban spaces? However, locative technologies invoke an additional use for the signpost. In an age where information is increasingly organised by location (Frith, 2015a) it is not only the data layer that renders the city legible by creating digital landmarks – the geo-located city also renders the data layer legible by enabling the sorting of information according to what is nearby.

As Howes (2005) notes, "the perceptual is cultural and political," and as such it draws an incomplete portrait to speak of the politics of urban representation – and practices of mediation – without considering the politics of urban perception. Throughout the history of the city, various attempts have been made to purify urban spaces of unwanted sensations (Degen, 2008; Howes, 2005). These attempts have been particularly aimed at those sensations – such as odour and noise – which tend to permeate boundaries and resist control. Meanwhile, considerable attention has been paid to the creation of "imageable" cities (Lynch, 1960), with branded facades fit for cultural consumption (Zukin, 1995). In the modern city, it is the visual that reigns, and seeing is knowing (Howes, 2005: 324; Urry, 2000: 389). This coincides with the ascendancy of the gaze in the tourist consumption of places, wherein attaining the "proper" view on a space or attraction is associated with gaining mastery over that space (Urry, 1990).

The sensory environment of the city has arguably been denuded by these attempts at managing perception. Edensor (2007) argues that processes of sanitisation and aesthetic control have "produced an increasingly sterile urban environment" (17) that is tied to patterns of urban redevelopment for cultural consumption (Zukin, 1995). The realisation of city-as-shopping-mall, Edensor (2007) notes, relies upon creating "blandscapes" of repeated (and thus familiar) images, limited aromascapes, designed soundscapes, and smooth surfaces (19). The stylised and sensationalised cities of the late consumer capitalist "experience economy" (Pine & Gilmore, 1999) are increasingly in the business of selling ambience (Degen, 2008: 30), meaning that designer sensescapes are now being delineated within the city for tourist consumption. Arguably one of the most interesting facets of locative tourism applications is the extent to which they may endeavour to add "texture" back into these smoothed-over urban facades – laying select multisensory landscapes over the city in lieu of those sensations that have been edited out. However, as we will discuss in Chapter 2, the sensescapes of the city are already more varied and less disciplined than the imagining of "city-as-shopping-mall" would suggest (and indeed, as we will see throughout this book, it is often the lingering texture of the city that breaks through the smooth, glossy surface of the app).

Our ways of moving in the city – like our ways of sensing – are temporally, culturally, and spatially situated (Cresswell, 2010). The surge in the development of transportation and communications technologies beginning in the mid-19th century (from railway systems to the telephone), followed by a huge array of other systems (automobility, air travel, mobile phones, computers) emerging throughout the 20th century made circulation a driving factor in modern urban life – a pattern of movement, branded as a "public good," that dovetails nicely with the accumulation of capital (Sheller & Urry, 2006: 6–8). The smoothing over of urban environments serves to facilitate uninterrupted movement (Edensor, 2007: 219), and the modern city's cold, hard exterior seems to remind the urbanite at every turn that the streetscape is designed for moving through, not for lingering (Degen, 2008: 42; see also Lynch, 2021). The development of mobility as a public good and a sign of productivity is reflected in leisure practices as well, informing the cultural value attached to travel (Sheller & Urry, 2006; Urry, 1990). As such, examining the processes that shape the act of "touring" – that is, consuming a place by moving through it – can help us understand broader patterns of mobility and urban waymaking. Furthermore, wireless information technologies and the use patterns of mobile, technologically extended bodies have contributed to the erosion of some of urban sociology's favourite dichotomies; modern urban public space is at often at once digital and physical, public and private (de Freitas, 2010; Frith, 2015; Gaye & Holmquist, 2006; Sant, 2006; de Souza e Silva, 2006). Consequently, the examination of locative tourism apps offers a timely contribution to broader discussions of the way urban environments are being reshaped by and for mobile technology.

Locative media and the construction of augmented destination space

Locative media

Locative media broadly refers to a genre of site-specific platforms that use GIS (geographic information systems) and location-aware mobile technologies to enable and explore the convergence of digital content and "real" geographies (Farman, 2012; Frith, 2015; Hemment, 2006; Reiser, 2009; Tuters & Varnelis, 2006). Locative media emerged over the early 21st century as "a response to the decorporealized, screen-based experience of net art"

(Tuters & Varnelis, 2006: 357), aiming instead to facilitate the embodied interplay of digital and geospatial worlds (Farman, 2012). Locative applications play upon the appeal of site-specificity – that is, their "emphasis on the unique qualities of a particular location that cannot be transferred to another place" (Farman, 2014: 3). The app is an enticement to go to the (physical) place, as the information is only released to those who "commune with the surroundings" (Oppegaard & Grigar, 2014: 24). In other words, locative apps trade on the currency of the idea that where you are matters (McCullough, 2006a: 29) – that there is an "experiential value" to being in a place which amplifies the impact of media (Farman, 2014: 6), and that media can, in turn, add a certain value to the experience of space through real-time representation (Verhoeff & Cooley, 2014: 122). Many early locative media projects involved creative subversions of the map, and, taking cues from surrealists and Situationists alike, explored the critical and transformative possibilities of moving "otherwise" through the world (Tuters & Varnelis, 2006: 359). Locative media has thus been noted for its capacity to "turn ordinary spatial experiences into extraordinary ones" (de Lange, 2009: 67), arguably reenchanting space by reviving local value (McCullough, 2006a: 26) in areas that may otherwise have taken on the distinct – or, rather, indistinct – character of the postmodern blandscape (Edensor, 2007: 19; see also Sorkin, 1992; Zukin, 1992). What started out as a series of playful and interventionist mappings and geospatial annotations driven by artists and do-it-yourself technologists (Hemment, 2006: 349) has been taken up by a tourism industry on the hunt for ways to enliven destination spaces and capture tourists' attention in an increasingly competitive global market.

An emerging cohort of researchers have been investigating the use of locative and augmented reality (AR) technologies in re-presenting space for approximately a decade (Farman, 2012), with the bulk of locative media research coming from the field of new media arts and media geography (Wilken & Goggin, 2014: 4; see also Thielmann, 2010). However, these studies have dealt almost exclusively with locative applications as artistic or critical interventions in space (Farman, 2012; Germann Molz, 2012), leaving a gap in the literature surrounding the growing commercial implementations of the technology. Sample (2014) argues that locative media (in its more widespread forms) are not currently being used to their full potential as platforms for renegotiating space, instead taking the form of "gimmicky entertainment coupon books and glorified historical guidebooks" (76). My preliminary examination of a variety of tourism applications suggested that Sample's assessment of the popular locative landscape was somewhat reductive. Regardless, while more "pedestrian" applications may not explicitly set out to subvert the city as we know it, their booming presence in the urban tourism landscape demands our critical attention. The existing literature on locative media pinpoints several key areas for consideration as we move forward, particularly in the areas of urban inscription and authorship and questions of connection and disconnection in the embodied performance of locative applications.

The augmented city and the informational layer

While the built environment has long been augmented by information – as McCullough (2008) notes, inscriptions ranging from grand stone facades to humble street signs have "characterized almost all cities in history" (n.p.; see also Crang and Graham, 2007: 792) – the real-time, site-specific digital augmentations of locative media offer a somewhat novel means of engaging with the urban world (Graham et al., 2013: 465–466). Locative applications introduce what Frith (2015a) calls an external, multimedia "informational layer" to the world – one that, unlike those layers generally introduced by reading a book or listening to music, is explicitly designed to work with a particular location (22; see also de Souza e Silva & Frith, 2012). The app's media – which, thanks to the "indexicality" of mobile platforms (Verhoeff & Cooley, 2014) can take a wide variety of forms[1] – makes up one "layer of composition" within the locative narrative (Oppegaard & Grigar, 2014), while architecture and the physical environment form another (Ritchie, 2014: 53).

The use of the term "layering" – a common metaphor for mixed-reality experiences where digital information is intended to augment physical-spatial information (Verhoeff & Cooley, 2014: 122) – may appear to problematically imply that the mediation can be peeled away to uncover some unmediated version of the space (rather than acknowledging that spatiality is "always-already mediated" [Leszczynski, 2014: 729; see also Galloway, 2012; Lynch, 2013]). As a counter to this problem, Verhoeff and Cooley (2014) refer to the process of digital augmentation as a "thickening" of the informational layer (113–114), a metaphor which complements Pink and Hjorth's (2012) assertion that locative media's cartographies are not only overlaid but "entangled" with locations and their existing representations (145). The narrative of the locative app interacts with a variety of other inscriptions and mediations to contribute to what McCullough (2008) calls "urban markup" – the ongoing and contested representation of the streetscape. We need to examine how the sociopolitically charged stories told by the built environment interact with the equally loaded stories woven by our devices and broader cultural narratives to shape the touristic experience of space. As such, questions of authorship – of who makes and remakes locative media and how these platforms are used and repurposed – become a crucial consideration (Galloway & Ward, 2006).

Urban markup: (co-)authoring the layered city

One of the primary allures of the "thickened" informational layer (Verhoeff & Cooley, 2014) is that it ostensibly expands the possibilities for storytelling within a given space. Crucially, "mobile media offer the possibility to layer multiple – even conflicting – stories onto a single space" (Farman, 2014: 8).[2] As such, locative apps at their most interactive arguably have the potential to "level out the hierarchy of composition" between creator and consumer

(Oppegaard & Grigar, 2014: 19) and go beyond mere representation to enable creative, co-authored engagements with urban space (including with its human and technological others) (Crang & Graham, 2007: 807–809). However, this aspirational outlook for locative media may tend to overestimate the neutrality of the genre. Augmented reality apps have the dual issue of presenting content that obscures its own authorship and operating through code that often goes unnoticed and otherwise appears as a "neutral platform" for enabling augmented spatial relations (Graham et al., 2013). Providing resources for audiences to contribute to the narrative is a possibility but not a precondition of locative media (Ritchie, 2014), and the option may seem less appealing for content developers who are aiming for a branded urban aesthetic. Furthermore, as Leaver and Lloyd (2015) argue, the average user of these apps may not have the requisite digital literacy to become a co-producer of content rather than a simple consumer (167).

It is important to remember, however, that the form and function of locative narratives are driven by a variety of considerations. The technological infrastructure – both in the form of personal devices and broader communication networks – that locative narratives build upon have particular affordances and constraints (Ritchie, 2014). Farman (2014), following McLuhan (1964), notes that a medium "will often impact the ways a story is told, distributed and experienced" (8). A long story is, for example, ill-suited to a small screen (Farman, 2014: 8), while headphones may have an "individualizing" impact on the experience of mobile media (Frith & Ahern, 2015: 496; see also Bull, 2004; 2007). The demands of the interface, the existing architecture of historical space, and dominant cultural scripts combine to constrain the possibilities of locative narratives (Farman, 2014; Ritchie, 2014). Both authors and users are encountering technological challenges that are frustrating the locative endeavour (Oppegaard & Grigar, 2014; Ritchie, 2014). For example, gaps and lag in GPS coverage may interrupt the planned flow of the tour, inserting pauses where moments of transition were intended and disrupting the sense of "objective" orientation provided by embedded maps (Farman, 2015: 87). In a roundabout way, however, these gaps between the digital and physical layers point to the fact that – regardless of the extent to which users are invited to co-author it – the narrative woven between the informational layer and architectural space is dynamic because it is performed (often imperfectly so) by the techno-mediated body (Peacock, 2005: 129–130).

Connecting and disconnecting (or, being in two places at once)

While performing the touristic spaces made possible by locative apps is arguably an exercise in making connections (Oppegaard & Grigar, 2014), Farman (2014) notes that we often talk about mobile media in terms of disconnection from "meaningful" experience (6; see also Oppegaard & Grigar, 2014: 25) – a discussion that parallels broader debates within tourism studies about what constitutes an "authentic" experience of place (see Cohen & Cohen, 2012; MacCannell, 1973). It appears likely that, as Hess and Herbig (2013) note, "[t]he use of technologies such as smartphones in physical places paradoxically increases both connection and disconnection" (2209; see also Germann Molz, 2012). Perhaps the better question to ask, then, is what kinds of connections are enabled or disabled by using locative apps for touring? Some have argued that mobile interactive experiences can "reconnect users in new ways" (Oppegaard & Grigar, 2014: 26; see also de Souza e Silva & Sutko, 2008) and encourage engagement on a level that is not demanded of them by, for example, a more typical museum exhibit (Oppegaard & Grigar, 2014: 27). Rather than merely whisking the user away into an imagined and/or virtual land, the design of locative media is to "transport participants *into* their physical surroundings" (Barber, 2014: 107; see also de Souza e Silva & Sutko, 2008).

However, numerous authors suggest that one of the more productive possibilities of a locative app lies not in seamless transition, but in its seams – that is, the possibility of tension between the digital layer and architectural/physical space (Greenspan, 2011; Hight, 2007; Khaled et al., 2011). As Oppegaard and Grigar (2014) put it, when using a locative app, "A participant's foot is in both worlds (worlds, it should be noted, that are never completely separate)" (24). This means that the locative app user has to go through the process of comparing the "real world" to the app's narrative; thus, Greenspan (2011) contends, "opening up real space to imaginary alternatives" (24). This function means that – rather than offering a simple distraction from the site – these apps may actually refocus users' attention on the world around them as moments of serendipity, matching, and contrast demand a "toggling of awareness or focus between the fictional and real worlds" (Khaled et al., 2011: 131).

What is productive here is not collapse between the application content and historical space, but rather the distinction. Hight (2007) argues that users of immersive apps are "at all times aware of being in two spaces at once"; like a diver submerged in a pool, the outside world does not disappear (Hight, 2007: n.p.). The enchantment of submersion – in pool or app – therefore relies on the knowledge of other-than-ness within the familiar. Similarly, Sobchack (2004) argues that any potential "transcendence" that technological augmentation offers is grounded in the body – in our "'material premises' for making sense" – because it is, as she puts it, "my lived body that provides me the material premises for the playful irresponsibility of my imagination" (Sobchack, 2004: 172–173). Our awareness of our own bodily limitations is what gives the experience of "escaping" these limitations its allure. Consequently, the "material premises" of the technologically augmented body are also sites of tension, where app users might experience the unease of disjuncture between the physical world and "display events"

(Peacock, 2005: 132). Observations about this tension make clear the need to further investigate the agency and experience of tourists as they endeavour to perform the locative tour with one foot in both worlds.

Directions for research

Hemment (2006) notes that locative arts respond to the emergent capabilities of GPS and location-aware technology by asking, "what can be experienced now that could not be experienced before?" (349). The movement of locative technologies into mainstream tourism – into the realm of habitual performance and the staged destination space – prompts us to ask the same thing of tourist practice. In light of locative media, what can the tourist experience be now that she could not experience before? What varieties of sensory experiences and mobilities do these tours enable or disable? What kinds of narratives do they set in motion, and how do the maps of meaning they layer over the streetscape interact with the dynamism of life in the city? What elements of the urban encounter are foregrounded in this augmented reading of the city as a destination space, and what – or who – gets framed out in the process? Can performing a locative tour evoke in the user an awareness of his or her own role in authoring destination space? All in all, what does it mean to "do tourism" with a locative app in hand?

What rises to the top of the combined existing literature on urban spaces, touristic practices, and locative interventions is the fact that the sites in question are *not* virtual spaces of absolute control (McCullough, 2006a). Rather, these are embodied and enacted spaces that (by necessity) dance with pre-existing urban imaginaries, embodied conceptions of place, and the conditioned but far-from-predictable performances of tourists, urbanites, and urban*ities* alike. *Locative Tourism Applications* is, at its root, an exploration of what happens to the touristic experience of the city when locative applications meet what McCullough (2006a) calls the "messy multiplicity of street level" (26). Thriving in the "fold between virtual and physical, data space and geographical space" (Hemment, 2006: 354), enabled by the at-once intimate and public collision between site, data layer, and techno-mediated body, locative tourism technologies have made "other places" available to us within the city. As such, the contours of these spaces and the tourist encounters they facilitate cannot be fully determined by simply adding what we know about locative technologies to what we know about urban spaces and tourist practices. While tracing these threads can certainly provide invaluable pathways for exploration, they can take us only so far, and not far enough.

Tourism's map is a contested and shifting one, but one in which locative media already has a place – in practice, if not yet in theory. As I have demonstrated here, locative media is an emerging domain of practice, with considerable implications for how we think about the performance of tourism spaces. It is time to put locative tourism studies on the map.

Notes

1 As Oppegaard and Grigar (2014) note, "Mobile devices have absorbed the specialties of just about every medium – newspapers, television, radio." Thus, "McLuhan's mantra of the 'medium is the message' grows once again in ramifications" (23).

2 Hess and Herbig (2013) demonstrate how this potential for coexisting, paradoxical accounts manifests itself in divergent online and offline experiences at the app-mediated 9/11 memorial in New York City.

2 Orientations

In this chapter, we turn our attention to the practice of sensing the city, which – for our purposes in this book – offers an opportunity to reflect on both the idea of "sense and the city" as theory and "sens*ing* the city" as method before we hit the proverbial pavement (phone in hand) to examine locative tourism apps as "extensions of the senses" (Howes & Classen, 2014; McLuhan, 1964). This chapter offers a brief history of the senses in the city – namely the ocularcentric, rationalist design of the modern city (meant to see and be seen) and the practice of "othering" particular urban sensations – and, indeed, ways of sensing. We will also touch on the unruliness of some urban sensations; as later chapters will further demonstrate, the city is often surprisingly resistant to modernity's demands of standardisation and sanitation (Zardini, 2005).

This brief introduction to the history of the urban sensorium paves the way for a discussion of the locative tour as a particular "way of sensing" (Howes & Classen, 2014) – a culturally situated mode of perceiving the world, an embodied means of encountering the city that at once speaks to cultural norms of knowing and styles of mobility. More artistic variations on locative media have aimed to tap into its power as an embodied spatial practice, embracing the necessarily unfinished character of the locative story (Barber, 2014; Farman, 2012). In the context of an "experience economy" (Klingmann, 2007; Pine & Gilmore, 1999), using the body of the tourist to "flesh out" the locative narrative opens up the possibility of framing the city for all the senses. Yet – as we will shortly see – thanks to its own precarity and contingency, the locative tourism app as a medium often has trouble telling only one story about the world around it, so prone is it to encountering other and conflicting modes of urban life.

Finally, this chapter reflects on the potential for a (multi-sited) sensory ethnography of app use to illuminate the mediated urban sensorium – with its peculiar rhythms and narrative entanglements – as experienced through the locative app. As a field centred on questions of site-specificity and the value of "being there," I argue that a turn towards multi-sited ethnography (and particularly sensory ethnography) has a lot to offer locative media studies. Similarly, this method offers a fruitful venue for tourism studies in applying its sensory or performative turns to new technologies. While

DOI: 10.4324/9781003142386-4

I acknowledge that locative apps themselves frequently come and go, my goal in situating the specific apps studied in this book within broader cultural practices of mediation – and, perhaps more importantly, foregrounding the value of sensory ethnography for understanding those practices – is to allow this book to continue to offer valuable insight for future researchers and practitioners, long after the last of the apps discussed herein has faded into obsolescence.

Sense and the city

As Degen (2008) argues, "A focus on the senses offers a way of analysing the relationship between built form and social relations, as senses provide the framing texture for the material and social bond in public spaces" (10). Reflecting on the sensual life of cities can add context to our understanding of how people relate to the city and its multitude of others (with or without an app in hand).

Early sociological analyses of the city are marked by a tension between responses of attraction and repulsion to the intensity of sensory difference offered by urban life (Edensor, 2007: 17; Park, 1915; Simmel, 2010/1903). In more recent accounts, many authors have argued that sensory diversity is being designed out of the modern city, with regimes of aesthetic control and sanitised urban development producing "an increasingly sterile urban environment" (Edensor, 2007: 17; see also Sennett, 1994). However, this aesthetic control is never complete – even in the most "spectacularly banal" spaces of tourism – as the senses themselves often reveal.

Sight and the (modern) city

Sight became associated in the modern age with scientific inquiry; in other words, for modern science, seeing is knowing (Howes, 2005: 324; Urry, 2000: 389). However, we now often think of "the gaze" as maintaining a particular distance between people and places in the society of the spectacle; increasingly the (mediated) gaze is also derided as superficial – as "getting in the way of real experiences" (Urry, 2000: 391). Nevertheless, drawing from Simmel, Urry (2000) notes that, given the association between seeing and knowing in modern life, looking at someone "produces extraordinary moments of intimacy" (389). As such, sharing anything more than a fleeting gaze with a stranger can be felt as intrusive. There is an inherent tension, therefore, between the ways we think about sight in the city: a sense at once intimate and distancing, penetrating and superficial (Urry, 2000: 390–391).

The role of visibility in modern urban planning, however, generally relies on a more straightforward understanding of the gaze as the best way to apprehend reality (Hayward, 2004: 42–43). Le Corbusier viewed open sightlines as modernity perfected, and described a city planned around geometry, repetition, and visibility as the pinnacle of human-made geography (2010: 29). These ideals gained renewed traction with the emergence of fortress cities and defensible spaces, where CCTV cameras elevated the power of the gaze to an eye in the sky (Davis, 1992: 166–167). Those elements of the city's visual character that seem to resist visual penetration – for example, darkness – are treated with suspicion, and efforts are made to design them out of the environment (Edensor, 2017).

Like the city's sightlines, the haptic or tactile geographies of the city have also been reshaped by the rationalisation and commodification of space, although in divergent ways. Some urban spaces have been smoothed over and levelled out – a process whereby textures, contours, and waste matter are removed from these environments to facilitate uninterrupted movement (Edensor, 2007: 219) – while others have had textures and contours added to make them as uncomfortable as possible (Davis, 1992: 160–161). The urban tactile environment cultivates in citizens a bodily awareness of the city's inhospitable character (Davis, 1992; Degen, 2008). The hardness of pavement and the chill of concrete, for example, give us the sense that the city street is designed for moving through, not for lingering (Degen, 2008: 42). Due to the density of the modern city, however, the "fear of touch" that may help drive this ethics of spatial mobility (Sennett, 1994) is perpetually at odds with the near inevitability of touching other bodies in the crowded metropolis (Urry, 2000: 395).

The ease of association between the gaze and rationalist planning initiatives is perhaps related to the level of control which people can exert over their gaze. Sight is a sense that can be "shut off" – one can usually look away, look selectively (making, for example, a habit of studying others' shoes on a crowded subway), or close one's eyes altogether (Degen, 2008: 43). However, some of the other sensory dimensions of the city do not lend themselves so easily to purification and control (Classen, 2005; Degen, 2008). The sensescapes of sound and aroma, for example, are much harder to discipline along modern lines (Degen, 2008: 43–44).

Unruly sensations

As urban life intensified, so, too, did the variety and volume of sounds in the city (Steward & Cowan, 2007: 14), to the point of being considered a nuisance. Despite the management of urban sensescapes, sounds and odours frequently cross boundaries, although cities have at various points in their histories attempted to manage these "pollutions" of space. Thompson (2005), for example, describes New York's noise-reduction efforts in the 1920s, "the decade that roared," as largely unsuccessful in muting the city (190). Arguments for noise reduction are often mobilised around "quality of life" (Thompson, 2005: 198), depicting an unrestricted soundscape as potentially harmful. While noise abatement continues to prove challenging for cities, the soundscape of the city is not inescapable; many people now experience the "sound of the city" to a soundtrack played in their own heads (Thompson, 2005: 198). The emergence of earlier mobile technologies like the Walkman and mp3 player opened up the potential for personalising the aural experience of the city (see Bull, 2004, 2005, 2006) but may have had a dampening effect on sound's critical capacity to provoke spatial reimagining through exchange.

Scents are also difficult to avoid, not least because odours do not respect boundaries and are thus difficult to regulate (Classen, 2005; Degen, 2008: 44–45; Urry, 2000: 393). The ambiguous character of aroma is likely part of the reason urban smells have historically been allocated a moral dimension: in the industrial city, "it was widely believed that dirt, immorality, and poverty were a natural combination" (Classen, 2005: 294). Associations between marginal populations and dirt have long been used to exclude these populations from society (Sibley, 1995), giving new meaning to the term "cleaning up the streets" (Classen, 2005: 294). In addition to being viewed as pollution, scents also have an intimating effect – not only do they announce the proximity of something or someone, but they can also call forth distant memories (Degen, 2008: 45; Edensor, 2007). Consequently, aroma not only forges connections between people and places but across times as well, and as such, resists the modernist ideal of "everything in its place." The introduction of deodorising technologies and the crafting of commercial (pleasurable and consumable) aromascapes has exerted some control over scents of the city (Edensor, 2007; Urry, 2000). However, as Diaconu (2011) argues, no matter how much regulatory power cities throw at them, "odours are likely to remain the last citadel of 'freedom' and 'indiscipline': smellscapes ... are the result of all living beings in a city – and these cannot be subject to tight regulation" (236).

The tastes of the city offer further diversity, reflecting the global exchange of the modern metropolis. However, the variety of consumable (literally edible) cultures available within a city is not stripped of politics or contention. Law (2001) examines the gustatory place-making practices of Filipino domestic workers in Hong Kong, who remake a small piece of home ("Little Manila") in the centre of the city through tastes and vibrant associations. Law (2001) argues that Little Manila, although in some respects carnivalesque, is not simply an extension of the society of spectacle, but the sensual, embodied negotiation of marginality in the multicultural city (267). Domestic workers – often forbidden from cooking Filipino food in their homes of employ –reclaim a sense of belonging and connection by gathering in public space for a "taste" of home (278), thus layering the central city (and its tourist destinations) with a sensescape at once personal and political.

This is just a taste of the sensory history of the city, the fullness of which is beyond the scope of this text, but has been well illuminated by sensory scholars such as Classen (2005), Degen (2008), Kenny (2014), Mack (2015), Zardini (2005), and others (see also Howes [2018b] for a primer on the history of the senses). However, this sampling does emphasise for the reader a few key elements in the history of sensation (and its regulation) in the city.

First, the urban – thanks to the close proximity of others and the sensory overload that Simmel (2010/1903) identified – has long served as both battleground and test case for humanity's desire to master its sensory environment. Relatedly, this negotiation of sensation in the city is far from apolitical (Howes, 2005); the purification of the sensescape – tenuous though it may be – involves powerful cultural judgements regarding what sensations, ways of being, and ways of knowing are acceptable in a "modern" city (Classen, 2005; Mack, 2015; Zardini, 2005). However, while the sensory experience of the city can be curated by both developers and individuals to some extent (Bull, 2004; Zukin, 1995), thanks to the unruly quality of certain sensations and the constant dynamism of the city itself, sensing the city will nearly always be a moment of encounter – of sensing, being sensed by, and sensing with, the other.

This unruly nature of urban sensation demands that we speak not only of "urban sensations" but of *ways* of sensing the urban – to consider sens*ing* as practice, and more directly, locative tourism as a practice of sensing (and being sensed by) the city.

Sensing the city

Locative media as a practice of "sensing the city"

The proliferation of mobile media has led to the twinned proliferation of "hybrid spaces" in our daily lives (de Souza e Silva, 2006), or geographies that are overlaid with digital inscription (Saker & Evans, 2020). Locative narratives are one such form of digital inscription, and, importantly, these narratives are assembled across space through mobility (Hight, 2006; see also Barber, 2014) and through the body of the user. Barber (2014) makes clear that locative narrative – far from disengaging the user from the space – relies upon the space outside the frame, and the user's embodied interaction with that space, to fill in the gaps in the story:

> The flaneur is seen as the wandering but engaged participant-observer involved in the creation of narrative experiences/interactions within sites of historical or cultural interest. The mobile telephone, a device of convergence, engenders this interaction by prompting the creation and sharing of narratives that are at once site-specific, mobile, and aurally focused, thus leaving the visual and tactile senses free to provide additional, layered, sensory input.
>
> (98)

To this layered sensory input we might also add the neglected senses of taste and smell, as we will explore in the coming chapters. But the point stands that locative narratives become cohesive stories only when they are (literally) fleshed out and set in motion. The stories they tell rely on the user navigating the environment, yes – but also sensing it.

Jason Farman's (2012) *Mobile Interface Theory: Embodied Space and Locative Media* –in its second edition as of this writing – remains a foundational exploration of this embodied interaction between the user, the site, and locative media. Farman implicates the body in the production of locative media and in the socio-spatial relations they enable, and also interrogates the data politics of this kind of mobile placemaking. As he notes, "Our bodies sense the world as a collaboration between material and digital spaces while simultaneously interacting with the cultural inscriptions written into the experience, such as the privacy implications of disclosing your location to businesses and other users" (45). Farman and others have expertly untangled many of the more pressing implications of making meaning through location (see also Farman, 2014; Gordon & de Souza e Silva, 2011) and of narrative practices of "writing while walking" (Didur & Fan, 2018; Fan, 2017).

In the coming chapters, I aim to mobilise this fertile conceptualisation of locative meaning-making as embodied, emplaced, and in motion, to help understand what is increasingly one of locative narrative's more common – and, certainly, more bankable – genres: the locative tourism app. Furthermore, I set out to extend that discussion by situating locative tourism within broader historical and modern practices of urban sense-making (as illuminated by the anthropology of the senses), expanding the technological and more-than-visual dimensions of tourism studies in the process.

It can be tempting to think about locative or augmented reality tourism applications as putting a "wall" of representation and technology between the user and the space, manufacturing a sort of "tourist bubble" (Edensor, 2001: 64). Almost undoubtedly, tourism applications, like any other media, may enable some sensory experiences of space while disabling or downplaying others (Germann Molz, 2012; McLuhan, 1964). However, in some respects, these technologies also "extend our senses" (Howes & Classen, 2014; McLuhan, 1964; Parrinello, 2001), acting as a technological prosthesis (Parrinello, 2001: 210) which increases our mental and sensuous capacity by allowing us to access digitally embedded spatial knowledges (Germann Molz, 2012; Hemment, 2006). Richardson (2007) further argues that, because the cell phone has become a nearly constant presence on our persons, our relationships with micro-screen interfaces "impact upon our body limits, shifting the variable boundaries of embodiment, and altering our sense of having a body" (207). From this perspective, it becomes apparent that the body we are seeking to reintroduce to tourism theory comes with accessories – it is thoroughly entwined with the technological. In the case of locative media, attention must be paid to how the affordances of the medium extend the body – in other words, what sense ratios they privilege (McLuhan, 1964) – and how they shape the apparent possibilities of tourist space (Germann Molz, 2012).

It is with this context (of the app as "extension of the senses," or as techno-sensory prosthesis) in mind that I aim to demonstrate the value – indeed, I would argue, the necessity – of taking a sensory ethnographic approach to the study of locative media. To that end, we arrive now at a key question: what is sensory ethnography?

Sensory ethnography

Sensory ethnography is an established methodology for creating knowledge about the embodied experience of communications technology and other forms of media (Alper, 2018; Bull, 2006; Lynch et al., 2020; Nakamura, 2013; Pink, 2009; Van Doom, 2013). As Lynch et al. (2020) note, "the practice of sensory ethnography involves attending to the body and cultivating its capacities as a sensor – precipitating a shift from the conventional social scientific method of participant observation to one of participant sensation" (194; see also Howes, 2003, 2015; Pink, 2009). This practice of "sharing in the sensible [*partage du sensible*]" (Laplantine, 2015: 2) involves practicing a "sensory embodied reflexivity" in which the researcher is critically aware of his or her own sensory experience and the cultural context of the way that sensory information is perceived, interpreted, and valued (Culhane, 2017b). The theoretical threads of sensory ethnography situate ethnographic knowledge making as "co-creative" and assume that "ethnographic knowledge emerges not through detached observation but through conversations and exchanges of many kinds among people interacting in diverse zones of entanglement" (Culhane, 2017a: 3). Sensory ethnography also imagines the ethnographer as "emplaced" (Howes, 2005) and increasingly acknowledges non-human actors, atmospheres, traces, and imaginaries as among the constitutive factors of these "zones of entanglement" (Culhane, 2017a; Lynch et al., 2020; Springgay & Truman, 2017).

For this study, doing sensory ethnography with the locative tourism app meant paying attention to not only the sensations of encountering the city – in terms of the interplay of the five senses, or even, at times, the sixth – but also to the rhythms, structures, and atmospheres of enacting the locative tour. As Soyini Madison (2006) argues, "Ethnography is as much, or more, about bodily attention – performing in and against a circumscribed space – as it is about what is told to you in an interview" (401, quoted in Culhane, 2017a: 11).

Although this book has been informed by cultural geography – particularly by the insistence of early cultural geographies that representations of space *matter* (Anderson, 2010; Cosgrove, 2008; Jackson, 1989) – as well as by the tradition of studying locative media as a genre of narrative, it diverges somewhat from those earlier trajectories which focused on "reading" space. While my approach to this ethnographic study was sensitive to representations of the city (both in terms of urban branding, and the stories the city tells about itself through the streetscape and other in situ representations), I took care to interpret the city not as something purely to be "read" but, rather, as something to be experienced. In this respect, my work follows sensory anthropology's rejection of the textualisation of both the ethnographic endeavour and studies of mediation (Howes, 2019; Jones, 2018). Instead, this book considers mediation as a relational and embodied practice of co-creation.

Multi-sited sensory ethnography: the importance of "being there" with locative apps

In addition to sensory attunement, the practices of digital tourism – increasingly both mobile and networked (Germann Molz, 2012; Larsen, 2008) – demand a type of ethnography that can, well, go with the flow. As Larsen (2008) puts it, given the increasing mobility of both human and non-human actors and the complexity of connections that defines modern touristic practice, "it is critical that ethnography engages with the mobilities that connect fields across distance" (153). Enter multi-sited ethnography, a type of ethnography which "move[s] out from the single sites and local situations of conventional ethnographic research designs to examine the circulation of cultural meanings, objects and identities in diffuse timespace" (Marcus, 1995; see also Larsen, 2008: 154). As Larsen (2008) notes, "Multi-sited ethnographies are 'designed around chains, paths, threads, conjunctions, or juxtapositions of locations' to follow the physical, virtual, imaginative and communicative journeys of humans and non-humans" that not only span but increasingly define both material and virtual worlds (154; see also Wittel, 2000).

The use of mobile devices connects practices, places, and imaginaries across time and space (Hjorth, 2008), from the global to the local, and from the touristic to the mundane. Understanding these "convergences" and the particular aesthetic orderings, which they both rely upon and reinforce (Hjorth, 2008), required an approach to studying locative tourism that was similarly light on its feet. And so, I endeavoured to take sensory ethnography on the road.

Contrary to appearances, my globetrotting approach to studying locative tourism applications was not merely a bit of barely disguised wanderlust. Having done some preliminary research with these apps around Europe after a conference, I quickly realised that locative tourism apps were far more varied in their design and use than the literature suggested, and that an initial descriptive survey stage (where "survey" is used in the geographical sense of providing multiple data points) would help map the contours of locative media as a touristic phenomenon while also setting the stage for further analysis. It would – to beleaguer the map metaphor a moment longer – offer a lay of the land. So, in 2015, I began my sensory ethnographic exploration, using locative tourism applications on site in 10 cities (London, Dublin, Derry-Londonderry, Edinburgh, New Orleans, Toronto, Seattle, San Francisco, Hong Kong, and Melbourne) across four continents. (For a list and brief description of the apps studied in each city, see the Appendix.) I focused my attention on city-sanctioned applications – that is, apps that were either promoted or funded by urban or regional tourism organisations – to allow me to better contextualise these apps as part of a given city's broader tapestry of sensory marketing, brand imagery, and other such markers of the city-as-destination-space.

From there, I fixed my sights on two additional cities (Montreal and Christchurch) that appeared to be particularly interesting locales for analysing how locative tours help users make sense of the city. These case studies, which allowed prolonged and repeated encounters with locative tours – and tourists – in Christchurch (see Chapter 5) and Montreal (see Chapter 6), were an attempt to get a better feel for the place of the tour – to reflexively trace its sensations and register its rhythms "in [my] muscles and bones" (Tuan, 2001: 183–184). These focal points also allowed me to think between the "Concept City" of the tour – the abstract, rationalised space of city planners (de Certeau, 1984) – and the lived experience of the site, in order to better understand the role of designers, urban development, and tourists in the co-production of that place. This included collecting data – interviews, but also media releases, pre-recorded interviews, documentaries, artist statements, and published papers – about the visions behind *High Street Stories* and *Montréal en Histoires/Cité Mémoire*, as well as the processes involved in bringing these projects to life.

As part of the case studies, I also analysed the locative tourism app alongside local tourism and urban development plans in each city, with a particular eye towards unifying statements or brand images (whether for pertinent neighbourhoods or for the city as a whole). Including urban development plans in my analysis was an acknowledgement that cities are designed and built with particular readings already in mind (Hayward, 2004; Zukin, 1995). As such, the sites which the tours are mediating are already laden with meaning in the form of their architecture, infrastructure, commercial development, and public spaces. Attentive to the power of traces and absences in the urban environment (Edensor, 2005b; Gordon, 2008; Lefebvre, 2004), and bearing in mind the works of Malcolm McCullough (2006b) and Rosalyn Deutsche (1998) on the productive interplay of urban inscriptions, I also analysed the content of the applications in relation to a variety of other urban markup (including signage, advertising, public sculpture, street art, and graffiti). While this practice may not reflect the average user's experience of the tour (at least consciously), it did offer a valuable window into the milieu of urban markup (Farman, 2014) and contested meaning making in public spaces, of which the tour is only one part.

Sensory ethnography on the move: rhythm, mobility, and the co-production of the locative tour

Sensitive to urban performances, structures, and flows (de Freitas, 2010), this book is a story about *touring with* locative apps as much as it is one about the *content* of locative apps. This position reflects the inextricable link between the content of the app and the people and places of the city, which both animate and are animated by the tour to various degrees (Didur, 2014; Fan, 2017). My ethnographic practice of touring was also informed by Henri Lefebvre's (2004) *Rhythmanalysis*, which emphasises the polyrhythmic qualities of urban tourism spaces, where the cyclical rhythms of the tour interact with the alternating rhythms of everyday life to animate the streetscape (30). Lefebvre also notes the importance of not only paying attention to the overt narratives of the streetscape, but attending to the city's background and making sensible the traces of what is absent from that streetscape. "[The rhythmanalyst] will listen to the world, and above all what are disdainfully called noises, which are said without meaning, and to *murmurs*, full of meaning – and finally he will listen to the silences" (19).

Performing the map also allows a better sense of the tension between the fixed quality of cartographic representation and the fluid qualities of navigational practice (Verhoeff & Cooley, 2014: 123), the latter of which is, when it comes to the performance of locative media, highly contingent and prone to interruption/disruption (Fan, 2017). My work is thus positioned within a rich field of literature which has taken a sensuous approach to the study of urban rhythms (for examples, see Degen, 2008, 2012; Edensor, 2010; Edensor & Holloway, 2008; and Lefebvre, 2004; Truman & Springgay, 2019).

In the early stages of fieldwork for this book, when I was on my globe-trotting tour of applications, I often walked the tour routes myself, but I rarely found the experience solitary. Part of that is doubtless that very little is solitary in a tourist zone (and many of these apps managed to "hit the highlights" even when they overtly took a road less travelled by). Nevertheless, my fieldnotes from that time are populated by a chorus of guest stars – unscripted "others" who routinely coloured my experience of the apps. From crickets frantically whirring their legs together at the entrance to a bird market, to faulty wireless towers and hidden rooftop sensors that stopped and started my progress, to slick cobblestones and soupy-hot Louisiana nights that settled under my skin – even if had I never met a soul while on my journeys, I would still suggest to the reader that the locative tour can never be fully scripted. As an encounter with the city, the locative tour is always a co-production. Incorporating an autoethnographic approach allowed me to attend to the moments of correspondence and tension between the app and the city as sensed through my "material premises" (Sobchack, 2004: 172–173) – exploring the potentialities of the space opened up by the collision of my body with the data layer of the tour and the dynamic stage of the city.

Still, I did meet other people on my journeys, and want to speak here briefly on the value of walking methodologies – in my case, walk-along interviews and participant sensation – when it came to examining that co-production of the locative app as a matter of sensation. Walk-along interviews involve interviewing participants while out in the field – in this case, while performing the locative tour. Walk-alongs are an established method for exploring the experience of urban space (Jones et al., 2008; Truman & Springgay, 2019), and combine the "strengths of field observation and (sit-down) qualitative interviews" by adding immediacy to location-based discussion (Carpiano, 2009: 271). Tourists are, by nature, a transient crowd, so I took my participants where I could find them – in hostels, and along the tour route. Navigating the tour routes with these participants, and asking them to reflect on their experiences of the app and the city as we went, I was struck by the connections participants drew between the app content, the cityscape, and their own histories while walking. Incorporating a walk-along approach complemented the site-specific nature of the application content and allowed me to "place" my interactions with participants. Whether through walk-along interviews or more informal encounters, touring with participants allowed us to do that essential "performing in and against a circumscribed space" together (Soyini Madison, 2006) offering invaluable embodied perspective in the co-creation of both place and knowledge. Acknowledging that, when it comes to interviews, context shapes content (Culhane, 2017a: 12), I also tried wherever possible to conduct any sit-down interviews on or near the tour route. (In the case of several *High Street Stories* interviews, this involved eating at the C1 Café, which grows its herbs and microgreens in the streetscape outside – allowing us to ingest a bit of High Street while we talked about it).

Walk-along interviews (and other participant encounters on-site) also offered me a better sense of the traces that users found in the environment, not only through their experience of the mediated city, but in the frames of reference and urban imaginaries they used to interpret and contextualise what they were experiencing. As Morretti (2017) puts it, "Walking tours are exercises in the imagination" (101), and walking along with participants gives us access to other ways of imagining the tour (and the city it mediates). Part of using walking as a methodology, Morretti continues, is accepting the interruptions that come along with it as part of the social experience you are attempting to capture (101). This rang especially true when studying locative tourism apps, in which gaps and seams in the mediation offered moments of critical reflection on both the practice of touring and the practice of being with the rhythms of the city and tour at once.

Locative tourism on a shifting stage: methodological challenges and reflections

I consider it worthwhile to reflect briefly on some methodological challenges I encountered over the course of this ethnography. While this study has embraced locative media's focus on the importance of "being there," the on-site analysis of locative apps resulted in some challenges that were particular to the time and place of this fieldwork. For one thing, I have never felt quite so at the mercy of nature; tours were frequently rained out, or too cold for the technology to function. Towards the end of my fieldwork in Christchurch, I awoke one night to find the floor of my room rolling like the deck of a ship, as a 7.8-magnitude earthquake had rocked nearby Kaikoura. Within days, the city's hostels – where I recruited most of my participants for that case study – were full-up with tourists who had been evacuated from Kaikoura on container ships. Some had campervans and rental cars stuck in the impact zone and had to bide their time before their cars could be retrieved – the only access roads to the north and south had been buried under landslides or torn to shreds, respectively – and, unsurprisingly, none were particularly eager to tour an earthquake zone (nor would I press them). Even my own ethnographic fieldnotes from High Street in the days after that earthquake are marked by the queasiness of the aftershocks – the sense of being knocked just a little off balance. My remaining time there gave new meaning to the concept of the locative app as staged on shifting ground.

Most shifts were far less dramatic but still put a spotlight on the precarity of the locative tour. Apps that looked promising online were sometimes borderline obsolete by the time I arrived for data collection (the free preloaded devices at the tourist information centre for Derry's *Walk the Walls* app were no longer available by the time I arrived, for example). Many were discontinued not long after data were collected, like the more narrative *Discover Hong Kong* apps, which were shelved in favour of a single app that overlaid aggregated shopping, dining, and attraction information onto the Hong Kong street view. Christchurch's *High Street Stories* was scaffolded onto an older app called *CityViewAR* – which included an augmented-reality street view, but the 3-D reconstructions of buildings, though still working during a preliminary scouting visit, were glitchy at best by the time fieldwork began in earnest several months later (as maintenance on the latter app had been discontinued). Some apps were the victims of their own success – *Detour* was bought out by Bose in 2017 with the aim of creating an audio-focused AR platform to compete with the more visual-focused augmentation of the (launched and then unlaunched) Google Glass. Those apps with greater staying power often engaged with rolling sponsorships in order to stay active (which, as we will explore in the *Montréal en Histoires* case study, shifted the way they mediated the city).

Though this research took up the question of whether locative apps aimed to "pin down" the shifting flows of urbanity, engaging with these apps was itself often an exercise in glimpsing the ephemeral. My personal experience of the precarity of the locative tour – along with my experience of the contingency of co-creating the spaces of the city with others and the app – heavily informs the analysis in the chapters that follow.

Part II

A tour of locative tourism apps

Between gaze and performance

We now begin our tour of locative tourism apps. In the following chapters, we will wander between cities and criss-cross continents in an effort to understand the variety of ways that locative tourism apps can mediate the city, both in terms of how they extend the senses of users and in terms of the encounters with the urban that they help produce. As in the literature from which these chapters – "Gaze" and "Performance" – draw their names, there is considerable conceptual overlap between these two themes. But then, as we will see, that entanglement is entirely the point.

Chapter 3's title, "Gaze," is in some respects a misdirect. This chapter does discuss the importance of the gaze – the tourist gaze, the directed gaze, the extended gaze – in locative tourism. However, it also examines how locative tourism engages with the more-than-visual elements of sensing the city. Through these apps, the city is touched (and touches back), the walls are made to "speak," the urban brand is smelled and tasted, and even the user's sixth sense can be activated. As such, while this chapter considers how locative apps frame the view of the city and manage its brand image, it also examines how the extended gaze offered by the locative tour is entangled with other (at times conflicting) senses of the city.

Chapter 4, "Performance," turns its attention to the stage of the tour, and to the hazards and potentialities of performing the augmented map. In many ways, this chapter is a study of rupture – of discordant rhythms, disorientation, narratives of urban change, and the "others" who pierce the veil of touristic enchantment offered by locative apps. And yet, this chapter also traces moments of serendipity and reorientation – moments when performing the app prompts the user to experience the city otherwise.

Rather than an exhaustive account, these chapters offer a glimpse of the experiential possibilities of locative tourism. This is a tour of what can happen when the maps of meaning offered by locative tourism apps meet the living, breathing stage of the city through the technologically extended body of the user. The conceptual "signposts" of locative tourism that we trace here – the "alignment work" required to conjure the magic of the app, the polyrhythmic quality of performing the locative tour, and the contrasting narratives and ghostly traces that the app encounters, to name a few – will serve to orient the analysis of the comparative case studies in Part III.

DOI: 10.4324/9781003142386-5

3 Gaze

This chapter explores how locative tourism apps both extend the tourist gaze and engage users in more-than-visual experiences of the city, particularly where a "feast for the senses" is part of the urban brand. We begin with a section on "Framing the City", which discusses the aesthetic implications of taking the museum to the streets using apps like London's *Streetmuseum*, before moving on to an analysis of the gamification of the tourist gaze in Edinburgh's *World Heritage City* app. Finally, this section examines how "time travel" apps – like New Orleans' *Historic NOLA* – position the user in particular ways and reflects on the implications of this positioning for what is "in place" or "out of place" within the frame of the tour. The following section, "Constructing (and Contesting) the Urban Brand," discusses how urban branding shapes the content of the locative tour, primarily by looking at how Derry-Londonderry's *Walk the Walls* app directs the user's gaze away from more problematic parts of the city's history (and how the traces of those other histories peek through). Section 3 focuses on "Sensing the City," and begins with considering how Seattle's *Space Needle* app technologically extends the tourist gaze by augmenting the panorama. We then consider the "othered senses" in tourism by exploring how locative tourism apps in cities from London to Hong Kong provoke the user – intentionally or otherwise – to encounter the city in a more multisensory way than the concept of the tourist gaze might suggest (including, in the case of New Orleans' *Wicked Walks*, by activating the tourist's sixth sense).

Framing the city

Taking the museum to the street in London

In *The Cultures of Cities*, Sharon Zukin (1995) argues that post-industrial cities are shifting to a symbolic economy, a twinned (re-)production of urban space and symbols that offers coherent images of the city and its lifestyle for consumers to buy into (not to mention *buy* in). Museums are part and parcel of this shift towards the "cultured" urban – where "culture suggests the coherence and consistency of a brand-name product" (Zukin, 1995: 12); they serve as regeneration machines. Given this, what is one to

DOI: 10.4324/9781003142386-6

make of the trend towards turning the street itself into a museum? Is this a rehabilitation the streetscape's tarnished identity, the moment of its own shift into an "item of cultural consumption"? (Zukin, 1989: 3). If, as Zukin suggests, museums are stabilising points for the revitalisation of neighbourhoods, what better way to regenerate the street in the eyes of the tourist-consumer than to turn that very street into a museum?

It would be disingenuous to say that these apps turn the journey into the destination (most intersect with common tourist attractions in the city), but they certainly aim to make the journey part of the destination by multiplying the points of interest in the city. Touring with the locative app turns the very streets you walk into a destination space, rather than some gauntlet to be run (Christopherson, 2008) on one's way between cultural attractions. The city is reframed through technotourism into an exhibition space that blends past and present-future projections of what the city was, is, and is becoming through the anchor point of mobile technology.

What are the benefits to the museum of taking its wares – and with them, the ownership of archival and artefactual ways of knowing about the city – into the streets? In many ways it can be interpreted as a pushback against the aesthetics of the white cube – a movement that has been taking hold as much within the museum as without (Jones, 2018: 220). (Indeed, as Constance Classen [2017] points out, the normative ordering within the museum is often more diverse and transgressive than it is given credit for – historically, people have not only seen but touched and tasted artefacts.) Moving into the city allows museums to tap into the "experience economy" (Pine & Gilmore, 1999) – and thus into the trend towards selling multisensory and seemingly more "authentic" experiences of place. What happens, then, to the normative aesthetic ordering of the museum – where, as Edensor (2005c) suggests, the user is positioned at an optimal viewing distance from the object of her gaze – when the museum becomes a StreetMuseum? What implications does this aesthetic reorganisation have for the production and consumption of urban spaces and imaginaries?

Organised by the Museum of London and released in 2010, London *Streetmuseum* was one of the first touristic uses of locative media formats. The aim – as the name would suggest – was to take the museum to the streets of London by enabling archival material to be embedded in places throughout the city, particularly in the immediate area around the museum. An updated version – called *Streetmuseum Londinium* – was released in 2014, partnering with the History Channel and adding 3-D elements to the experience, as well as the simulation of touch (users could "dig" for buried treasures on their screens at various locales). *Streetmuseum* has likely been the most thoroughly analysed locative app (see, for example, Forsyth, 2011; Jeater, 2012; Morais, 2016, Wang et al., 2012), and its relatively simple design has spawned many imitators. In the wake of Streetmuseum's success, many locative tourism apps have taken a similar approach to the "museumization" (Wang et al., 2012) of the street – embedding archival images and stories in the digital streetscape. *Toronto in Time* is one example that follows the

Streetmuseum model – although it uses a more thematic approach to re-embedding archival collections and thus directs users' paths through the city to a greater degree than *Streetmuseum* – and New Orleans' *Historic NOLA* app is another.

For *Streetmuseum*, the Museum of London partnered with a London advertising agency, and the app was designed to be – in some respects – in situ advertising for the museum itself, with its creators hoping to raise awareness and drive traffic into the museum (particularly amongst younger demographics) (Ellis, 2010). Later uses of the technology, however, have leaned more towards branding the city itself (and promoting the interests of brands within the city), rather than aiming to draw users into brick-and-mortar museums.

Streetmuseum's advertising strategy hints at how the application is sold to potential users – through, for example, the tagline "Take a trip to the London of yesteryear" – as offering the potential to "travel in time" and exist between worlds. Promotional images of *Streetmuseum* in use (see Figure 3.1) illustrate how locative apps rely on the physical environment around them to animate their content; many locative apps draw their magic

Figure 3.1 Taking the archive to the streets in *Streetmuseum*.

(Image credit: *Streetmuseum*, © Museum of London).

from providing a sense of being in two places (or times) at once (Greenspan, 2011; Hight, 2006; Khaled et al., 2011). In order to capitalise on the enchantment of this liminal quality, designers cannot fully eclipse the city as it is – it cannot be blocked out. Users must have a foot in both worlds to fully experience the app.

While these apps rarely seem designed to destabilise users' visions of space – indeed, they rather seem designed to anchor perceptions of the city – the inherent precarity involved in positioning users between two worlds leaves the door open for potential slippage (Khaled et al., 2011; Tuters & Varnelis, 2006). That very liminality and precarity makes it possible for alternative ways of knowing and sensing space to upend totalising narratives about the urban.

These kinds of apps are at their most effective – that is, they can most seamlessly blend these two worlds – in relatively controlled environments, where the animating characteristics of the space (the scaffolding upon which the tour is built) are relatively stable. Take, for example, the application at Dunluce Castle, which offers users 3-D CGI reconstructions of the castle as well as audio and visual depictions of what life was like within the walls (*Dunluce Castle*, 2013). Mapping the app onto the castle benefits from the fact that – rather like an open-air museum – access to the space is controlled and the ruins that the app augments can be relied upon to hold steady. It serves, therefore as something of an interesting point of comparison to apps set in urban (living) streets, a kind of pseudo control case for taking the museum out of museum walls. The *Dunluce Castle* guide has the benefit of being able to anchor its augmented content in the "real" through numbered points displayed on small placards throughout the castle, easing users' navigation by telling them where to stand. The ruin of the castle – exposed though it may be to the elements – is a curated ruin. It has one overarching interpretation, and its occupants (save the odd heritage worker) are all visitors taking in the exhibit. As such, it holds up to augmentation very well.

Certainly, many museum scholars would take issue with any description of the museum as a completely controlled environment; in fact, as Classen (2017) points out, while normative ways of looking may still outwardly rule the museum, there is a long history of transgressive touch and even taste involved in experiencing exhibitions. In addition, numerous authors have described how the museum – often pointed to as the epitome of the distancing, "look, don't touch" aesthetics of ocularcentric modernity (Edensor, 2005c) – is increasingly opening up other realms of sensory experience for visitors (Binter, 2014; Clintberg, 2014; Howes, 2014a), often mediated by digital technology (Howes, 2014a: 263). Similarly, to conceptualise the street as free from control would be naïve. However, it does not seem controversial to suggest that the city street is a far more dynamic and shifting stage upon which to stage any exhibition. The following sections will begin to examine how locative tourism apps mediate users' experience of urbanity on just such uncertain ground.

Gamifying the tourist gaze in Edinburgh

At face value, locative tourism applications often appear to solidify what Urry (1990) called the Tourist Gaze – movement around nodes in the city that act as signposts for what "has to be seen." The user is encouraged to carve a path between these must-see nodes in order to get the "right" shot of the city. As you move throughout its historic streets, *Edinburgh's World Heritage City* app turns this type of mobility into a game (see Figure 3.2). This is a practice known as "gamification," which "concerns the mobilisation and implementation of ludic elements… in order to manage 'serious' and 'real' issues" (Vanolo, 2018: 320) – in this case, the preservation of built heritage. The app awards points based on visiting a place, taking a photograph, and uploading that photograph for other users to see. Points are also awarded for taking a quiz about the app content, so the user is encouraged to listen to the audio narration as well, but the points pale in comparison to those the app awards for going to, photographing, and disseminating images around these given nodes. This application enhances, therefore, a sedimentation of photographs around particular locations (since part of running the application is showing others your best shot). Using the app thus inculcates the practice of photographing

Figure 3.2 Gamifying the tourist gaze in Edinburgh.

(Image credit: *Edinburgh World Heritage City*, by Edinburgh World Heritage).

a place. Nevertheless, this sometimes reveals other ways of looking at a site, as the collective gaze unveils details one might otherwise have overlooked. For example, a fellow user spots – and photographs – a date carved into a corner stone, prompting me to look closer. However, this, too, enhances the portrait of the site as an object worthy of the tourist gaze. By "turning urban spaces into playgrounds to be explored," *Edinburgh's World Heritage City* seizes on gamification's potential to enhance connections between people and places (Vanolo, 2018), albeit in a very familiar way.

Though the possibility of user-created content is often billed as one of the counter-normative potentialities of the locative app, *Edinburgh World Heritage City* incorporates user content in perhaps the most normative way possible. By encouraging users to take and then geotag photographs at destination points around the city, the app furthers the sedimentation of imagery around particular nodes – it solidifies the tourist gaze. However, if the object is to multiply the city's destination points, then *Edinburgh World Heritage City* has a clear "in" to what counts within a gaze-centric imaginary of the city: manufacturing an imageable site.

In and out of frame in New Orleans

Tourism, for its part, has long held a particular place for the subject and for the object – the tourist and the toured, the gazer and the gazed-upon, respectively. These subject–object positions were mediated and reinforced, as Urry (1990) notes, by the presence of the camera, which required that the tourist–photographer remain at the appropriate distance from the object of his or her gaze. After all, the point was to signify his or her journey by capturing signposts – indicators that the site had been properly seen – and to do so required that the site be properly "in frame" (Urry, 1990). We can think about this process of "getting the shot" as a form of cultural dressage (Lefebvre, 2004): the branded image of the city is created by photographers repeatedly taking up this same view from a distance (with slight variations) and then circulating these images as proof of their well-travelled lives.

Similarly, applications that rely on users lining up archival photographs with the world around them most often require the user to stand in a very particular spot. Owing to this precise orientation, it becomes a bit of a game to line up the edges, to position oneself exactly where another photographer had stood and see the scene through both their eyes and your own. This manoeuvring is a form of what Licoppe (2016) refers to as "alignment work," in which the user of locative media has to reconcile the many possible ways of considering her surroundings into a cohesive whole. This alignment work exposes the extent to which the body is an "active framer of the image" (Hansen, 2004), and of the locative tour more broadly. Locative tourism apps might offer the tantalising prospect of standing between two worlds or seeing across the expanse of time, but it is the movement of the body that "makes it real" for the user (Hansen, 2004: 41). Furthermore, this alignment work frequently exposes gaps and seams between the app content and the physical environment (Licoppe, 2016: 103). These gaps and seams are on full display when using New Orleans' *Historic NOLA* app.

In New Orleans' Jackson Square, the *Historic NOLA* app directs my gaze past a homeless man sleeping under a squat, spiny palm of some variety. I am attempting to line up a view of the St Louis Cathedral with a nearly identical view of the cathedral from decades before – a carbon copy of the building in front of me, only in black and white. Because the views are so identical, and because lining up the old photograph with the view ahead puts the rough sleeper squarely "in frame," *he* becomes what is new and noticeable about the space. Deeper into the square, at the corner of St Louis Cathedral and the Castillo, construction scaffolding blocks me from standing at the proper distance required to line up the app view with the streetscape, and the effect is that of a world cast in miniature – everything on the screen is just a little bit smaller than it ought to be. Further down the street, a door opens behind me just as I am about to take an overlay screencap of the city's Armory, and the image winds up eerily askew, with pedestrians and piles of garbage caught in frame, wandering somewhere between the old image and the new (see Figure 3.3).

Figure 3.3 The Arsenal, askew (overlay of archival image with street view, created using *Historic NOLA*).

Image credit: "The Arsenal," The Charles L. Franck Studio Collection at the Historic New Orleans Collection.

Some apps give more guidance to the user in this process of world-melding than others. Take, for example, *Montréal en Histoires*, which offers users a detailed AR overlay (which traces the basic contours of the buildings on a given site – see Figure 3.4) to help them "line up" the virtual tableau on screen with the world around them. The app also complements its geo-location and AR overlay with a signature pair of yellow feet stamped across the sidewalks of Old Montreal, the latter acting as both signpost and seemingly ideal viewing spot for the tour's night-time projections. (These standing spots have the further benefit of helping users re-sync with the rhythm of the tour, as we will discuss in Chapter 6.)

This practice of lining up the contours of the real with the digital projection – the "alignment work" (Licoppe, 2016) of positioning one's body exactly so that the magic of the app can happen – is often more than a little confounding. Nevertheless, this discomfort exposes just how embodied and kinaesthetic the practice of synthesising new media worlds can be (Hansen, 2004). Alignment work makes the user acutely aware of how the app positions them in the city – and brings into focus anything that gets in the way or is not, evidently, meant to be seen.

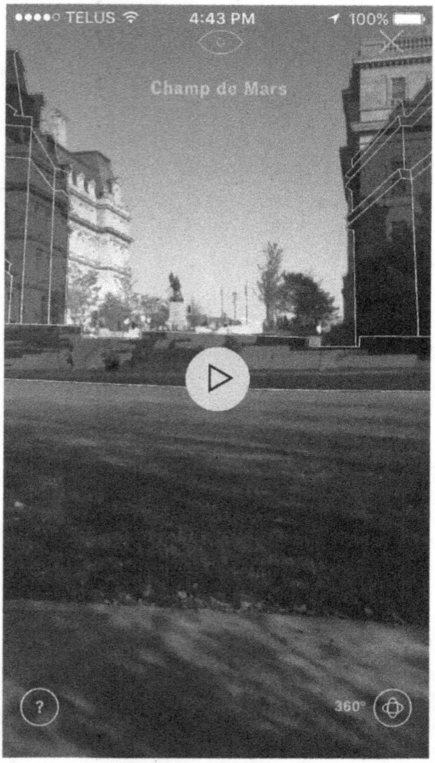

Figure 3.4 Positioning the user in Montreal – a navigation overlay helps users line up the augmented reality feature with the world around them.

(Source: Image created using *Montreal en Histoires*).

Constructing (and contesting) the urban brand

In this section, we will shift from considering practices of imaging the city to the brand image of the city – and how the tourist industry attempts to "fix" the meaning of certain destinations. While it could be argued that locative tours are an ideal medium through which to attach a theming frame to a dynamic space, this section will also argue that branded spaces are contested, and that tourists and their destinations are not always so easily pinned down.

Re-presenting the branded city

The surge in urban redevelopment around cultural consumption that Zukin identified (see also Logan & Molotch, 2007; Zukin, 1989) was accompanied, she argued, by a Disney-fied approach to urban growth based on the construction of orderly, spectacular-yet-sanitised spaces for consumption (Zukin, 1995: 54–76). Culture became a brand that could be sold. Elsewhere, a multitude of other authors have described how urban space has been redeveloped to offer the safe, familiar experience of a suburban shopping mall (Crawford, 1992; Jackson, 1989) mixed with the spectacular sameness of a theme park (Boyer, 1992; Sorkin, 1992). The tourism strategies of many destinations, especially cities, are increasingly being organised under overarching themes (Dinnie, 2011; MacCannell, 2001; Urry & Larsen, 2011). Many have raised concerns about the extent to which city life is being smoothed over and repackaged into unambiguous products (Boyer, 1992; Soja, 1996; Zukin, 1995), how those who do not fit with the brand image of the city are being excluded, and how public space has been increasingly privatised to facilitate that exclusion (Boddy, 1992; Kohn, 2004; Smith, 1992; Zukin, 1995).

Theming makes a space legible for the tourist; it creates a sense of familiarity by containing a fractured and changing landscape within a unitary narrative frame (Dinnie, 2004; Lukas, 2007a; Manovich, 2006; Urry & Larsen, 2011). Since this thematic organisation of space is intended to attract and facilitate consumption, themed spaces might also be thought of as "branded spaces" (Dinnie, 2004; Dinnie, 2011). Urry and Larsen (2011) argue that theming reflects the broader "Disneyfication" of spaces, wherein landscapes are increasingly composed in a style of inauthentic pastiche designed for consumption by the tourist gaze (120; see also van Hoven, 2011). These bubbles of themed space (MacCannell, 2001: 26) are also frequently typified by privatisation and surveillance (Urry & Larsen, 2011: 125), since it is easier to police the meaning of a space which is not strictly public. One way to arrange space for theming is to create extra divisions; countries are broken up into themed zones – such as "Last of the Summer Wine Country" or "Bronte Country" in England, or the regional theme of "Maritimicity"[1] in Canada (Urry & Larsen, 2011: 125). In this way, the practice of branding or theming space is a negotiation between creating a unitary story around a space and dividing the landscape into sections small enough to support these grand narratives.

However, tourism destinations must walk a fine line between sameness and difference. Differentiation is key, particularly in the increasingly competitive tourism market, and amongst destinations that now boast many of the same scenic attractions (Hudson & Ritchie, 2009: 217). Faced with the tall order of standing out on a global stage, destinations and their "stage managers" – industry workers and guides – now actively seek to "reinscribe difference in places" (Coleman & Crang, 2002: 3). For many, this has meant a move away from focus on the spectacle and towards appeals to the emotional and sensual (Dann & Jacobsen, 2003; Howes, 2011; Hudson & Ritchie, 2009). The curation and promotion of sensescapes – part of the broader trend towards hyperaesthesia or the commodification of experience (Howes, 2005) – is a growing part of tourism branding efforts (Howes, 2011: 64). Vienna, for example, advertises itself as "A Journey Through Time for All the Senses" (Howes, 2011); Seville is similarly promoted as a "joy to the senses," all orange blossoms and sunshine, while favela tours in Rio, taking a different approach, offer travellers the opportunity to smell the slums (Dann & Jacobsen, 2003: 18). The theming of smellscapes (Dann & Jacobsen, 2003), tastescapes (Everett, 2009; Germann Molz, 2007) and soundscapes (Edensor & Holloway, 2008: 489–490) have all been acknowledged as key to managing the commodified heritage of a destination and helping it remain "on brand."

Since theming is a limited "approximation of place, time, event, culture or person" (Lukas, 2007b: 272) – so the brand image of a place necessarily filters out a variety of other interpretations of and ways of being in the city – it is a sociopolitically charged exercise in inclusion and exclusion (Little, 1991: 150). The nearly unparalleled success of the glamour-raunch branding of Las Vegas, for example, relied upon suppressing other imaginings of the city that were "confusing the message" (Hudson & Ritchie, 2009: 219; see also Dinnie, 2011). The branding of spaces is often a contested process, and the act of (re)branding can bring dividing lines into stark relief. For example, the attempted rebranding of New Orleans after Hurricane Katrina met with resistance in the prevalent counter images of the "Big Easy" as a city in crisis, with global attention focused not only on the storm damage but on the deep-running socioeconomic inequalities of the city (Gotham, 2007).

Media play an important role in the management of brand identity around tourism destinations. Tourists carry a variety of popular representations into these spaces with them, whether in hand (through the map, the guidebook, and now the app) or in the form of circulating urban imaginaries (Lagerkvist, 2008). These representations both shape and are reinforced by the normative practices of touring (Lagerkvist, 2008; Urry, 1990), casting a veil of touristic enchantment over certain spaces while obscuring other pathways and interpretations of the city.

Augmented-reality tourism applications can be thought of as facilitating consumption and consumer satisfaction by overlaying the "brand image" with the product (the destination space), stabilising the thematic narrative of already mediated spaces (Allen, 2008: 27). However, like maps and guidebooks, these applications run into the problem of image-destination contrasts, making any disjunctures between the tourist imaginary and spatial experience even more evident (Allen, 1996; Farman, 2012). Herein lies the primary challenge for branding space: even when the messaging manages to be consistent, the spaces these brands frame and the tourists they invite are not particularly easy to pin down (Gotham, 2007: 25), as one locative tour in Derry makes clear.

Directing the gaze in Derry

What happens when the brand image of a place relies heavily on smoothing over of tensions? The city of Derry-Londonderry has its history of conflict built right into the name. Derry is the town's more colloquial name, though Londonderry remains its official name – one which cannot avoid (and, depending on the usage, actively courts) association with British control. Some of the bloodiest moments of the Irish Troubles – a civil conflict between opposing nationalist (mostly Catholic) and British loyalist (usually Protestant) factions over British rule in Northern Ireland – took place in Derry. Most notably, the city was the site of the infamous "Bloody Sunday," which saw dozens of unarmed civilians in Derry's nationalist Bogside neighbourhood shot at the hands of British soldiers as recently as 1972. The Irish Troubles continued to make news well into the 1990s, shaping international perspectives of Northern Ireland as a conflict zone, and the evident tensions in the town are still scrawled along the Derry streetscape (see Figures 3.5 and 3.6).

However, Derry has another name for itself: the UK City of Culture for 2013. Having been declared a UK City of Culture after a successful bid in 2010, the city of Derry set about rebranding itself, investing in modern redevelopment projects and heritage initiatives that rarely mentioned the city's recent history of conflict (Doak, 2014). The (short-lived) *Walk the Walls* application was an offshoot of this City of Culture injection, and users were provided with the app on pre-loaded devices for a time at the local tourism office. The *Walk the Walls* application guides users along the walls that once enclosed the medieval city, all the while relating stories of the 17th-century sieges that the town survived behind those walls. In making the walls themselves the object of the tour's gaze – rather than the fairly panoramic view of the city they provide – *Walk the Walls* is an atypical tourist app. Most tours rarely lose the opportunity to tell the city's story from high ground, where it is easiest to imagine the space as telling a somewhat unified story.

The era of the city's history which *Walk the Walls* opts to narrate hardly seems accidental, especially given the city's recent rebranding initiatives. The 17th-century sieges, by virtue of their relative historical distance, have less of the sting (and sense of imminent danger) that the Troubles still carry.

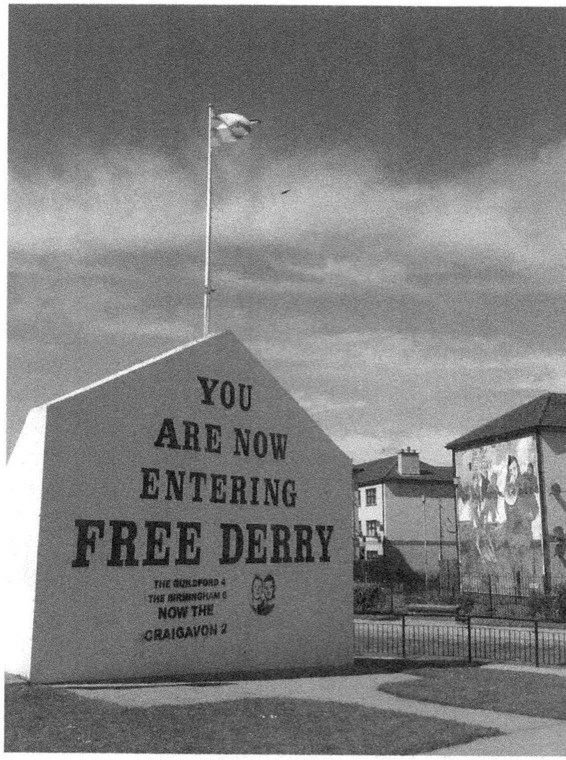

Figure 3.5 An iconic sign just below Derry's history city walls (in the Bogside neighbourhood, a historically Catholic/Nationalist stronghold) reads "Welcome to Free Derry."

The app describes the "thundering anger" of the walled city's cannons during the 17th-century sieges, painting a heroic image of a city united and steeled against a common foe. However, as you walk around the walls, Derry unveils its more troubled histories in a myriad of ways (see, for example, Figures 3.5 and 3.6). So much of the view on offer when using *Walk the Walls* is of a city scarred by more recent histories, all of which go largely uncontextualised by the app.

If we compare the united portrait of the city as experienced through *Walk the Walls* to a tour offered by a local guide – notably one who hails from the Bogside, typically viewed as the nationalist part of town, and the actual site of the Bloody Sunday massacre – we can start to see past the comforting veneer. Though we walk nearly the same path around the city walls – and our guide points out the majestic Guildhall, also a key feature of the *Walk the Walls* app – the view of the city presented in this local tour could hardly be more different. The guide points out the last remaining "Peace Wall" (or border wall) that runs perpendicular to the ancient city walls – its rather garish and mundane green a stark contrast to the medieval fortifications (Figure 3.8). As the

Figure 3.6 A sign visible from the city walls (in the traditionally protestant/Unionist west bank of the city) declares the area "still under siege."

Bogside stretches out before us, "Free Derry" is written on the rooftops (not to mention on a prominent sign; see Figure 3.5) broadcast across the hills in the sunlight.

We step off the city walls and into the Bogside to visit the memorial to the lives lost on Bloody Sunday, which sits just at the foot of the walled embankment. From here, tourists can see the outside of the famous walls where they were just walking. Scrawled across the side are the words "End British Internment" – a mark of persistent conflict, of a city less united under siege than still (at least in part) divided amongst itself. Walking away from the old town, it is impossible not to notice the colours marking the edges of the sidewalks – blue, white, and red for Loyalist neighbourhoods; orange, white, and green for the Nationalist ones. Even as the city's soaring Peace Bridge (see Figure 3.7) – a powerful symbol of a hard-won period of calm in the city – has made it into the local tourism logo, the pavement still tells the story of a fractured past. So, too, does the remaining border wall – an unmistakeable architectural scar from the Troubles that still cuts the streetscape in two (Figure 3.8). Derry's streetscape is an ever-present reminder that the routes we take (and are taken on) are not only made political in the act of walking them or of narrativising them – they are marked by, and conveyers of, their own stories, of the political and cultural values that they whisper at every turn (if you know how to look for them, and if, indeed, your gaze is not directed elsewhere). Some spaces resist the creation of unified narratives (Friedrich et al., 2018).

Figure 3.7 Derry's symbolic Peace Bridge, which is integrated into the Derry tourism logo.

Sensing the city (with app in hand)

The position of the tourist has always been, to some extent, simultaneous. The tourist must be at once inside and outside, to be in place – to go there, to be there – and out of place at the same time. Managing one's out-of-placeness is a way of obtaining a "higher ground" on the site, affording the necessary near-distance for making sense of things (Strain, 2003). In many ways, then, the tourist in her ideal role is like the (ostensibly) less-critical cousin of Lefebvre's (2004) rhythmanalyst on the balcony – close enough to the action to claim experience, yet far enough away to gain perspective. The goal, then, is to examine how that practice of making sense is conditioned, and how particular configurations of "sense" are privileged over others in these practices.

As we explored in Chapters 1 and 2, the sensory history of (particularly Western) urban life reveals a tension between efforts to control the sensescapes of the city – through sanitisation and commodification – and the extent to which the senses resist this purification of urban space. In light of that literature, the remainder of this chapter starts to piece together how the uneven, multisensuous experience of the city is framed by the locative app, beginning with a discussion of how Seattle's *Space Needle* app augments

Figure 3.8 Derry's remaining border wall, visible from the route of *Walk the Walls*.

the panoramic view of the city and technologically extends the tourist gaze. We will also explore here how using locative apps modulates touch in the city, both by simulating touching the city through the screen and by mapping out moments of permissible touch in users' encounters with the city. Finally, this section examines the experience of apps that invite users to explore the city in increasingly multisensory ways – whether through paranormal pub crawling in New Orleans or offering up a feast for the senses in the cosmopolitan consumer buffet of Hong Kong.

As we start to examine how locative tourism apps manage and extend the senses, we begin (as befits the title of this chapter) with the gaze. Sight became associated in the modern age with scientific inquiry; in other words, for modern science, seeing is knowing (Howes, 2005: 324; Urry, 2000: 389). Science and "polite" society embraced the gaze as *the* modern way of knowing, seeming as it did to offer "intimate" knowledge at a distance that was safe from contamination (Howes, 2005: 324; Urry, 2000: 389). In the context of tourism, gaze remains a key driver of tourist mobility, but has acquired something of a reputation for producing superficial experiences – and obscuring more authentic encounters with destination space (Urry, 2000: 391).

We have also explored how the ascendancy of sight aligned with rationalist urban planning initiatives – the city of vision was the city of planners (Steward & Cowan, 2007: 8). As de Certeau (1984) reflected from atop the World Trade Center in New York, the panorama offers perhaps our best glimpse of the orderly viewpoint of city planners; it offers a view of the city that, absent the "mess" of its inhabitants and mundane goings on, *makes sense*. While the majority of apps encounter the city at street level, taking our cue from de Certeau, let us now take a brief detour to take in the totalising view from above – to further consider how sight (and especially the panoramic view) can be extended by the locative app.

"If you see one thing in Seattle, see everything": augmenting the panorama

The promotional material for Seattle's Space Needle makes no bones about the particular configuration of urban sensemaking that it offers. As the pamphlets on offer inside the door read: "IF YOU SEE ONE THING IN SEATTLE, SEE *EVERYTHING*." The *Space Needle* and *Space Needle 360* apps seem a logical extension of the rationalist gaze, seeking to offer as much information – and as many varied sightlines – as possible in order to make the city below "knowable" at a glance.

The entranceway to Seattle's Space Needle offers historical context for the tower's construction, and pains have been taken to make the building – both in terms of its scale and its view – sensible to visitors from above and below. A curved display in the ramp up to the tower's elevators describes the process of building the Needle. While the *Space Needle* app does not necessarily revel in time travel the way many other locative tourism apps do, the entryway to the tower does offer a real-world approximation. A mock vintage radio set invites small hands to "turn the dial back – it's 1961 today." Doing so sends music of the era filtering out into the lobby. Farther along the ramp, the board invites users to turn the crank, touch a giant bolt ("imagine turning a bolt like this"), and spin the wheel to reignite the torch. Children delight in touching these mechanisms as we move along – although one suspects the diversion is more important to them than any sense of time travel. Placing a giant bolt at child level does a compelling job of making the scale of the tower (in all its marvel) perceptible through the fingers, rather than just through sight.

The entry board also provides some context on the history of in situ media use in the tower. After all, while the technology that enables information to be digitally embedded in place is new, the concept of using media to help tourists gain a perceived "higher ground" on their destinations is as old as the practice of mass tourism itself (Spring, 2006). As the curved entryway describes, "In 1962, diners looked at the back of the cocktail menu to identify landmarks as the restaurant revolved." Even in the 1960s, diners experienced an augmented panorama in the Space Needle – albeit with a cocktail, rather than an app, in hand.

The *Space Needle* app offers users a number of ways to augment the experience of the tower, each of them involving seemingly superpowered extensions of sight. The first is an "enhanced panorama," which uses the direction your camera is facing to give you a sense of what you are looking at as you circle the observation deck. This is the much-sought-after "view from the top" (de Certeau, 1984; Strain, 2003), only magnified and annotated. When the distant mountains are blanketed in clouds, the app can still conjure points of interest, seemingly out of thin air. Around me, people are searching for Mount Rainier ("She said that one wasn't Rainier" / "I want to say Rainier is that way"), while the app informs me precisely where it is (or, at least, I assume it does). At one point the app tells me I am looking at Canada – in which case the app projects sight out well beyond human capacity. *Space Needle 360* serves as a virtual reality sister app to the *Space Needle's* augmented reality. That app proffers visitors an eagle's-eye view from beyond the edge of the observation deck, thus offering the tourist a view of the city which is only ever available through technological extension.

Yet another capacity of the *Space Needle* app pushes these techno-mediated superpowers a step further, allowing users to see through the floor. Like most of the magic of the *Space Needle* app, this superpower revolves around the use of "space spots": large circular stickers on the floor of the observation deck that essentially function as dressed-up QR codes. Using these QR codes to centre the app allows *Space Needle* to overcome some of the issues with GPS positioning that plague other apps (particularly those with multiple waypoints over relatively short distances). Hover over a space spot with your device's camera, and you will either send a projection of the Space Needle soaring before your eyes (see Figure 3.9) or punch an apparent hole through the observation deck (see Figure 3.10).

The views down indicate another potential use for a locative tourism app – sprucing up an aging attraction to compete with similar offerings in other cities. The view of the city below (see Figure 3.10) seems designed to compete with the glass floor in Toronto's CN Tower – offering a precipitous view of the pavement some 160 metres down, and made to look lifelike by animations of passing clouds and the elevator whizzing up the tower (otherwise, one supposes the view might be indistinguishable from a picture, ruining the illusion of being able to see through walls – or, rather, floors). Another such hole shows you an animation of a dining area below – though, strangely, one full of empty tables. Conceivably, it is meant to lure you down for a meal and a view in relative solitude, should the smell of overpriced hot dogs wafting over the crowded observation deck not tempt you enough.

Perhaps the *Space Needle* app's greatest trick is solving the dilemma of cities with iconic high-rise buildings everywhere. After all, the Space Needle suffers from the same affliction as the Empire State Building and the Eiffel Tower: it offers a panoramic view of a city skyline without its most famous landmark. The app conjures a holographic overlay of the Space Needle before you, repositioning the landmark within the frame of the panorama

Figure 3.9 An augmented panorama, with an animated Space Needle front and centre.

(Image credit: the author, using the *Space Needle* app).

that landmark enables. Ill-content to provide just one view of the Space Needle, however, the app has several. You can choose to see the tower projected out before you in the rain, or even a retro-futuristic rendering of the tower as it might have appeared on the Jetsons. Hover over another spot, and animated fireworks paint the sky behind the tower, exploding across your screen (see Figure 3.10) and, seemingly, over the heads and backs of those looking out over the city. That is, until a father chases his daughter across the Space Spot, and the projection flickers and then disappears. (Indeed, as will be discussed later, these applications often encounter "people problems," and their seamless use often depends on a vision of the city without its inhabitants).

Touching the city

Like the city's sightlines, the haptic or tactile geographies of the city have also been reshaped by the commodification of space, although in divergent ways. Some urban spaces have been smoothed over and levelled out – a

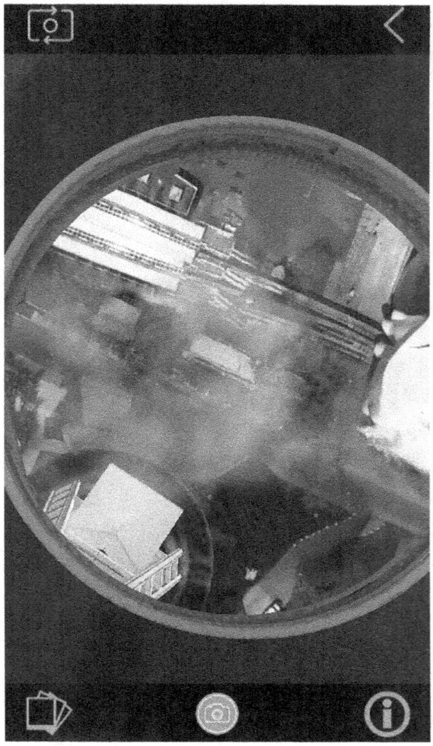

Figure 3.10 Extending the tourist gaze with the *Space Needle* app: the augmented "view below" through a "space spot."

(Image credit: the author, created using the *Space Needle* app).

process whereby textures, contours, and waste matter are removed from these environments to facilitate uninterrupted movement (Edensor, 2007: 219) – while others have had textures and contours added to make them as uncomfortable as possible (Davis, 1992: 160–161). The urban tactile environment cultivates in citizens a bodily awareness of the city's inhospitable character. The hardness of pavement and the chill of concrete, for example, give us the sense that the city street is designed for moving through, not for lingering (Degen, 2008: 42). Due to the density of the modern city, however, the "fear of touch" that may help drive this ethics of spatial mobility (Sennett, 1994) is perpetually at odds with the near inevitability of touching other bodies in the crowded metropolis (Urry, 2000: 395).

The practice of touring the city likewise involves a complex negotiation between touching and not touching (Merchant, 2011) – between the furtive pleasure of touch and its status as transgressive act (Obrador-Pons, 2009) – something that can become fundamental to the way destinations are explored. Tourists employ all manner of tools to negotiate touch in nature, for example – from sunscreen, to clothing, to walking trails and other modes of transportation (Markwell, 2001). In museum studies, the negotiation of touch in touristic endeavours has been identified as a key pathway for practitioners and researchers seeking to reduce the alienating qualities of the gaze, since the experience of touching and being touched enhances our sense of "withness" with other people and other things (Clintberg, 2014: 320; van Hoven, 2011: 43; Obrador-Pons, 2009). This courting of touch has interesting implications for the practice of taking the museum to the street.

Launched as a companion to the successful *Streetmuseum* app we previously discussed, *Streetmuseum Londinium* aims to unearth Roman London for its users by not only staging AR tableaus around historic points of interest, but also offering users the chance to dig for the past. The premise of *Streetmuseum Londinium*'s "digging for the past" is that the user can uncover digital representations of artefacts (based on the Museum of London's actual collection) in various places around the city. Clicking on a "dig" icon at these sites, you run your finger over the image of an unobtrusive plot of dirt until you eventually unearth an artefact (see Figures 3.11 and 3.12). There is a "collect them all" element to this feature (to reference another popular locative app, *Pokémon GO*), and the anticipation of unveiling these artefacts – and the satisfying trumpet's herald that sounds whenever an item is uncovered – lends itself to the gamification of the tourist experience.

The version of touch offered here lacks nearly any resistance – or even a sound that would suggest resistance, like the grating of sand over a clay pot

Figure 3.11 "Digging" for the past with *Streetmuseum Londinium.*
(Image credit: *Streetmuseum Londinium*, © Museum of London).

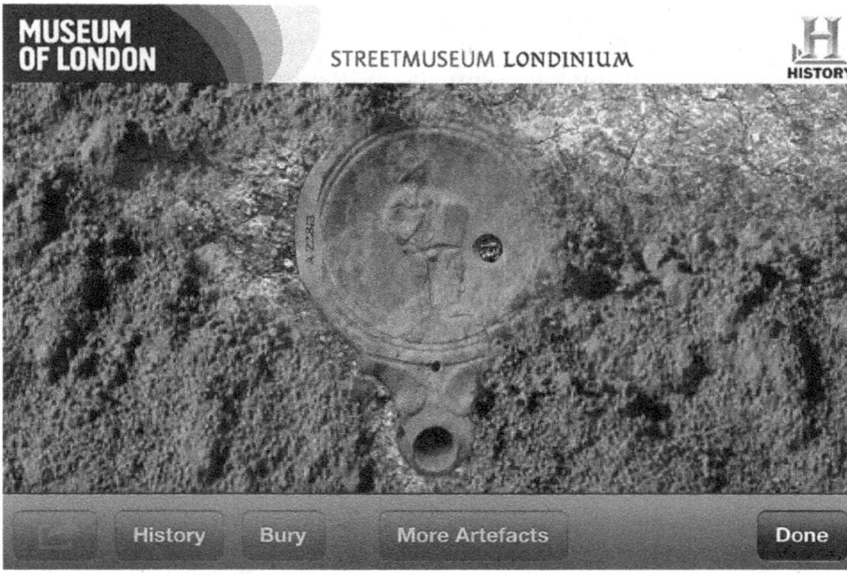

Figure 3.12 An artefact is (virtually) revealed on the site as the user sweeps away the digital dirt with their fingers.

(Image credit: *Streetmuseum Londinium*, © Museum of London).

or metal object. The experience of uncovering the artefact is unhindered – smooth. The subtle drag of skin over glass is all that is encountered. Touch is an essential part of archaeological discovery and the process of contextualising objects, right down to rubbing the soil in a bit of spit to determine its composition (clay is sticky, silt is soapy, sand is gritty). By comparison, the technological re-contextualisation and re-discovery of artefacts – or, rather, their digital ghosts – seems rather impoverished, converting a rough texture into its smooth simulation. This corresponds to a variety of other technological actions that have been "smoothed out" when they are folded into the capacities of the smartphone and its glassy exterior. As Howes and Salter (2018) put it, we live in a "touch-impoverished world" (382) wherein most touch devices:

> actually keep all of their content behind a smooth pane of glass, and that content is not addressed to the fingertips in any ways, but to our eyes and ears. There was a lot more tactility to the old rotary dial or even touch-tone phones. The iPhone, which is designed to be "intuitive," has taken all the resistance out of touching things, and rendered communication textureless.
>
> (383)

Digging for the past in *Streetmuseum Londinium* is thus an extension of existing practices of easing resistance and the smoothing out of activities on the phone – from the rotary dial to the archaeological excavation. It also speaks to how the experience of touch in the city has, itself, been smoothed out and sanitised (in this case, virtualised); the focus on mobility in the modern city leads to the urbanite being whisked between sites in such a way as to minimise contact (Sennett, 1994). At the same time, *Streetmuseum Londinium* makes the past – something rather resistant to touch – "touchable" even by approximation, in the same way that a person might touch the glass case of an artefact when displayed inside the museum (Classen, 2017), evoking connection and leaving a digital fingerprint. Of course, one might argue that the average tourist is highly unlikely to encounter an open-air excavation – particularly in the middle of a city street – so this smoothed-out approximation is likely as good as it gets.

This smoothed-out re-enactment does speak to the value that has been attributed to "exploration" and engagement of users in re-enchanting historical objects (by situating them in place). The gamified element of the experience (which requires user interaction and offers an audio reward) also adds to the interactive quality of the experience, and transforms what would likely be just one small part of a display of assorted artefacts – to be glazed over and ambled past behind glass – into unique waypoints worthy of individual attention. By a combination of their recontextualisation and the fact that they must be touched to be seen, these objects are re-enchanted, and thus become worthy of sight. (If the Museum of London has its way, perhaps even in person.)

While the smoothed-out version of touch in *Streetmuseum Londinium* seems partly designed to re-entrench the "empire of sight" within museums, touch also gets incorporated into a variety of other tours. There is the touch of the dead and passing spirits, which is a key part of locative ghost tours (which we will examine shortly), but several of the apps studied also invite users to touch the city through what might be thought of as lucky objects. Lucky objects are not uncommon in tourism practice. For example, rubbing David Hume's toe for luck is a necessary part of any Royal Mile tour in Edinburgh (see Figure 3.13). The burnishing of these lucky objects through touch, interestingly enough, seems to invite more fingers to caress them. (Hume's golden toe sticks out like, well, a sore thumb, drawing in passers-by). Where an object has been obviously touched by others, it transforms into a site of permissible touch in a city that often seems designed for the eyes, rather than the fingers.

Locative apps can play a role in enhancing the acceptability of touch in these sites. Rachel the Piggy Bank – one of the geotagged destinations of the *STQRY* public art tour in Seattle's Pike Place Market – is a favourite to rub for good fortune, or for children (and one imagines the odd adult) to climb atop. The idea of touch as bestowing luck is on even more obvious display in the city of Dublin, where a great stone inside St Audoen's Church is regaled as a famous well of good fortune that people graze, rub, and even hug in search of luck (*StoryMap Dublin*). The *StoryMap* narrator of St Audoen's great stone compares it favourably to the more famous Blarney

Figure 3.13 Traces of others on Hume's (lucky) toe, Edinburgh.

Stone, which visitors must literally bend over backwards to kiss. The stone at St Audoen's, he notes, has all the luck and none of the pesky potential contamination involved in kissing the stone; his story thus conveys both the value and the dangers of touch in one shot.

Locative apps can therefore play a role in giving users "permission" to touch objects where touch might otherwise be taboo, as can be the case with gravestones and public artworks. As such, they help script which parts of the city are for touching and which are best apprehended through sight alone.

There are all manner of incidental and even necessary versions of touch involved in touring as well, which contribute to the atmosphere that tours attempt to build but are not necessarily part of their overt narratives. The most notable example is the notion of the city sensed through the feet (Crouch, 2000; Crouch & Desforges, 2003; Ingold, 2004). Feeling the contours of cobblestones through the soles of my leather boots – worn thin by years of locative walking tours – is a painful if necessary reminder that I am constantly "in touch" with the city while using these apps. For me, walking cobblestone streets with the app thus (literally) grounds the "time-travel" experience. Not unlike Hume's burnished toe, pathways can also betray traces of people who came before us – the aura of time and of others – through places that get worn underfoot. Take, for example, the sill stones on the threshold of Edinburgh closes, marked by deep grooves that betray the passage of countless feet and considerable time. Beyond what the app tells you, you can sense these flows through the uneven streetscape beneath your feet. When the locative narrative of a place is bolstered by history sensed through the soles, it gives new meaning to de Certeau's (1984) concept of the street as stories told on foot.

Other(ed) senses in tourism

Since our tour of locative tourism apps will shortly take a multisensory tack, it seems worthwhile to address the role of the other – and other(ed) senses – in tourism. Beyond the gaze – extended or otherwise – taste is the sense to which tourism studies has arguably paid the most attention. Food tourism "writes the body into tourism" and is a multisensory tourist performance that includes but does not privilege the gaze (Everett, 2009: 337). Food tourism often allows tourists to consume landscape and the produce of that landscape simultaneously – for example, eating seafood while overlooking the harbour – forging stronger connections between body and land (344), and between bodies eating together (Calvino, 2005: 307). However, Germann Molz (2007) argues that food tourism is less about consuming a particular place or culture than "performing a sense of adventure, adaptability and openness to any other culture" (77). Food tourism also turns the gaze back on the tourist. Everett (2009) notes, for example, that culinary destinations often contain viewing windows for watching people eat (338), while Germann Molz (2007) describes Beijing bug vendors giggling in delight and anticipation at seeing tourists consume their wares (85). In addition to taste and sight, smell is also crucial to the experience in food tourism, not only because of its centrality to taste but also because it helps create immersive experiences (Everett, 2009).

Smell has also been given some attention in tourist research because of its connection to memory (van Hoven, 2011: 43). An overemphasis on the gaze can mask the way that aromas give tourist destinations a unique character (Dann & Jacobsen, 2003: 3). The smell of a place can also disrupt the sanitised image of the gaze, since smells do not always live up to expectations. One traveller recalls the Coliseum, for example, smelling like "one big urinal" (Dann & Jacobsen, 2003: 15). Consequently, the management of smellscapes has become a key element in making tourism spaces more attractive for consumption. Heritage tourism destinations are expected to maintain the infrastructure of their past while banishing the more "malodourous" qualities of the times they reference (Dann & Jacobsen, 2003: 17). However, not all tourist smellscapes are managed or inauthentic, and distinct smells can be one of the aspects of a place that make it most memorable (van Hoven, 2011: 33). Furthermore, smells that might otherwise be considered widely unpleasant – such as the smell of bear faeces – can be recontextualised in the tourist endeavour to be exciting when they signal promised attractions (i.e., bears) (van Hoven, 2011).

Soundscapes are another component of the way tourists navigate and experience spaces. Since listening is spatially situated (Waitt & Duffy, 2010: 466), soundscapes can have a strong impact on the way tourists make sense of spaces. The altered qualities of sounds underwater, for example, can disorient novice divers (Merchant, 2011: 227). At other times, silences within a tourism landscape are crucial for shaping its perception, as when contentious or otherwise "off-brand" elements of the landscape pass without commentary in a guided tour (Edensor & Holloway, 2008: 492). On a more multisensuous track, Waitt & Duffy (2010) note how the experience of the music festival is not only audiovisual but also a "fleshy experience," threading sound vibrations through body and space and sending tingles up tourist spines (460–467), creating intimate (if brief) connections between people caught up in a fleeting moment of sensory experience (470).

As we discussed in Chapter 1, the realisation of the modern ideal city-as-shopping-mall relies upon creating "blandscapes" of repeated (and thus familiar) images, limited aromascapes, designed soundscapes, and smooth surfaces (Edensor, 2007: 19). As a result, the stylised and sensationalised cities of the late consumer capitalist "experience economy" (Pine & Gilmore, 1999) are increasingly in the business of selling ambience (Degen, 2008: 30), meaning that designer sensescapes are now being delineated within the city for tourist consumption. Arguably one of the most interesting facets of locative tourism applications is the extent to which they add "texture" back into these apparently smoothed-over urban facades – layering select multisensory landscapes over the city in lieu of those sensations that have been edited out. These curated sensescapes then bump up against the sensory diversity in the city that has not quite been designed out. Things get especially interesting when the "texture" these apps offer is cut from an otherworldly cloth.

Engaging the sixth sense in New Orleans

Any experience of the tourist districts in New Orleans is bound to be strung together with music. Jackson Square, a popular photo destination and the starting point for most horse-drawn carriage tours of the city, nearly always dances to the music of buskers, horses' hooves on the pavement and the sounds of chittering birds (sugared up, no doubt, on the spoils of beignets from Café du Monde across the street). I have come at the beginning of Mardi Gras season, and brassy marching bands pepper the soundscape throughout my wanderings.

Bourbon Street – the most touristy street the app leads me down – is an all-out assault on the senses, even in the early afternoon (when just a ghost of the city's famed nightlife remains). Bar employees act as modern-day town criers, calling out two-for-one shots over a mash of college frat party music blasting from the mostly open street side windows. Doors and windows flung open, New Orleans is a permeable city. Just across the Quarter, on Frenchmen, the music similarly tumbles into the street, but the effect is rather less chaotic – an assortment of jazz numbers that seem somehow complementary, remixed by the porous New Orleans streetscape.

New Orleans' *Wicked Walks* app is effectively a techno-mediated paranormal pub crawl; it aims to guide users through a series of supposedly haunted bars in New Orleans' historic (and tourism-oriented) French Quarter. According to dark tourism scholars, the origins of psychogeography and the Situationist International can likely trace their roots to Parisian pub crawls, so I am in good company on my mission here (Morten et al., 2018). Whereas it has been noted that the role of the tour guide in a more traditional ghost tour acts is to act as a kind of surrogate believer – performing the act of apprehending ghosts in the tourist's stead (Thompson, 2010) – the *Wicked Walks* app invites users to conjure up ghosts with their own bodies. This effectively involves calibrating the body to be a good conduit between worlds – the lifeworld, the app world, and the otherworld. All with a helping hand from a strong cocktail or two.

At times this calibration involves shifting how one sees. There is a particular way of looking involved in animating the ghost tour – less of a tourist gaze than what might be called a tourist glance (Gibson, 2006; Larsen, 2001), a persistent catching of the world out of the corner of one's eye. Typically, the tourist glance (or "travel glance") is discussed in the context of mobilities studies, as a way of looking that is specific to the tourist on the move. When ghost hunting via a locative tourism app, however, the precarity of position that creates the glance is one of standing on the precipice of experiential worlds, and the sense of an object that can (or does) dematerialise when subject to the full focus of the gaze.

Essential to the adoption of such a glance is the creation of a mood or atmosphere. Buser (2017), examining another ghost-story app that haunts the walls of Bodiam Castle, notes that designers there used things like overlapping sounds and a narrative of urgency to enhance the feeling of in-betweenness and help set the user on edge (10). Haunted-ness is a kind of electric charge of possibility that hangs between the user and the space itself, which primes one to look for things on the periphery of one's vision (quite in opposition to the directness of the tourist gaze). Mirrors and reflective surfaces cause a start and a second glance. Two ethnographic vignettes describe some of the ways that the building of atmosphere in the *Wicked Walks* tour helps calibrate the body towards hauntedness.

On the night *Wicked Walks* brings me to Pat O'Brien's, there's a dampness in the air – it's been raining all day in New Orleans. I sneak a peek on the way in at the fire fountain in the courtyard, where (I'm told) a macabre face will sometimes appear in the flames, but no such ghost appears. After a few sips of the app's recommended cocktail – the bar's famously strong Hurricane – I do feel slightly more suggestible. The dampness in the air and the breeze from the courtyard has me very aware of my skin, the humid New Orleans weather furthering the app's ghost hunt, and making me conscious of every passing chill. Animated by the atmosphere *Wicked Walks* lays over the bar, the dampness in the air takes on spectral qualities when it hits my skin.

At Muriel's across town the next day, the notion of a haunted bar takes on a more lush texture. I am sipping on my cocktail as I make my way up the stairs to "hear" (as *Wicked Walks* puts it) the opulent velvet and tassels of Muriel's séance lounge. The séance room is decked in pillows, mirrors, even more velvet (see Figure 3.14). Reflections bounce across the picture frames and mirrors of the space, one of them slightly askew, and the mood set by the app prompts me to look a little too fast in corners here. I catch a glimpse of a figure in one of the mirrors out of the corner of my eye and do a double take, before realising that I have been spooked by my own reflection and bursting out laughing, the spell now broken.

While ghost tours often rely on building mood through storytelling to turn tourists' bodies into believers (Buser, 2017; Thompson, 2010), *Wicked Walks* overtly prompts the user to employ other-than-visual ways of sensing to achieve that goal. More than once, I find myself smelling for Faulkner's pipe smoke outside a bookstore at the app's suggestion. By my second visit to the author's haunt, I am all but convinced that I can smell it. Either way, the experience is unique – how often does one visit a place just to sniff it? Attuning your attention to your skin – searching for the chill of a passing ghost – also has the unexpected consequence of revealing the oppressiveness of the humid air; New Orleans is a city that is constantly touching you, getting under your skin.

The app does, at times, fail to conjure up the atmosphere required to summon ghosts. As much as the app stirs up the sensory imagination, at times the

Figure 3.14 Feeling for ghosts at Muriel's séance lounge in New Orleans. (Image credit: the author).

user encounters moments of discord that break the spell. The app describes Lafitte's bar, for example, as a pirate haunt lit by candlelight, where glowing red eyes might be seen peering out of the fireplace. When I arrive at the bar on a rainy night, the place is indeed lit by candles, but it is also lit by an electronic jukebox and a handful of televisions broadcasting college basketball. The fireplace is there – mercifully, given the damp weather outside – but no beady red eyes can be seen over the harsh blue light of the television screens. The beer is a local draft, served out of plastic cups, and the atmosphere is decidedly more college hangout (albeit a very old one) than pirate haunt.

Wicked Walks is also intriguing for how little photographic evidence it provides for this paranormal history of the city. It is not that photographs of haunted places do not exist. (I ask the bartender if he has any ghost stories – and he proclaims with a smirk that he has ghost *pictures* – and promptly whips out his phone. One, a vaguely smoky face peering out from the top balcony of a closed museum, stays in my mind.) The app, however, seems to take the perspective that believing is better than seeing when it comes to activating the sixth sense.

Performing place pastiche in Hong Kong

By actively constructing layered, simultaneous spaces, locative tourism apps can take on an element of pastiche. Many applications, for example, promise an experience of time travel, offering tourists the chance to see places as they were, or hear the past by layering images and sounds from times past over places in the present. Various authors have noted the "aesthetic pastiche" quality of sensory tourism – that is, the meeting of various times and places in one space by way of the senses (Dann & Jacobsen, 2003; Everett, 2009; Howes, 2011; Lagerkvist, 2007). For example, Lagerkvist (2007) describes tourist practices of eating the past (or at least a nostalgic representation of it) while gazing towards the future (the technologically advanced skyline of Pudong) in Shanghai (162). The pastiche quality of tourism spaces and representations has been posited elsewhere as contributing to postmodern spectacle space (Urry & Larsen, 2011: 125) and the nostalgic, disembedded quality of photographs (Sontag, 1977). These gaze-centred accounts have tended to describe pastiche as producing a kind of placelessness; however, Lagerkvist (2007) notes that the performance of pastiche often draws upon a variety of senses (including the gaze) in order to summon other times and places into the tourist's experience of a place in the present. As such, these experiences of the virtual are very much emplaced and embodied. There are likely few better places to experience techno-mediated sensory pastiche than in Hong Kong.

Hong Kong's *City Walks* app – produced by the Hong Kong Tourism Board – invites you to "explore Asia's world city" by

> allowing you to experience the busy downtown streets and the colours, sounds and aromas of local markets. You can also find serenity in a

centuries-old temple, get immersed in a bygone era and then step into this dynamic 21st century city to savour the rich contrast of the ancient and the modern.

(*Hong Kong City Walks*)

We can see here the variety of experience – the atmospheric and the sensory – which is supposedly on offer in these walks. This is very much Brand Hong Kong; lacking much in the way of "natural tourism resources," Hong Kong's tourism brand plays up "shopping, dining and cultural heritage," along with its sheer diversity of activities, as its main strengths (Loo et al., 2011).

Firmly on-brand, Hong Kong's locative tours offer a city of polytemporality, of contrast and pastiche. Like the ferries that connect one side of the city's harbour to the other, Hong Kong's attraction lies in the blending of worlds – east meets west, past meets present, old meets new. "Cosmopolitanism" is not only the name of the game – it's the name of one of the tours (*Hong Kong City Walks*). This blending of times and cultures is very much designed to be experienced through the body.

The first locative tour I take in Hong Kong travels through the city's various specialty markets. Not content to be simply the object of the consumer's gaze, the wares of these various markets impose themselves on you as you work your way through the tour. Along the Traditional Medicine Street, aromatic ginseng can be found drying in baskets along the sidewalk that you must dodge as you go. In the flower market, storefronts sprawl out across the sidewalk in a sensual cacophony, demanding that you weave in and out of a mosaic of colour. The flow of pedestrians is halting, and petals and trimmed greenery blanket the sidewalk underfoot – your footsteps are softer here, your path stickier and more fragrant than the concrete before. Scents of the fresh flowers wash over you in waves, none of them waiting its turn. By contrast, the smell of the fish market on a 40-degree-plus day is pungent enough to nearly stop you in your tracks, but you wander in anyway, entranced by the plump tactility of the walls of plastic bags that house the smaller fish – like an overgrown sheet of bubble wrap with tiny captives inside (see Figure 3.15). Vats of boiling oil simmer away with fried delights inches from the sidewalk, breaking up the smell of landlocked fish with something a bit more appetizing.

The real and the fake intermingle at Cat Street (an antiques market), where time-worn novelty playing cards – peeling at the edges from too many hands – are sold alongside scores of identical dragon's-head door knockers that are obviously newly cast but have been given an aged patina. Familiar Hong Kong knickknacks sit alongside merchandise branded with seemingly every American logo possible, chopsticks comingling with a McDonald's Coca Cola smartphone case. The old blends with the new, the "fake" with the "real." A vendor selling carved stone coasters invites me to hold each in my hand and pick the one that feels right to me, that speaks to me. I choose a blue stone dragon – luck and power, he declares, and I wonder if – like a

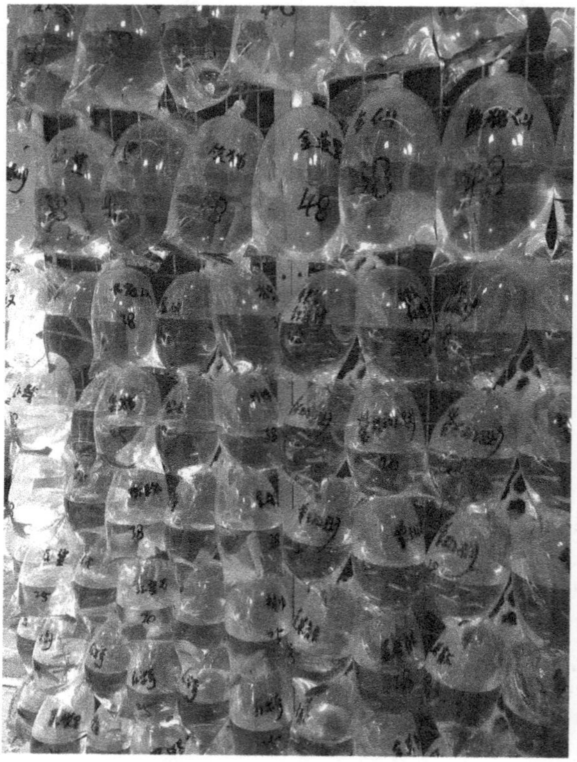

Figure 3.15 Small fish hang in water-filled plastic bags along the stalls of the Hong Kong fish market.

soothsayer in New Orleans' Jackson Square – he reads this less from what is in my hands than what is in my face. The jade market, by comparison, is surprisingly sedate, its cool wares mostly tucked away behind glass, save for a few small beads in baskets by the door for the overtly tactile. This marks a sharp contrast in textures with the raw meat hanging exposed on hooks in the corner butcher stall.

Of the varied markets which the app traverses, the songbird market is the most like entering a different world. The sonic geography changes the moment you walk through the stone pillars into a courtyard. The sound of traffic dims and gives way to a trill of birdsong. Stacked cages of hissing crickets and other feed bugs near the entranceway send a wave of noise sluicing across the courtyard, loud enough to break through the audio narration, demanding that you remove at least one headphone to see what the ruckus is about. (Some environments, it would seem, elicit a reorientation of one's relationship to the technology, rather than the other way around). The space feels walled off to some degree from the rest of the city, with tall trees arching over the market's proceedings. These trees house their own birds, some of which seem to be answering the calls of the

Figure 3.16 Parrots in the Hong Kong bird market – for looking and for listening to, but not for touching.

songbirds in cages below. The app invites users to listen to the songbirds and admire the vibrant plumage of the parrots, but it warns them not to touch (likely to avoid contamination) (see Figure 3.16).

The apps can also engender moments of encounter with the private, particularly in local temples, which is the theme of the second tour I take. The most famous among them, the Man Mo Temple, is fairly well accepted as a tourist destination, but some of the other temples feel much more like an invasion to enter, let alone to photograph. Encounters with incense in the temple feel intimate to an unfamiliar traveller: it invades the nose, it stings the eyes, and one finds oneself touched by the traces of absent worshippers (see Figure 3.17). Owing to the transgressive nature of smell – that is, the extent to which it resists containment (Classen, 2005; Degen, 2008: 44–45; Urry, 2000: 393) – these sacred spaces spill out over their boundaries and out into the streets. Because of that, towards the end of a tour spent hopping in and out of temples – not all of which are spectacular from the outside – you learn to smell your destination before you can see it. By the end, you, yourself, are scented by a thousand absent prayers.[2]

Figure 3.17 Incense hangs in the air at Man Mo Temple.

Exploring Hong Kong through these themed locative apps leads to an embodied experience of cosmopolitanism and difference – a sensorial performance of pastiche. Hong Kong's *City Walks* app weaves these varied sensations together into Brand Hong Kong – a city where all the world's sensations are on the market.

In taking the museum to the street, locative media takes some of the museum's normative aesthetic ordering with it. Users often must adopt a particular position in space to get the app content to line up with the cityscape before them, but, for their trouble, they gain a technologically extended gaze that might peer into the past or through solid walls. Locative tourism apps can often appear to solidify the practices of the tourist gaze – amplifying the sedimentation of photography around particular nodes in the city and directing users to filter out conflicting interpretations of the branded cityscape. However, as some of the apps surveyed in this section demonstrate, locative tours can also provoke users to experience the city in surprisingly multisensory ways (particularly when the cities they mediate are jostling for top ranking in the experience economy).

Notes

1 What McKay calls "a peculiar petit-bourgeois rhetoric of lobster pots, grizzled fishermen, wharves and schooners" that seems to mark Canada's (east coast) Maritime Provinces as a collectively themed space.
2 The same could likely be said of a long day on the fish market street, but it makes for a slightly less poetic description.

4 Performance

In this chapter, we turn our attention to the stage of the locative tour, exploring how the city and its inhabitants "act back" in relation to the mediation of the tour. The first section, "In Place, Out of Sync," explores the embodied rhythm(s) of locative tourism, including the glitches and discordances that tend to occur when the app confronts other rhythms circulating in the cityscape (be they touristic or more mundane). The next section, "Ruin and Mastery," examines conflicting narratives about urban change and development in locative apps like Melbourne's *Lost! 100* and *Along the Yarra*. Finally, "Encountering the Other in Layered Space" describes how performing the locative tour can reveal othered histories (and othered people) within the city, effectively multiplying the readings of the map.

In place, out of sync: the rhythms of the locative tour

Orientation and disjuncture

Most of our discussion of how locative apps extend the senses and modulate spatial experience has focused on correspondences – cases where an app mediates the environment in a relatively seamless way. However, as I have hinted at, much of the experience of locative tourism apps is punctuated by instances where things do not go as planned – instances where the digital and geographical layers of spaces cannot be merged by the body of the user (or, at least, not without some effort). These gaps and seams in the locative tour can expose some interesting elements of touristic and broader spatial practice – especially as regards the polyrhythmic quality of urban spaces – that might otherwise fly under the radar.

The potential for disjuncture between the content of locative apps and the environments they mediate is well acknowledged in the existing literature on locative apps as artistic interventions (McGarrigle, 2010; Townsend, 2006; Tuters & Varnelis, 2006). In fact, some locative projects examine the critical potential of courting that very possibility of disjuncture and disorientation, by, for example, layering the maps of entirely other cities over a given city and asking the user to navigate the urban using that map, tracing, say, the geography of Baghdad over the streets of New York (Flanagan, 2007).

DOI: 10.4324/9781003142386-7

The intent behind these types of apps is often to invoke the "other ways of walking" so prized by the Situationists and psychogeographers (Tuters & Varnelis, 2006). Within these artistic interventions, disorientation is conceived of as a state of being which is (potentially) productive of creative reorientation and reimagining of space. By intentionally disorienting participants, locative artists have attempted to spur users to think about, use, and imagine the spaces of daily life otherwise (Flanagan, 2007). This is not to say, however, that locative media is inherently subversive. Taking play onto the pavement is not, as Flanagan (2007) puts it, "a defacto act of empowerment" (7).

While some notable artistic interventions have used locative technology to get users to rethink spaces and spatial practice (Flanagan, 2007; Tuters & Varnelis, 2006), disorientation in the locative tour rarely seems to be intentional in nature, let alone revolutionary. Rather, the disorientation experienced here is a product of what we have previously discussed as the "alignment work" (Licoppe, 2016) required for the app content and the city street to meet in the technologically extended body of the tourist.

Locative media's transition from artistic interventions (often bent on unsettling the map) to commercial applications (which depend on the smooth intersection between city and map to facilitate pleasurable user experiences) has been far from an easy one. Technological challenges – including gaps and lag in GPS coverage – can often disrupt the taken-for-granted "objectivity" of the locative map (Farman, 2014; Oppegaard & Grigar, 2014; Ritchie, 2014). Furthermore, experiencing disjuncture with the map can expose the changeability of the locative narrative, the latter of which is fundamentally dynamic because it "relies on the negotiation of the user between material and digital spaces, selves and representations" (Didur & Fan, 2018; see also Fan, 2017; Peacock, 2005). Thus, even if the disorientation these gaps and seams provoke is unintentional, the resulting disjuncture between the app world and the street world can bring both the technology and the space it mediates into sharper focus. We can begin to understand the affects of this discordance by attending to the rhythm of the locative tour.

Rhythms and the city: falling out of place and out of pace

As discussed in Chapter 1, the way we move through the city is shaped by a dominant socio-spatial ethos which has branded mobility as a public good (Cresswell, 2010; Sheller & Urry, 2006) and has increasingly smoothed over urban environments to facilitate uninterrupted movement (Edensor, 2007: 219). The design of the city often cultivates in its citizens an embodied awareness that public space is for moving through, not lingering in (Degen, 2008: 42; Lynch, 2021). The cultural value attached to tourism reflects this idea of mobility as a public good (Sheller & Urry, 2006; Urry, 1990). As such, examining the processes that shape the act of "touring" – that is, consuming a place by moving through it – can help us understand broader patterns of mobility and urban waymaking.

One of the key ways that scholars have tacked the multisensory experience of urban mobilities is through an analysis of rhythm (see, for example, Edensor, 2007; Hetherington, 2013; Hornsey, 2010; Lefebvre, 2004; Wunderlich, 2008). In *Rhythmanalysis*, Henri Lefebvre (2004) notes that the everyday is awash in nested cyclical and linear rhythms, a dialectical relationship through which time and space reinforce one another (8–9), and in processes of repetition that maintain the normative flow of society (6). Nevertheless, Lefebvre suggests that rhythms reveal to us an order – a production of the world wherein political power can be found (32). We learn the habitual rhythms of societies, and thus how to come together and be together in particular ways through repetition – or what Lefebvre calls dressage (41–43). Bearing this concept in mind, we can examine how locative tourism conditions certain ways of moving through the city, but also how the rhythms of those locative tours clash with other rhythms that simultaneously pulse through urban life (bearing witness to what Lefebvre [2004] referred to as polyrhythmia).

Tour sites often have distinct rhythms, bound by the cyclical movement of groups in and out, shaped by streetscapes designed for mobility and consumption, and channelled around photographic hotspots (Edensor, 1998). Take, for example, an Old Montreal street. The pace of foot traffic here, especially in the summertime, is ambling. People tend to walk at a pace that luxuriates in the atmosphere of Montreal. Walking down the touristic thoroughfare of St Paul Street, the streets and sidewalks are too narrow to allow the bob and weave of someone on a mission, and if you are used to walking quickly, this can be an infuriating experience. People – particularly women in heels – traverse the uneven cobblestones with care, while children – loathing to be held by hand – stretch their bodies across the paths and crane their necks. This is a place that sells the allure of being there – where walking the street is meant to be part of its charm. This is hardly the urban gauntlet of Mike Davis's (1992) imagining, where the city "bristles with malice" (154), but it is nevertheless a site where the only real places to stay are places to buy. Tuck into a shop, by all means – but stop in the middle of the street, and one quickly finds oneself an obstacle in a slow-moving wave.

This is not to say that the rhythms of touristic movement are unitary or uniform. There is polyrhythmia here, as well. Authors such as Edensor and Holloway (2008) and Farías (2010: 389) have argued that, even in most "scripted" or "staged" forms of tourism mobility, improvisation and interruption can be found. Elements of the less-extraordinary often intrude into the "montage of attractions" (Farías, 2010: 396; Edensor & Holloway, 2008: 492), and pauses – whether planned or unplanned – work with flows to craft the uneven rhythm of the tour (Edensor & Holloway, 2008: 499). Farías (2010) notes how traffic jams interrupt the flow of sightseeing bus tours and force tour guides to improvise, incorporating more mundane, less "signposted" elements of the environment into the fold of the tour (396). The less-than-spectacular is thus always intermingled with the spectacular, just as mobility is interspersed with moments of immobility.

One of the easiest ways to sense the contrasting flows of the tourist environment is to simply walk the streets of a tourist district. Tourist rhythms can be more chaotic than one might expect, owing to the combination of distracted gaze, people following the traffic rules of their own respective countries, and stopping for photographs. This is such a persistent problem that apps like Melbourne's *Museum Victoria Tours: Walk Through History* advise tourists in the app guide to keep to the left of that city's (mixed-use) sidewalks to avoid running into others.

Locative apps can also vary significantly in the way they move users through space. In fact, the chief allure of several apps I encountered lies in the fact that they adopt different rhythms and pathways to the conventional tour. Apps like San Francisco's *Detour* market themselves as moving off the beaten path within cities – with creator Andrew Mason dubbing his app the "un-tour."[1] Compared to many of the tours studied here, *Detour* relies more heavily on audio than on visual augmentation and also has built-in audio cues that condition users to walk their tour to a given particular beat. This dressage (Lefebvre, 2004) comes in two forms, one more direct than the other. The first is the music that often plays behind the action as you walk. This music is used to signal the "time travelling" journey of the app – *Detour*'s "Haight-Ashbury" tour makes the shift from brassy big band to the electric grooves of the swinging sixties, for example, to temporally signify the cultural revolution unfolding on the neighbourhood's streets. The second form of built-in dressage is a series of audio cues that urge you to keep moving. Walk in the wrong direction, and the audio narration stops. Stay too long in one spot, and the narrator will urge you to continue. Movement is what beckons the narrative – if you want to learn more, you have to keep moving. *Detour*'s location-based capacities of are among the most sophisticated and seamless that I encountered during my fieldwork, and yet it seems primarily to use those capacities to keep users moving along the route of the tour.

In Dublin, meanwhile, the authors of that city's *Story Map* have enabled what are called "rambles" in their app. While users can explore the map and the app's geotagged stories at their leisure, *Story Map* allows users to choose two given points on the map, after which the app will generate a route of stories between those two points – a ramble. It is worth noting that the term "rambling" evokes not just a manner of walking, but the Irish concept of a rambling house – a temporary venue for local storytelling and other entertainment (Lyden, 2006). Commonsensically, one can either ramble through the city or "ramble on" about it – in this case, both. "Rambles" are thus a particularly apt, and particularly Irish, way of describing a tour that merges storytelling with walking – a tapestry of yarns woven together on foot.

As Tom Rowley, one of the *StoryMap's* authors, describes it,

> Walking around the city – everyone has their own stories that they remember on certain streets, stories that flavour their personal experience of the city, that they tell on to friends. We thought it'd be exciting

> to pool those stories in one place, like one big pub where everyone shares their stories, creating a sense of what the city means to Dubliners.
> (*StoryMap*)

The taste metaphors here are notable – stories add flavour to streets and can be drunk in the digital watering hole of "charm and character" that *StoryMap* was designed to provide. The designers also describe it as a "collective vision" of the city – that is, a view of the city from a variety of local perspectives – and evidently one that is meant to be savoured.

Consequently, touring the *StoryMap* invokes a particular rhythm – not only in the exploration of the map, but in the telling of stories. The stories are not especially streamlined – many of them revel in detail; they are meant to take the long way around. Your rambling guides lead you down alleyways, in and out of churches, and sit you down for a solid half-hour tale – long enough for a pint – with some local characters in a corner pub in the Liberties (a local working-class neighbourhood, somewhat off the beaten track from Dublin's usual tourist haunts). This pace and manner of walking is, in that respect, as much a commentary on the culture of Dublin as the stories themselves.

Step inside a building, and you may find yourself encountering yet another rhythm or two. For example, *StoryMap* includes a section about the Great Stone in St Audoen's Church that leads me inside the church. There, as I pause to look at the exposed rafters arching overhead, I find myself (inadvertently) on another tour altogether. A guide inside the church sees me perusing the stone walls and peering up at the rafters, hunting for a great stone with app in hand, and inquires whether she can help me find something. We strike up a conversation over the 3-D map of the churchyard, and before I know it, I am on another tour altogether. The local tour guide adds a considerable variety of other "points on the map" to my locative tour – rather than making a pit stop, I wind up wandering around the church, carefully sidestepping the grave markers which the guide points out beneath my feet. By the time I make it to the great stone again, I have already heard one version of its tale.

Not all such overlapping rhythms are so easy to reconcile, however. The *STQRY* public art tour of Seattle's Pike Place Market assumes that you can stop in the market to admire various small pieces of public art. However, on a Sunday in May – Mother's Day, to be precise – the market is packed to the gills with people, and fragrant with endless supplies of flowers that spill out of its walls. Tulips, peonies, seasonal flowers fill my nose, and the crowd funnels me past a piroshky place that smells good enough to make my mouth water. During pauses in the app narration, the market's chit-chat blends together in a persistent hum. The art tour, as it turns out, highlights a fairly mundane visual attraction within a place where visuality is only part of the appeal. At the produce stands, people palm, turn, sniff, and gently squeeze. The stands themselves offer a pointillist tableaux of brightly coloured produce, and slabs of roasted meat and cheese stand displayed on rounds and pillars like edible sculptures (albeit ones still begging to be carved). Neon signs overhead point the way to various gustatory exhibits (see Figure 4.1). Perhaps it is because I am on a public art tour that the neon signs remind me of the neon signs in the entry hall of the Centre Pompidou in Paris, directing visitors to the art museum's various attractions.

Pike Place is part market, part exhibition – a self-aware attraction that is meant to be seen. It has an art museum's halting pace as people stop before stands to admire the goods (though not, as it would happen, before the art I am hunting). The app directs my gaze to several small murals that are by far the least arresting part of a market that boasts singing fishmongers tossing their large wet wares across countertops. I can feel the flow of the crowd, ebbing and rushing onwards between points. It does not know to ebb and flow with the rhythm of the app.

Mobile media has contributed to the eroding boundaries of what were once understood as distinct social realms; modern urban public space is both digital and physical, public and private (de Freitas, 2010; Frith, 2015; Gaye & Holmquist, 2006; Sant, 2006; de Souza e Silva, 2006). The content of a locative app is not accessible to all, and thus the experience of space it offers functions more like the private bubble of a "personal soundtrack" (Thompson, 2005) than it does an organized tour.

Figure 4.1 From market to museum – neon signage points tourists towards the main attractions in Seattle's Pike Place Market.

(Image credit: Taylor Rooney).

Considering locative tourism as a pseudo-private experience of space sheds further light on the clashing rhythms that users encounter. A user who has had the entirety of the street converted into a museum for his or her pleasure will encounter many more points of interest than the tourist exploring the more conventional "signposts" of the imageable city (Urry, 1990). As such, the app user may often be at odds with the conventional rhythms of the urban street, especially in areas where the primary flow of people is not for tourists at all (for example, along Christchurch's High Street, which, during weekdays, is more commonly used as a construction zone – see Chapter 5).

The extent to which the locative tour bumps up against contradictory rhythms can also vary wildly over the course of a single day. Various authors have noted that the movement of coach tours through destination space tends to follow a cyclical schedule, and those rhythms come to infuse the atmosphere of tourist attractions (Edensor & Holloway, 2008; Farías, 2010). Take, for example, the Shrine of Remembrance in Melbourne, which features in that city's *Heritage Vic* and *Our City* apps. The Shrine is evidently a place that looms large in the imagination of the city, and – to look upon its stately exterior (see Figure 4.2) – there is little wonder why.

Figure 4.2 Melbourne's stately Shrine of Remembrance in a moment of quiet between tours. The Shrine is a common stop on tours of the city – locative and otherwise.

The site conveys its own import with the manicured grounds and pathways leading up to the tiered steps, atop which the Shrine sits regally, decked in classical architectural flourishes that leave it looking something between a mausoleum and the Parthenon. (According to the *Our City* app, the Shrine was, in fact, inspired by the ancient Mausoleum at Halicarnassus). The apps note the solemnity of the site as well as the status of the monument as an object of real affection amongst the local populace; it reportedly "reflect[s] the community's ongoing need for a public expression of grief and commemoration" (*Heritage Vic*, Department of Environment, Land, Water and Planning, 2016).

At night, floodlights bathe the Shrine in warmth – a golden jewel amongst Melbourne's greenery on the south side of the Yarra River. In addition to its imposing architecture, the Shrine offers a few other attractions to the tourist – there is a museum in its guts, and the view of the Melbourne skyline from the Shrine's steps is hard to beat. User-uploaded images on the *Heritage Victoria* app often showcase these dramatic sightlines back towards the downtown. Near dusk on one of the days I am visiting, I look out at the skyline, golden and blue, and the courtyard warming itself by eternal flames. The space is all but deserted, peaceful, and its pathways uncluttered except by the odd pedestrian who seems to stroll through on their way home from work.

That is, until a tour bus arrives. Suddenly the pathways from the street are full of people, stopping and clotting in uneven rhythms – sometimes just to look, often to take photos. Eventually, many of the tourists make their way up to the steps beside me to pose with the stone lions that guard the Shrine. Others have their friends take photos as they jump (repeatedly) before the stately columns, aiming for a perfectly curated shot of "spontaneity." The solemn atmosphere curated by both the architecture and the app is broken. Tourists – en masse – bring their own atmosphere with them.

Performing the glitch

If we accept that technology "becomes visible in the moment of breakdown" (Suominen et al., 2018), then moments of glitching simultaneously expose our connection and disconnection from the technological networks within which we are enmeshed. The glitch exposes not only our relationship to the mobile device (as an imperfect approximation of ourselves) but also to the wider technological networks that facilitate global positioning (Wi-Fi, cell towers, and satellites) and to the brick-and-mortar elements of the environment that can inhibit seamless connections to those networks (tall buildings, for example). Glitching involves not only falling out of step with the rhythm of the street, but falling out of sync with the technological network – to be misplaced according to mechanical sensors and experience the tangible disorientation of being not so much lost in the city as lost *to* the (smart) city.

The glitch as a potentially productive disruption of rhythm has been explored by media artists – using the medium of the CD to make the conditions of the production of sound perceptible – to bring the CD into focus by, for example, scratching it and capturing the resulting discord (Kelly, 2009). "These artists took the passive and transparent tools of playback and manipulated, cracked and broke them into new forms for creating original compositions" (Kelly, 2009: 40). The tools of playback – the technology – thus came sharply into view (or, rather, into sound). Consequently, if we consider the city encountered through the locative app as a soundscape, glitches expose the technologies and the trifold "tools of playback" that bring it into being – the city, the body, and the mobile device. Much like the experiments with "productive" disorientation that were a key feature of early locative art, moments of glitching – of finding one's rhythm of movement interrupted by the jarring effect of being both lost *in* the city and lost *to* the city – can still offer critical potential even when they fail to conjure the desired effect.

Performing the glitch with the locative app tends to lay bare the intersection between the app, the body, and the urban environment. To experience being out of place within a locative app is to become aware of the (taken-for-granted) precision of GPS tracking and/or the imprecision of its application. There are times when the app places you across a wide city boulevard, or where tall buildings mean that you cannot "pick up" a virtual object or activate a pin because the application believes you are not "in place" – even when you are. (Farman [2014] describes the disorienting experience of a map mis-placing him in Boston, for example). This forces users to reposition themselves in such a way that they reconcile the app with the environment. This reorientation illuminates how the technology is not simply an extension of the self, but rather the extent to which the user is an extension of the technology, and a conduit between digital and physical space – responsible for "giving birth to the world" (Hansen, 2006: 5).

There are thus felt contradictions between the "fixity" of apps and the rapidly changing urban environment. We experience obsolescence through our bodies, feeling the difference between the city described and the city encountered. While many locative tourism apps fail to account for their evolving settings – and suffer the glitchy consequences – some apps opt to engage directly with these processes of urban change and development.

Ruin and mastery: narratives of change and development

Rapid change is a defining feature of urban life. In their book *Urban Fortunes*, Logan and Molotch argue that the development of the city is neither neutral nor inevitable, but driven by the capitalist mantra that growth equals success, no matter its demands or effects (Logan & Molotch, 2007: xv; see also Molotch, 1976). Under this model, place as a whole is commodified and places in particular become stratified according to the "ease with which they can attract capital" (Logan & Molotch, 2007: 12). The city under advanced capitalism needs to create new markets for consumption within the metropolis (Castells, 1976; see also Christopherson,

2008: 414). This need for new markets, particularly in the economic climate of the post-Fordist city, has driven a surge of urban redevelopment around cultural consumption (Logan & Molotch, 2007; Zukin, 1995).

We can think of the architecture of the city as engaged in the ongoing re-presentation of its past and present (Sorkin, 1992; Zukin, 1989, 1995). Heritage organisations have given shape to this urban narrative, acting as an authority on what parts of the city's history should remain constant throughout rapid change and redevelopment (Zukin, 1995). As the heritage of the city is selectively preserved, its streets begin to tell a cleaned-up version of their own stories – the fragmented histories of the urban smoothed over in favour of picturesque streetscapes full of "historical character" (Zukin, 1995; Sorkin, 1992; Boyer, 1992). However, this process of development and selective remembrance rarely goes uncontested.

This section examines some of the stories that locative apps tell about the development of cities like Melbourne and San Francisco over time. These diverse narratives expose contrasting perspectives on the perils (or virtues) of redevelopment and shed light on how cities developed for cultural consumption perform claims of authenticity for tourists.

Contrasting narratives of development and change in Melbourne

Although the changing metropolis often disrupts the narrative rhythm of locative tours, not all apps treat disjuncture between the 'real' and digital layers as hazardous. Rather, for some, the rapid rate of change within the city is entirely the point. Take, for example, *Melbourne's Lost! 100* app, commissioned by Victoria Heritage, which uses the locative app's favourite trick of layering old photos over new sightlines to make a point about the erasure of heritage buildings from Melbourne's shifting city landscape. The heritage buildings in *Lost! 100* are cast as an threatened species (down to a category of "endangered" buildings. The app also takes full advantage of the ghostly nature of its projections, allowing users to change the opacity of the image to allow the buildings' replacements to peer through. This visual trick enhances the sense of loss, while the use of black-and-white photos (even for the more contemporary buildings) lends credit to the notion of heritage and the value of time (see Figure 4.3).

Melbourne's Lost! 100 also marks another possibility for the locative app when it comes to avoiding obsolescence. Users can submit their own stories around particular sites, a feature which evidently caters more to locals than to tourists, but which helps lend a sense of a lived-in authenticity and richer oral history to the buildings in question. One man, for example, relates the story of his father taking him to the top of a given building to look out, thus imagining the view from that building as part of its loss. This feedback tool allows users to point out elements of disjuncture between the app and the environment, effectively updating the app as they go along. When one of the endangered buildings falls prey to redevelopment, one user simply writes, "another one gone!"

Figure 4.3 Heritage haunts the streetscape in *Melbourne's Lost! 100*.
(Composite photo created using *Melbourne's Lost! 100*. Archival image credit: "National Mutual Building north side, upper central Collins Street, Melbourne, 1965, 2" by Wolfgang Sievers, © National Library of Australia).

For *Melbourne's Lost! 100*, these new narratives of loss usually serve to strengthen the app's overarching narrative. At times, however, this user-created content injects an element of precarity into the narrative, fracturing the unifying vision of the tour. While many of the stories that users attach to *Melbourne's Lost! 100* take the same reverent and mournful tone as the app towards lost buildings, some of them undercut the value that has been assigned wholesale to heritage buildings. The "Gas and Fuel Corporation Building," for example, evidently had a reputation exactly as glamourous as its name would suggest, given the number of derisive comments attached to the entry. As one user writes: "Boy am I glad that this ugly edifice faced its extinction, the square has a better and more meaningful hub these days" (Joseph, user, *Melbourne's Lost! 100*)

The smell of progress

Smell (and its attempted eradication) is part of the civilising narratives that many heritage-based apps forward. Museums Victoria's "The Golden Mile" tour in Melbourne, for example, discusses an early point in the city's history (1890) where the city was still lacking in sewers, when "male tenants were obliged to relieve themselves in corrugated iron urinals at the back of the ornate, Gothic-style Rialto building. Bad smells and rampant typhoid inspired one wit to re-christen the city 'Marvellous Smellbourne'"

(Museums Victoria, 2016). Nevertheless, the urinals were preserved by Victoria's Heritage Council. Across other apps in Melbourne, the portrait of the city's characteristic alleyways shifts from open-air sewers and drainage to quaint café culture hotspots that smell of flat whites and pastries. This purification of smell evokes a particularly aromatic narrative of change, one where the erasure of unpleasant aromas is seen as a definitive marker of progress (Classen, 2005).

Other apps also recall the smell of the city's past for users, in a move that seems designed to help visitors gain a more intimate feel – or, rather, smell – for the character of life in a given time and place. Not all such scent memories are particularly pleasant. Evocations of Christchurch's industrial past – before the intervention of heritage organisations smoothed over the space – mean that *High Street Stories* variously describes the putridity of an old meat locker and the pungent aroma of a bottle factory that used to permeate the neighbourhood. These descriptions sit alongside the more palatable descriptions of café culture along the street, each evocation mixing with the ambient scent of the street to form a real-imagined scentscape.

While *Melbourne's Lost! 100* views the development of the city and changing skyline as an unabashed loss (as is clear from its title), another app in the city takes a much more positive view on the shifting urban landscape. Melbourne's Yarra River is a notable gap in the map of *Melbourne's Lost! 100* – a gap made more legible when one considers that the Yarra was a long-underdeveloped site and essentially functioned as a waste reservoir for the city. *Along the Yarra* fills that gap by examining the (seemingly glorious) reclamation of the river – a place "upon which the city had turned its back." The app describes the recent development of the Yarra from urban/industrial wasteland to gentrified strip, notably through the voices of those who drove the neighbourhood's rejuvenation. The app describes how pedestrian bridges and public art works have been installed along the Yarra to aid in this process of gentrification. If the goal of these latter interventions was to drive foot traffic back into the neighbourhood – and thus to weave it into the narrative of the city "from below" (de Certeau, 1984) – the integration of a locative app could only help further this goal. After all, the locative tourism app can turn the experience a gentrifying district into a cultural object – an up-and-coming museum in the street. The positive spin on development in *Along the Yarra* stands in stark contrast to the mournful atmosphere developed by *Melbourne's Lost! 100.*

Absent in both views of Melbourne – that which mourns development and that which praises it – is the history of the Yarra that precedes its devolution into a wasteland. As Mitch Goodwin (2017) notes, the Yarra had served as the lifeblood of the Indigenous peoples native to that area - a conceptualization which is absent from the portrait of the river as having to be reclaimed, and of a city which had turned its back on the river. The exploitation of the river that led to that wasteland – and the subjugation and massacre of the Indigenous peoples that went hand in hand with this exploitation – haunt the background of its narrative. *Along the Yarra* may not engage with spectral imagery to the same extent as its heritage counterpart (*Melbourne's Lost! 100*), but it has its fair share of ghosts.

Nature, civilisation, and simulacra in the locative tour

Narratives of progress and development are not only confined to the built environment; the city's greenspaces are similarly subject to narration in locative apps as attractions and civic achievements. Here, we will briefly examine a variety of ways that locative apps treat nature in the city, from nature as something to be mastered, to nature as a marker of time and absent presences.

More and more, technology is a part of the way we connect with nature (Stinson, 2016; White & Wilbert, 2010). For example, apps are a growing means of identifying vegetation in urban environments (see apps like *PlantSnapp* or *PlantID*). Urban green space is also central to our conceptualisation of what makes a "civilised" or liveable city. Naturally, then, some green spaces have made their way onto the maps of locative tours, most often in the form of parks and public gardens. Apps that fold green spaces into their tours offer a window into the way we perceive and historicise nature in the city, and draw attention to the animating properties of nature and technology alike (Didur, 2014). By weaving the natural into grand tales of the urban, these apps can often illuminate the interplay between nature and civilisation, or what Hinchliffe (2007) calls "socionatures."

San Francisco's *Guidekick: Golden Gate Park* app takes a fascinating dive into the civilisation–nature debate. The app describes the work of "enterprising characters" of the city's past to build from scratch a grand park – modelled after Central Park – to function as the lungs of the city. Breaking ground on Golden Gate Park aimed to put to bed the city's Wild West reputation and mark San Francisco's entree into a "premiere metropolitan city" (*Guidekick: Golden Gate Park*). Man's mastery over nature is framed in the tour as metaphorical for his mastery of the self. This description is typical for the urban planning of the time, where planned green spaces were seen as essential to the development of a well-conditioned citizenry. Parks and other open spaces were not merely signs of civilisation – they were civilisation projects (Deutsche, 1998), not unlike the museum of the time (Classen, 2017).

The app highlights the "planned" nature of the park, with its manicured lawns, high visibility, and carefully curated landscapes, all built on sand dunes. At the same time, the park is depicted as a simulation par excellence; the artificial lake at the heart of the park (Stow Lake) was expertly crafted to, as we are told, "imitate nature" (*Guidekick: Golden Gate Park*, 2016). Walking around the banks of the river, the artificial character that the app ascribes to the park invites the user to look a second time at features like logs rimming the banks. How much of this is "real"? Or, to put it another way, how much of this is "natural"?

Around Stow Lake, the logs grow moss, the turtles (sold by the app as an attraction, described by the locals as an infestation) and the geese move in.

Water trickles over a (natural-looking) boulder, greening it with algae. Only later do I see the seats expertly carved out of the faces of these boulders, worn smooth with time. There are built-in groves for lounging, toppled trees for climbing. High above the lake, a local man points out a feature of the park not marked in the app – herons nesting in a lofty tree. The tall perches of the park's long-established trees have become a natural breeding ground. As time goes on, the 'real' and the 'fake' become inseparable; what exists is neither entirely artificial nor fully wild. Viewed through the app, the park takes shape as an ideal form of "socionatur" (Hinchliffe, 2007) – that is, it lays bare the entanglement of the social and natural worlds (wherein humans both shape and are shaped by nature).

Aside from its notable civilising character, nature in these apps also serves as a marker of the passage of time – something of a useful currency in apps that advertise time travel. The *Historic NOLA* app, for example, strips away decades of tree growth in Jackson Square to reveal the historic buildings behind. In Edinburgh, monuments to man and state alike are blanketed in velvet robes of moss, as plush as a velvet settee in a New Orleans séance lounge. Moss along gravestones obscures names, and water blackens the faces of monuments – securing lives lived firmly in the realm of historical monument. Nature's presence here thus transforms objects of mourning into places fit for consumption; the graveyard becomes a suitable place for touring in part because it is teeming with life.

Plants not only serve to communicate time – they also serve as staging points for other types of urban markup, and nature also becomes a screen for more intimate stories that run parallel to the augmentation of sites by locative apps. One particularly fulsome plant in the Melbourne Botanical Gardens, for example, becomes a site for inscription – where loves and absent presence are marked (see Figure 4.4). When the city and the app are co-authors, user-created content can take many forms.

Narratives of authenticity in San Francisco

In discussing nature, we have seen how apps can illuminate artificiality in their environments, but how might they wade into the fraught waters of "authenticity?" Authenticity has been a key concern of tourism studies since its modern genesis, with scholars like Boorstin (1961) and MacCannell (1973) interrogating the role of authenticity in driving tourism. MacCannell (1973) in particular argued that a search for authentic experience in a world lacking therein is what drove tourists to seek out far-flung destinations. As MacCannell (1973) went on to note, this search lent itself to the performances of authenticity by locals and the reshaping of places to give an illusion of the authentic – a "staged authenticity" (Knudsen & Waade, 2010: 25; MacCannell, 1973). Opinions continue to differ on whether tourists can ever obtain the longed-for authenticity (Knudsen & Waade, 2010) but some scholars have attempted to trouble the notion of a purely object-oriented notion of authenticity, instead expanding the question to

Figure 4.4 Nature as a canvas for other urban inscriptions in Melbourne's Botanical Gardens.

how authentic the internal experience of the tourist is (Wang, 1999). Locative tours – and especially the element of them that touts a "self-guided" exploration – can help tourists capture a sense of authenticity in place while still participating in the much-denigrated touristic endeavour. Media play a considerable role in both conveying this sense of authenticity to tourists at their destination and extending the value of that experience beyond the moment at hand (Knudsen & Waade, 2010).

Rather than moving across the globe to discuss how locative apps intersect with notions of the "authentic" in tourism, we can simply wander up the street in San Francisco, into the city's famed Haight-Ashbury district. Known as the locus for the counterculture movement of the 1960s, present-day Haight-Ashbury is one of San Francisco's biggest tourist draws–that is, an object of cultural consumption itself. The inherent tension between these opposing counterculture and culture-for-consumption identities is at the heart of at least one app mediating the neighbourhood.

The *Detour* in Haight-Ashbury ("Summer of Love") is designed to the reconstruct an "authentic" vision of the iconic neighbourhood – something the app makes no bones about, given that the narrator (actor Peter Coyote) informs you in no uncertain terms that he is going to show you *his* Haight-Ashbury. There is an implied intimacy to the narration – it presents as an eyewitness account to an age of free love and free-flowing drugs from someone in the thick of the counterculture and the neighbourhood as it is now. The *Detour* digs into the contradictions of a section of the city that became famous for counterculture – which now hawks an Instagrammable version of it ("Glitter Beards Here!") – and the extensive commodification of that sentiment in scores of overpriced hippy-lite shops with tie-dye in the windows and designer clothes lining the racks of thrift shops. Walking the *Detour* down Haight-Ashbury, the user confronts a drastically different organisation of space from the one Coyote describes. (*His* Haight-Ashbury revolves around the proposition "What if everything was free?")

Detour's Haight-Ashbury tour strengthens its claim on authenticity by openly denouncing the commodification and stereotyping of the narrator's erstwhile lifestyle. Claiming authenticity here also involves providing a counter-narrative to the writing on the walls – where, for example, the mural of George Harrison is undercut by Coyote's description of the former's evident disdain for the "scene" there in Haight-Ashbury. The mural is thus transfigured – a worthy memorial for a place looking to recapture signifiers of the 1960s without any of the soul.

Yet, the *Detour* cannot avoid the fact that, for all its narratives of authenticity, it is still a means of "selling" Haight-Ashbury, albeit to the visitor on the hunt for the "real" counterculture – as a tourist. The tension involved in walking this tightrope is on full display once the tour arrives at the juncture of Haight and Ashbury Streets, finding the iconic street sign bearing both names. "Go ahead," Peter Coyote all but sneers. "You can take a picture."

Encountering the other in layered space

Henri Lefebvre declared that "the most important thing is to multiply the readings of the city" (1996, in Edensor, 2005a). This section will explore how some locative tourism apps have attempted to do just that through innovative (if variously successful) practices of mapping and countermapping. Locative apps co-presence multiple ways of experiencing urban space, and, as such, open the door for users to encounter narrative "others" – be they other stories or othered bodies. As such, though locative apps may often serve to reinforce the distant gaze of tourism or forward reductionist, branded versions of a location, they also contain the potential for rupture and reorientation.

Multiplying the readings of the city: authorship, mapping, and countermapping

Augmented-reality apps have the dual issue of presenting *content* that obscures its own authorship and operating through *code* that often goes unnoticed and otherwise appears as a "neutral platform" for enabling augmented spatial relations (Graham et al., 2013). In light of this, Graham et al. (2013) argue that we need to make code, the fact of its authorship, and its embedded biases more visible, a task made difficult by the "distributed power of user-generated content" (467). The source of user-generated content is hard to trace, and although the authorship of these platforms is relatively open (in that, hypothetically, anyone could contribute), the "democracy" of the process is "belied by the disproportional power wielded by those with the time, inclination, education, resources and network positionalities necessary to make their ideas visible" (Graham et al., 2013: 469). Just because content is "user generated" does not necessarily mean that everyone's voices and best interests are equally represented.

Nevertheless, user-generated content can contribute to the multiplication of readings of the city (and thus to the contestation of urban spatial meaning) (Graham et al., 2013; Liao & Humphreys, 2015). Liao and Humphreys (2015) found that early adopters and content creators of the AR application Layar were using the app to create a multitude of private and public dialogues around space – to make things easier to find, to memorialise, to challenge dominant spatial meanings and exclusions, and to reinvigorate public space (8–12). Furthermore, they suggest that the creation of layers impacted the way users interacted with the physical landscape more generally, in some cases allowing users to see and engage with the multiplicity of narratives that could be built from the world around them (11).

Following the metaphor of performance, maps can be thought of as a type of "script" for tourist action. Like photographs, maps have often been conceptualised in tourism theory as a "classic means of directing the tourist gaze" (Rossetto, 2012: 1–2), and rely, indeed, upon the illusion of an objective gaze for much of their authority (Farman, 2010). However, the performance turn has moved away from the perspective that maps are closed media that "reduce visitors to passive executors of pre-designed routes" (Rossetto, 2012). Maps rely on tourist performance to be actualised, and the diversification of mapping practices (an influx of new scriptwriters, if you will) may help enable creative and reflexive performances of tourist space.

Mapping is a form of representation which straddles the contested line between "art" and "science." While, for a time, the popular study of cartography suggested that modern map-making had transitioned from subjective "art" to objective "science," cultural geographers and scholars of cartography now generally acknowledge that the practice of map-making remains value-laden and interpretive (Cosgrove, 2005: 51). However, like photographs (Sontag, 1977), the map has been invested with an "aura of authority" (Perkins, 2009: 126) – in everyday practice, we tend to treat the map as a factual reflection of the world (Cosgrove, 2005; Farman, 2010, 2012). Part of a map's power is that its representations are presented as functional, rather than interpretive; the map is expected to line up with reality, because that is the only way it is useful (Farman, 2010: 6; Perkins, 2009). Maps tend to submerge the power dynamics of representation and the contested meanings of spaces under the unitary guise of providing scientifically accurate, and thus useful, renderings of the world (Dwyer, 2003; Shields, 2003).

Conversely, a map is only ever useful if it is edited. In order to make a map legible, decisions must be made about what to include or exclude – at what scale to present information (Dodds & Joppe, 2001: 265). These issues of scale and inclusion and exclusion are nuanced by the introduction of technology – for example, digital maps can zoom in to show more or zoom out to show less, or add or subtract layers of information, putting some of the control regarding inclusion and exclusion in the hands of the user (Farman, 2010). However, the self-evident facticity of the map is seemingly increased when GPS and satellite photography come into play. The development of satellite-imagery-based mapping platform Google Earth, for example, gives the impression of finally being able to see "the world as it is" (Farman, 2010). However, Farman (2010) argues that the glaze of "neutrality" that satellite imagery lays over the map can obscure the ways these maps maintain the status quo by, for example, playing off the totalising gaze and layering (often contested) political borders over the satellite imagery (10).

Tourist maps, offering much-needed orientation for users who, by design, find themselves in unfamiliar landscapes, may lend themselves to particularly uncritical use (DeLyser, 2003: 104). In considering how tourist maps maintain this commonsensical quality, it is important to consider the interplay between various cultural renderings of tourist destinations. As Hanna and Del Casino (2003) note, tourism maps are intertextual – they reflect other spatial meanings that circulate through related forms of representation (xiv), from photographs and guidebooks to the branded facades of destination spaces. Bolstered by circulating representations that pinpoint "must see" attractions, tourist maps may tend to retain many key nodes and a consistent scale over time and multiple iterations. Generally speaking, tourism maps assume that the tourist wants a given scale of inclusion –the (branded) highlights – although "alternative" maps designed for particular tourism niches, such as urban green tourism, are increasingly circulating alongside more conventional versions (Dodds & Joppe, 2001).

However, it is important to note that maps are never complete, not only in the sense that they edit out aspects of the space, but in the sense that maps are performed texts (Perkins, 2009: 127). As Perkins (2009) notes, "spaces and mapping co-constitute one another, produced by and productive of, myriad corporeal practices" (127; see also Hanna & Del Casino, 2003). The ways that tourists perform destination spaces are thus both shaped by and shape the maps of those spaces.

Previous sections have laid bare some of the processes through which sociopolitical meaning is embedded in our representations of space. Looking to the conditions of production of map-making in these cities (as Lefebvre [1991] suggests) can help to contextualise what makes it onto the map and allow us to consider how certain brand identities of the city are furthered by these applications. As the case of Dublin's *Storymap* shows, the organisation of locative maps around the city's tourism brand is not always a purely top-down process.

Reorienting the map in Dublin

The use of Google Maps as a scaffold for many locative tourism projects means that conventional landmarks often lurk in the background, even as the map might attempt to expand the tourist's trajectory or to wander off the beaten path. More direct pressures can also lead to the re-centring of the app on the tourist geography. In developing *Storymap*, for example, the creators initially had planned to focus their storytelling primarily on places off the beaten track – away from the tourist magnet Temple Bar and the city centre. As previously noted, they wanted to keep the focus on personal, intimate storytelling, and one of the creators, Tom, tells me they were particularly keen on sharing the stories of their working-class home neighbourhood, the Liberties.

However, once investors got involved (such as Failte Ireland and the UNESCO City of Literature), many of those more common destination points were reincorporated into the map, and the map's wandering trajectory was snapped back towards the touristic centre. The authors still aimed to emphasise personal stories but frequently encountered challenges there as well. As it turns out, not so many people were willing to tell their own intimate stories of spaces in the city; Tom notes that they were much more obliging when it came to well-worn legends and historical tales, but relaying their personal stories to the world at large had many ill-at-ease. Consequently, the map came to be centred more on the touristic high points than on intimate geographies within Dublin as more stories were added (though the app does still include an admirable number of personal tales amongst the stories of "big name" attractions).

Queering the map in Toronto

One example of the way that locative tourism apps can multiply the readings of the city is in the use of locative apps to forward queer histories of locations throughout the city, as is the case in Toronto's *Queerstory* app. The designers of this app engage in a practice of countermapping, sometimes referred to as "queering space" (Sears, 2001). This kind of application has been deployed in cities from Ottawa to Glasgow, while – in a similar genre – online geo-located, user-generated narratives like Lucas Larochelle's (2018) *Queering the Map* have taken the intimacies of queer spatial storytelling to a global scale.

The gay body – whether conceived of individually or as a community – occupies an especially "urban" location in the popular imagination. Weston (1995) notes that both public depictions (media representations and the branding of gay communities for cultural consumption) and private narratives (coming out stories) tend to describe gays as "in place" in the city and "out of place" in the rural (254–259). As has been noted, there is a tendency when mapping the history of queer lives to cordon them off into acceptable spaces (which are, not surprisingly, then packaged as tourist attractions) (Adler & Brenner, 1992; Weston, 1995). The city is broadly imagined as a gay-inclusive space, whereas, in actuality, cities tend to ghettoise the history and visible presence of the LGBTQ+ community within designated "gay villages" (Adler & Brenner, 1992; Weston, 1995). This can have the effect of invisibilising queer history in other parts of the city.

Toronto's *Queerstory* application attempts to destabilise the ghettoisation of queer history in the city. While the app does engage with multiple points of interest within the Gay Village, the overt goal of the app is to demonstrate the queer lives and histories that echo through sites all around Toronto, and not just in the Village. Apps like *Queerstory* attempt to broaden the conceptualisation of where gay history happens by "queering" the urban narrative – and particularly, the urban map. Simultaneously, by adding intimacy and personalisation – rather than simply the iconographic rainbow flag – these apps can resist the tendency to erase diversity in favour of, as Weston (1995) calls it, the "unitary gay subject."

Even when using *Queerstory* as a standalone app, the extent to which it multiplies the narratives of the city is unmistakeable. The app's creators – non-profit media arts group Year Zero One – clearly meant for it to do just that: "Although Toronto is a city of firsts and an International LGBTQ hub, it has very few visual plaques to celebrate our struggles and triumphs. The *Queerstory* app fills this gap with a series of digital markers documenting our history" (Year Zero One, 2014). The app makes evident how landmarks in the city often overlook marginalized identities, wiping visible traces of their stories off the map. Here, making this history visible is a radical act (Truman & Springgay, 2019). However, it is worth noting that the relegation of such landmarks only to the digital layer marks only partial progress, given that these points remain invisible to any who are not explicitly looking for them.

The potential for these apps to multiply narratives of space becomes even more obvious when an app like *Queerstory* is experienced alongside a more generic "time-travelling" app, such as *Toronto in Time*. Walking routes through each app – first in *Toronto in Time* and then in *Queerstory* – I found myself revisiting certain sites, encountering points of intersection (and thus of layered meaning) between routes traced by each app. Take the example of the 52 Division police station. In the *Toronto in Time* app, this location is a hub for law-and-order narratives of the city. In the *Queerstory* narrative of the space, it was a locus for anger and protest in the wake of the bathhouse raids of the 1980s.

Encountering the other

Given that mobile tourism applications overtly create spaces of simultaneity, they also contain the potential for juxtaposition and rupture. Hetherington

(2013) has discussed this in light of the city as archive. What happens when the "memory" or "reading" of space that is conjured does not line up with the space in its present? What happens when the dynamism and flux of space cannot be held by its static representation? There is critical potential wherever the construction of the map or the archive – and its necessary oversimplification – is exposed by the landscape it proposes to augment (Hetherington, 2013: 28). That which is made "other" by these narratives will find its way in (30).

Among the most common "others" that these walking apps encounter is the homeless body. As I have noted elsewhere, "designing the city as an ideal, pleasurable space for consumption frequently means removing any 'sources of discomfort' for the consumer – including the homeless and panhandlers" (Lynch, 2021: 103; drawing from Kohn, 2004: 6–7). At major tourist sites, the erasure of homeless populations is often strictly enforced, but since locative media tend to multiply the points of interest across the city streetscape, the chances of encountering those who live on the street are high. Two of the apps in question engage with the issue of homelessness in their urban centres, albeit in somewhat tangential ways. Perhaps uncoincidentally, these apps belong to cities where the issue of homelessness is the most pressing and often the most visible; the US Department of Housing and Urban Development has both Seattle and San Francisco in the top 10 cities ranked in terms of homeless populations (US Department of Housing and Urban Development, 2018) – a dubious distinction that makes their presence difficult to narrate around.

Detour engages with the presence of the homeless throughout the two tours I encountered there. One tour ("Beyond the Painted Ladies") addresses it in a folksy way that seems designed to assuage user discomfort at encountering these people. As the app guides you up a pedestrian overpass, it reassures you: "Folks might be sleeping there, just walk on by." This has the effect of incorporating the presence of homeless people into the narrative whilst also smoothing that presence over, thereby facilitating mobility, rather than interruption. It also backhandedly acknowledges the permanence of people inhabiting certain spaces – that is, the sticking power of certain locales as nodes of homelessness, and the extent to which these locales exist in a permanent limbo between the private and the public. In this way, the private–public space of the tour intersects with the private–public space of the pedestrian bridge. This also necessarily raises the complex ethics of attempting to turn such spaces into sites/sights of consumption. One of the potentially unexpected consequences of moving the museum to the street is the need to account for places that are not simply for passing through – to encounter and narrativise the private lives of those who live in the street.

As Brian Greenspan (2011) notes, serendipity – or the encounter of unexpected correspondences – is one dynamic factor that gives locative media a great deal of its charm. Over the course of fieldwork, I had more than my share of serendipitous encounters. One has stuck with me above all the others, however.

Seattle's *STQRY* Public Art tour finishes its run outside of the Pike Place Market, in nearby Victor Steinbrueck Park. The park is a popular meeting place and hangout spot for many in the city's homeless population. Its location beside the popular market also means that this is a site where tourist and homeless populations merge. To one side of the park is a sculpture surrounded by a ring of benches – *The Tree of Life* – which marks the final destination of this tour. As I settle in on one of the benches, a little girl peers up at the Tree of Life and asks her mother what the statue is. The mother tells the girl, "It's a whale!" The girl, delighted, wraps her arms around the sculpture. The mother asks her to repeat the once-spontaneous gesture, so she can take a picture.

The *STQRY* app in hand, I learn a bit more about *The Tree of Life*, which is part of the Homeless Remembrance Project. The thick metal "whale tail" of the tree branches out from a glass base, the rebar roots of the sculpture visible underneath. The top of the tree is missing leaves – they are scattered on the ground around it, each bearing the name of a homeless person who has died. The tree is a testament to hope and loss, a gathering place, and a symbol of the human connection between "homeless and housed." The little girl did not know that she was hugging much more than "a whale," but in retrospect, the moment strikes me as incredibly poignant. I had stumbled across a moment of true serendipity, of the kind so prized by locative media's more artistic incarnations (Khaled et al., 2011). As a touristic experience, though, serendipity resists "pre-packaging," and so the locative tour's more impactful moments often rely on those ephemeral constellations of social relations (Massey, 1994) that make up a place at any given time. You just have to be there (app in hand).

As we have seen, because locative apps rely on users and the city around them to animate their urban narratives, they are prone to slippage – and that slippage can bring the "background" of the city into sharp focus. Users might find themselves at odds with urban rhythms, suddenly attuned to the flow of people around them. The shifting stage of the city and the embodied experience of the user can also offer a one-two punch that unsettles unitary narratives around urban spaces, allowing other ways of knowing and being in the city to make it onto the map. The following chapter will explore these characteristics in greater depth through a tale of two cities: a city of gaps and a city of screens.

Note

1 Creator Andrew Mason decries the practice of being guided around an unfamiliar city with a "bunch of strangers" and similarly rejects audio tours as "like walking through a museum." He sees the fluidity offered by walking with GPS-enabled content as an alternative (see Nolte, 2016).

Part III

A tale of two cities (case studies)

In Part III, we explore two of the studied apps – and the streetscapes with which they are entangled – in greater depth. The first, Christchurch's *High Street Stories*, was developed as a response to the levelling of the city's central business district by a series of devastating earthquakes years prior (and by the bulldozing for redevelopment in years since). Initially envisioned as a site for locals to collectively mourn their (nearly unrecognisable) downtown, *High Street Stories* was later advertised as offering locals and tourists alike a way to "walk the streets as they were" (*High Street Stories*). In Montreal, the city's 375th anniversary celebrations in 2017 drove the expansion of the once modestly scaled *Montréal en Histoires* app into a full-scale urban spectacle, with *Cité Mémoire* mounting towering nighttime projections (designed to work with the app) onto the sides of buildings throughout the city's Old Port.

Examining Christchurch's *High Street Stories* lets us explore the notion of locative media as scripting tourism on a shifting stage in maybe its most exaggerated and even literal form, as the city's regeneration after an earthquake means that the app narrates a streetscape which is being rapidly transformed. It also prompts users to trace the experiential contours of the urban ruin as outlined by the people who once inhabited it, and so *High Street Stories* offers an opportunity to consider how a locative app helps reinstate the normative aesthetic ordering of a tourist destination where there is "nothing to see." Additionally, we can see how the newly minted "Transitional City" creates a brand focused on temporary interventions – of which *High Street Stories* is only one – leading to a clash of urban inscriptions that colour the locative tour.

Looking at *Montréal en Histoires* offers us a unique chance to see what happens when the personal tour of streetscapes intersects with the creation of a mass-appeal spectacle – and the twinned but essentially different experiences of space that this intersection enables. *Montréal en Histoires* offers an example of the locative app as a branded content delivery system – where the content looks to manage not only the brand identity of the city/neighbourhood, but also of various sponsors. Finally, it gives us a glimpse of what happens when the locative screen is offloaded onto city architecture, and how the city, thus observed, proceeds to look back.

DOI: 10.4324/9781003142386-8

5 A city of gaps

Mediating the ruin in Christchurch

"Nothing to see here": tourism and place branding in the wake of disaster

Prior to the fall of 2010, Christchurch had a reputation as a charming, historic garden city. Along the town's High Street, the city's characteristic grid patterned streets were cross-cut by several diagonal through-ways, carving out unique triangular street corners that were often adorned with Gothic Revival buildings. The Christchurch Tram – a replica of the city's historical tramway system that was reimagined as a tourist attraction – ran the length of High Street and up to the nearby Cathedral Square. The Square marked the touristic heart of the town, the crowning jewel of which was the city's Gothic Revival Anglican cathedral. Christchurch Cathedral's imposing spire loomed large in the popular imagination of the city and in its promotional material, right down to the town's logo (which still prominently features the cathedral, now a haunted silhouette).

This pre-quake Christchurch branded itself as "the Garden City," a brand epitomised by the city's sprawling Hagley Park and Botanical Gardens. Christchurch sits on a flat and fertile watershed that makes the surrounding Canterbury area prime farmland, and the nearby Port Hills offered a pleasant afternoon's hike but little hint of the geological upheaval that carved the island's dramatic Southern Alps to the west. (The Port Hills are, in fact remnants of an ancient volcanic caldera that rings this part of the island, and like the volcanic field beneath Auckland that dots that city with grassy knolls, they whisper at New Zealand's place in the Pacific Ring of Fire from beneath a cloak of unassuming green). On the other side of those hills, cruise ships docked at regular intervals in the charming port of Lyttleton, their passengers a key tourism demographic for the city.

A series of devastating earthquakes in 2010 and 2011 fundamentally altered that postcard picture of the town. While New Zealand itself is no stranger to earthquakes, the Canterbury quake of 2010 (its epicentre just 40 kilometres north of the city in Darfield) exposed a fault line that nobody knew existed – shaking Christchurch to its core and causing considerable damage to infrastructure but, thankfully, not taking any lives. However, a second, far more devastating quake erupted below the city's Port Hills in

DOI: 10.4324/9781003142386-9

February 2011, bringing many of Christchurch's already-weakened downtown structures – including the historic cathedral's iconic spire – crashing into the streets (see Figure 5.1). Tragically, the second quake killed 185 people – many of whom died in a single failed building (the CTV building, located just off of High Street) – and injured thousands of others. Locals describe learning a new word: liquefaction, the process by which the ground was shaken so violently that it liquefied the Garden City's fertile soil, swallowing cars and bubbling into houses. In the aftermath of the quake, whole residential and commercial neighbourhoods of the city were "Red Zoned" – declared uninhabitable. The city lived through weeks without fresh water and endured months and then years of aftershocks (Smyth, 2011).

It is no stretch to say that the Christchurch I first encountered in May 2016 was a city still visibly recovering from trauma. The streetscape remained scarred by the quakes in many places – shattered buildings and hollowed-out lots sat vacant, stuck in limbo as they awaited resolution by insurers and landholders or redevelopment by the council. Nevertheless, the signs of the rebuild were everywhere – often quite literally, in the form of construction signs and road cones – and, by the time I returned to Christchurch four months later, the redevelopment of the downtown was in full swing.

Before I ever made it to Christchurch, however, I had heard whispers of what the city was like in the wake of the quakes. Friends who had been to

Figure 5.1 The ruins of the city's once-iconic Christchurch Cathedral, as they remained in late 2016.

the city remarked that they felt misled; they had been promised a garden city, and they found a town in ruins. When I tell my cab driver in Auckland that I am heading to Christchurch, he remarks that there's nothing to see there. "The gardens are nice," he admits, "but the downtown is still a bit of a ghost town." From the chatter in hostels, it is clear that I am far from the only person who has heard these whispers about Christchurch; the city's tarnished tourist brand precedes it. Most people who arrive here do so on their way elsewhere in the South Island, dissuaded from staying more than a night in the city by its reputation as a place with "nothing (left) to see." The main exceptions are those on working holiday visas, mostly tradespeople and architects looking for work related to the rebuild. The cruise ships that once brought waves of tourists into the city have been re-routed to the French colonial town of Akaroa to the south, with many of their passengers opting to bypass Christchurch entirely.

While not quite a touristic non-entity, Christchurch thus finds itself in the unenviable position of being a touristic non-place – a utilitarian place for moving through on one's way elsewhere (Augé, 2008). This effect is amplified by the transitional character of the space. In the city's downtown core, ongoing construction projects and uneven redevelopment do little to counter this image of the city as a non-place. When I ask tourists what they think of when they imagine the downtown, they unfailingly describe a city of "construction zones and parking lots." So much of what characterises the cityscape in the present – orange cones, barriers, construction signs, and scaffolding – is meant to facilitate what comes next. This is a place for moving through – and, moreover, a place that is always moving, always in flux,[1] difficult to capture and define, and often not especially photogenic. As such, it makes for a rather unconventional tourist destination; what is more, it lacks much of the "lived in" character that makes a space a place (Augé, 2008; Tuan, 2001).

The rebuild is the city's focus, and where it devotes most of its budget and energy – officials are clear that the needs of the local population and come before those of Brand Christchurch – but the rebranding of Christchurch as a destination remains an essential part of the recovery efforts (Coats & Ferguson, 2013). Tourism represented a substantial part of the local economy, one it could not afford to sacrifice entirely while also rebuilding the CBD from the ground up (Christchurch & Canterbury Tourism, 2014). Based on the city's own estimation, Christchurch lost 55%–60% of its tourist traffic in the period following the 2010–2011 earthquakes and acknowledged that it would take 10–15 years for the city to regain its standing amongst tourists without serious intervention (Christchurch & Canterbury Tourism, 2014). A persistent series of strong aftershocks throughout 2011 and 2012 also hampered rebuilding efforts. However, the ongoing aftershocks did not garner the same level of international attention as the initial quakes, and visitors often remark that they "thought things would have been farther along by now" (although that frustration is often openly shared by the locals, as well). "Not much to see here" is another common refrain ("CBD Christchurch," TripAdvisor, 2018).

This is not to say that a city rebuilding from an earthquake has no allure for the curious tourist. Natural disasters have long been a subject of fascination for the tourist, with the dramatic effects of Vesuvius on Pompeii serving as one enduring example (Skinner, 2018). Tourists who are motivated to visit a place in the wake of a disaster broadly fall into the category of dark tourism and often seek to either witness history, enacting a pilgrimage to commemorate the dead, or looking to encounter their own mortality, but they are rarely a discreet category of tourists (Seaton, 2018: 9–10, 27). Christchurch had its fair share of "rubberneckers" in the wake of the quakes, as Coats and Ferguson explored in their 2013 study on local perceptions of disaster tourists in Christchurch. Still, disaster tours also provided a way of contextualising the ongoing state of disarray in the city, preserving the memory of what Christchurch had gone through – and was still going through – for tourists long after news coverage of the quake had faded away (Coats & Ferguson, 2013; Tang, 2018: 429).

However, while memorials and educational exhibits – like the Canterbury Museum's "Quake City" outpost – do acknowledge the city's trauma, in general Christchurch has steered away from encouraging disaster tourism during the later transitional period, particularly as the city attempts to move forward. Instead, a series of temporary and innovative placemaking endeavours have been designed to act as cornerstones for transitional tourism in the city while the rebuild kicks into high gear (Christchurch & Canterbury Tourism, 2014). Christchurch in 2016 has a new brand identity: the "Transitional City," a brand designed to give coherence to the period between the initial crisis and recovery efforts and the unveiling of the (practically) new central city. Christchurch's iconic cathedral even has a transitional dupe – the Cardboard Cathedral a few blocks away, where the local Anglican congregation now worships, has become an attraction in its own right. Pop-up gardens, interactive art installations, and a plethora of public sculpture and street art murals now dot the landscape of the CBD. They are part of an active effort to re-inject colour and character into a cityscape still strewn with rubble and construction sites (Recovery Christchurch, 2016). These placemaking interventions serve the dual purpose of making the city more liveable for locals and more palatable for tourists in the transitional period. *High Street Stories* (Roland & HIT Lab NZ, 2013) exists within this milieu of recovery and rebranding.

Placemaking on High Street

In this section, I want to situate *High Street Stories* as one of Christchurch's transitional placemaking efforts, and explore what it means to make place in a ruined neighbourhood. *High Street Stories* is a location-based app that allows users to listen to stories embedded in the map of Christchurch's High Street, accompanied by photos of the street as it was. It was a companion piece to an online multimedia project of the same name, and it was also designed to work with the 3-D reconstructions of buildings in the CBD that were created for another Christchurch app, *CityViewAR*. The app was largely spearheaded by oral historian and academic Zoe Roland, who used local connections as well as a public Facebook page to crowdsource stories and photographs from people who had lived and worked along the street (and its connected alleyways). These oral histories were then recorded and curated by Zoe and were intended to be the backbone of the project's content (with the photographs and written elements meant to act as supporting players). Backers ranging from Heritage New Zealand, to cellular provider Vodafone, to the city's earthquake commission helped fund the project, but it remained relatively small in scale (particularly when compared to the app examined in the second case study). Although the designers had hopes of expanding the project to allow for more user-created content (Roland, 2013), those plans never materialised, and by the time I arrived to study the app for the second time, the app had begun a slow downward trajectory into obsolescence.[2]

On its website, *High Street Stories* includes the following mission statement: "The Canterbury earthquakes in 2010/2011 irrevocably damaged the High Street precinct, with Victorian and Edwardian streetscapes and lively laneways changed forever. This is a collection of stories about the people and places that made up High Street, Christchurch" (High Street Stories, 2016). The description clearly puts the focus on heritage streetscapes – namely Edwardian and Victorian architectural landmarks – as one might expect from an app sponsored by a heritage organisation, but it also includes a callout to the more recently developed laneways that had begun to inject fresh lifeblood into the street before the quake.

The app acknowledges Christchurch's High Street as a ruined space, to some extent; described in the past tense, High Street is framed here as a place to be seen *as it was*, not as it is. As the developers behind the website end of the project describe it, *High Street Stories* was designed to "provide a permanent 'collective remembrance' of architectural [and] social history and an engaging interactive journey for locals and tourists alike," allowing users to "relive the heyday (and the seedier side) of Christchurch's High Street" through stories unearthed from the rubble ("High Street Stories," NV Interactive, 2016). The app uses the earthquake as a frame rather than a focal point, focusing on stories of High Street before the quake as a means of helping users get a sense of what was lost. It does not (overtly) aim to immerse users in disaster or ruin, even if engaging with the ruin is a definitive part of experiencing the app. Instead, *High Street Stories* was designed to collectively recall and reanimate the previous lives of the street while walking through it. *High Street Stories* might thus be considered an exercise in haunted placemaking.

While disaster tourism often relies of the co-presencing of the tourist with the lost other (Skinner, 2018: 145), here the tour prompts the user to identify with the displaced, and to understand not only the structural damage and death toll of the quake, but also the loss of social connections which the mass displacement of the High Street community entailed. In that respect, an app like *High Street Stories* can be useful for disaster recovery, since – though it does not directly narrate the quake – it allows users to learn more about the human cost without asking locals to relive a traumatic experience for them. As such, while the photographic elements of *High Street Stories* speak to the app's mission of letting locals and tourists "walk the streets as they were" – where "as they were" takes on an objective aura through the app's use of historical photographs – the narration offered by the storytellers is more often about experiencing the streets "as they were" *for them*. The app is about provoking the user to share in a memory (and imagine its sensory entanglements).

The content designer and oral historian behind the app, Zoe Roland, was motivated to give the city a place for collective mourning and to re-establish a sense of place along High Street. She initially envisioned the app for "locals really – to remember what we had and find a collectivity within our almost entirely bulldozed city." It is worth noting that Zoe, her collaborators, and many locals I spoke to refer to the role of redevelopment in shaping the city after the earthquakes. The High Street of 2016 – largely a collection of parking lots, construction sites, and crumbling facades propped up by shipping containers, broken by occasional redevelopment "success stories" – reflects not only the damage of the 2010–2011 quakes but also a series of bureaucratic planning decisions in the interim. It is to those decisions – alongside the trauma of the quakes – that *High Street Stories* responds.

In attempting to remake place through stories, *High Street Stories* shares an animating ethos with soundwalks elsewhere, such as the LINKED soundwalk in London. Commissioned by the Museum of London and created by artist Graeme Miller, LINKED attempted to counter the disruptive and "sterilizing" effects of the M11 Link Road cross-cutting a community, broadcasting narrative fragments of the space "to elicit and connect with other memories and stories, including those of participants on the walk, so as to 'renew the narrative tissue of the neighbourhood'" (Pinder, 2016: 68–71). LINKED made clear that participants in sound walks actively contribute to re-making place along with the media, rather than simply layering the narrative over the landscape. Similarly, as we discussed in Chapter 2, the "magic" of the locative narrative arguably lies in the fact that it relies upon users to add flesh and bones to the skeletal structure of the narrative – to give it life and set it in motion (Barber, 2014; Didur & Fan, 2018; Fan, 2017; Farman, 2012; Hight, 2006). Furthermore, as Saker and Evans (2020) note, locative media can also encourage urban dwellers to follow alternate trajectories through their environments (53); here, crafting a route through – rather than around – the hollowed-out Central City rewrites it into the narrative of the place. What does it entail for users to help "renew the narrative tissue" – or re-make a place on foot – in a fractured city like Christchurch?

By placemaking through personal memories, *High Street Stories* also blurs the line between the public and private space (one already made hazy by the porous exteriors of ruined buildings) and offers a window into the intimate experience of the street. In that respect, it follows a long literary trajectory, as Yi-Fu Tuan (2001) notes:

> Many places, profoundly significant to particular individuals and groups, have little visual prominence. They are known viscerally, as it were, and not through the discerning eye or mind. A function of literary art is to give visibility to initiate experiences, including those of place.
>
> (162)

Zoe's focus on oral history – and particularly on stories that revealed the street's grittier textures and unsightly underbelly – serves to undercut the disjointed narrative of the hollowed-out streetscape. Listening to High Street through the app offers a narrative continuity that the landscape itself no longer provides.

What many of the stories do, therefore, is enable a type of placemaking through a surrogate sensing of the past – encouraging users to activate their sense memory (or sensory imaginations) to flesh out the skeleton of High Street. While tourists will never "register it in their muscles and bones" (Tuan, 2001: 184) quite the way locals do, this type of atmospheric storytelling – and embodied listening – allows the user to gain a sense of how High Street not only looked, but smelled, felt, tasted, and sounded. The sensory turns in both geography and anthropology have situated sensory knowledge and embodied experience as crucial to placemaking. As Howes (2018a) notes, focusing on the activity of the place can illuminate how "the space remains the same, but it is reconstituted by the sensory activity that goes on in it" (5). In other words, the meaning-making processes of placemaking hinge significantly on sensation. As such, the process of remaking place in Christchurch (through *High Street Stories*) is characterised by sensing the ruin through the frame of the app.

The act of taking collective remembrance into the street is also a significant one for the purposes of placemaking. This is a slow tour, characterised by a high density of content. The designers also chose to leave in much of the nuances of local speech – the pauses, the transitional phrases, the laughter, and moments of silent reflection – rather than edit them down (Roland, 2013). This destabilises the notion of Christchurch as a place for moving through (or avoiding entirely), rather than experiencing. Just by virtue of using the (at times inhospitable) construction site of High Street as a pedestrian and tourist space – by taking their time, ambling, and lingering – and by weaving together the amputated portions of the street on foot, these walkers are disrupting the rhythm of the space (Fan, 2017: 9). While it never proceeds evenly, walking the length of High Street and tracing its alleyways is arguably an act of placemaking.

Sensing the ruin in Christchurch

Sensory experiences of the urban are usually described in terms of sensory overload, as in Simmel's (2010/1903) early account, or as progressively regulated and "desensualised" (Edensor, 2018a: 159). However, the sensory regulation of the city is never total – as Edensor (2018a) puts it, the "unruly effects of sensory stimuli are always liable to break through the carefully guarded city" (166) and powerful sensations might still be found, particularly in the ruined spaces of the urban margins. Urban ruins, with their pungent odours, uneven and variously textured surfaces, and blurred aesthetics, can be "repellent but also delightful" (Edensor, 2018a: 166; see also Edensor, 2005a, 2005b, 2012, 2016).

Many parts of High Street are still riddled with marks of its past life – traces of past uses, inhabitants, and "modes of experience" that offer new affordances in the present day (Edensor, 2005a; Hannam & Yankovska, 2018). Any walking tour in public space offers the potential to encounter such traces (Morretti, 2017: 103), but communing with these "ghostly matters" (Gordon, 2008) are especially characteristic of wandering Christchurch's hollowed-out CBD, and *High Street Stories* manages to further animate and accentuate these spectral remains. As Morretti (2017) notes, such haunted public spaces – like the ruin – can "unsettle categories or emerge as ambivalent, contradictory locations" and thus "they may provide room for conversations, engagements or interrogations, because they can offer different associations or points of view" (103). Rather unlike Tim Edensor's (2005a) portrait of industrial ruins, where the multisensory qualities of decay in the urban ruin impose themselves on the visitor in a highly visceral way, the traces of both the "before" and the becoming of these sites are increasingly less overt – at least from the street level. In the immediate aftermath of the quake, locals described the sensory half-life of buildings being jolted into the present. Take, for example, the skate shop (once Knight's Butchery) that "when it fell down in the earthquake apparently you could smell the meat being shaken out of the walls ... people that didn't even know it was a butchery" (Roland, 2013). By now, however, most of the ruined buildings that remain here are fenced in, or hidden behind walls of repurposed shipping containers designed to keep their crumbling facades from tumbling to the street. As part of the tour, the ruined state of these spaces can only really be apprehended through the eyes.

However, at times the porous nature of the streetscape exposes the interior life of High Street and, along with it, the sensory afterlife of these spaces. The blown-out windows on the top level of an abandoned Indian restaurant offer glimpses of what seems to be poetry scrawled on the walls, only fragments of which can be seen from below. An open squat in the back of the building exposes discarded bottles and food containers ringing a bare mattress, buzzing with flies and offering any passers-by a ripe whiff. But the smell of decay here is mere metres from the heavenly aromas of the C1 café – one of first businesses to reopen on High Street after the quakes – which roasts its own espresso beans in the back of the shop and perfumes an entire corner of the street. These contrasting smellscapes emphasise just how unevenly Christchurch is being restored to the urban aesthetic norm.

Of course, *High Street Stories* does give these traces definition, albeit in a layered way. Therefore, it calms some of the unsettled qualities of the space. In the face of this, *High Street Stories* might be interpreted as functioning to restore the normative aesthetic ordering of the (street) museum, where everything – including visitors – is back in its place (see Edensor, 2005c). Even if the photos of old buildings were designed to be supporting players, grounding the oral histories of the sites, they were among the most striking parts of the tour for my participants. Functionally, layering the app's photos over their view of the streetscape gave tourists *something to see* on High Street. It also offered a way of experiencing the jarring aesthetics of ruins that were comfortably familiar. "It's like an outdoor museum," B., a British tourist and one of the participants, remarked on first impression.

In many places, however, the decay has been vacated – bulldozed from the street level to make way for the new – and thus presents very little challenge to the incoming sensory organisation of the space. As such, the locative content of *High Street Stories* sends the user on a hunt for traces of the city amidst a collection of fenced-off rubble and bulldozed sites. While in the average city, skyscrapers might send the gaze soaring upwards (Howes, 2014b: 28), here, the search for the (absent) skyline provokes the user to look down. A line of paving stones along the back of a parking lot, half buried under dust from nearby construction, whisper of an alleyway that used to run between buildings here. Up the route, a set of stairs leads off the street to a vanished destination. Amongst the grey stone gravel used to cover bulldozed lots, you can still find small chunks of red brick, splinters of wood, and shattered glass. Rather than the totalising understanding of a city from above, getting a sense of what High Street once was demands that the tourist get closer.

While evidence of the quakes is all around users, the app does not solely tell the story of Christchurch as it was in the moments before disaster struck. As *High Street Stories* makes clear, although the earthquake was by far the most rapid transformation of the street, it was hardly the first. The app also traces the neighbourhood's transition from colonial hub to a bustling warehouse district (of bottle factories, rubber plants, butcheries, and the like) to a "seedier" place populated by prostitutes, drug users, squatters, and students, who were themselves displaced by the revitalisation of the neighbourhood in the years immediately before the earthquake. However, the app's storytellers also recall traces of these former lives through the memoryscape. One local, who had moved a fashion business into the Old Knight's Butchery, describes the lingering "smell of death" on hot days, and how any alterations would bring with them the stench of the slaughterhouse (James Scott, "The Smell of Death, Carcasses to Couture").

Many of the app's more effective stories take care to conjure the atmosphere of the street for users. Take, for example, stories of the neighbourhood youth coming together for a rave in an abandoned Chinese food restaurant. The narrator of this story manages to convey the bohemian, devil-may-care attitude of the impromptu partygoers through his use of evocative detail, right down to the sonic qualities of their unconventional choice of decor:

> We found these boxes of Chinese takeaway trays, which at the time were aluminium, and there were thousands of them, so we just got a staple gun and covered the whole room in Chinese takeaway dishes. And then when the base hit the whole room rattles, it went "bwrzzzht, bwrzzzht." So yeah, it was kind of exciting, we just went for it. I think the whole thing ran for about 6 weeks until the authorities kind of copped on that perhaps we weren't fully legit.
>
> (Simon Kong, "Christchurch's 90s Rave Scene." In *High Street Stories* [Roland & HIT Lab NZ, 2013].)

Filling the space with the life of the past requires a sensory imagination that is activated by local description of not only the ways that the street looked (including elements that the black and white photos cannot capture – such as the contrasting colours of the street before heritage stepped in to repaint it in "acceptable colours") but also how it smelled (the visceral tang of the butchery, the acrid smell of the bottle factory and rubber band plant), how it tasted (in the corner cafés), how it sounded (the vibrant hum of the local music industry or the roar of a flaming car barrelling down the street for a movie), and how it touched (the negotiated intimacy of sex work, the pounding base of an impromptu rave, the brush of polyester puffer jackets crammed into too-small record stores). All of these imagined sensations settle over the fractured streetscape like so much (GPS-enabled) fairy dust, reminding us – as Hjorth (2011) writes of locative games – "places are constructed by an ongoing accumulation of stories, memories, and social practices" (84; see also Wilken, 2019: 101),

Of course, all of this accumulated sensory imagining happens alongside (and with) the High Street of 2016. While many of the sensations described in the app have vanished – some of them having been purified in revitalisation efforts before the quake even struck – several distinct others have taken its place. There are the scattered restaurants that leech ambient music and food smells into the street, of course, but there's also just the taste of High Street itself, which, thanks to fine dirt and construction debris stirred up by the city works, is best described as a bit dusty. The most striking contrast, however, is with the sonic atmosphere of contemporary Christchurch.

With the rebuild in full swing, the High Street of late 2016 is an exceptionally loud place during the day, the deep hum of machinery punctuated by the piercing qualities of bandsaws and jackhammers. It is easy to see – or, rather, hear – what Caroline Jones (2018) means when she describes the modern city as a "giant, resonance-making apparatus" in which the "machine-laden urban streets themselves became an aural medium" (233). With the street still in transition, these constant sounds have not yet been defined as "noise" to be purified from the civilised urban sensorium; these are the sounds of progress. This sonic atmosphere did complicate the staging of the app's audio. During the day, the street was an auditory assault to walk through, and the sound of a bandsaw would cut through the portable bubble of headphones quite as efficiently as the tool itself. Many users found it difficult to understand the audio narration at times over the constant noise of construction.

By contrast, the street – no longer a thoroughfare – often lulls into an almost eerie quiet in the evening, in the gap between when the construction workers leave and before the nightlife of the space begins. Even in these quiet moments, the sounds of the space are magnified – a penny board clattering against a bench-turned-makeshift-ramp echoes across the deserted street, any obstacles that might have impeded or absorbed its sound having long since fallen away.

Making sound in this place also takes on a different quality. Most tourists who can be spotted here in the evenings walk around in virtual silence, talking (when they do) in murmurs. There is a reverence due this place for them, evident in the way they talk, and which turns the act of touring into a solemn performance. Many of my participants observe a similarly reverential tone, albeit with a few adjustments to be heard over construction. This nearly always changes at the same point – when High Street intersects with Manchester Street, users are treated to stories of a burning car barrelling down the street for a movie set, the aforementioned story of the impromptu rave, and the tale of a box of unknown human ashes that was toted around the local bars as a last hurrah. These stories are almost always good for a chuckle from participants, if not a straight-up guffaw. I learn to anticipate it. In my internal map of High Street, the bench at the intersection of these streets becomes marked by laughter.

Many of *High Street Stories*' points on the map mark ephemeral moments never captured on film, which render the storytelling component of the app essential. That same storytelling component accounted for unevenness in the emotional connection that the app forged with users at various points along the tour. Some storytellers were better at compelling attention than others, which reshaped the map away from what would seem to be the overt "highlights" of a tour – at least from the perspective of an imageable space – with users spurning some of the still-standing buildings to stare at empty parking lots and listen. (Empty, that is, save for the photographic overlay, which was rarely held in view for the length of a story). The most vividly described spaces are often not even on High Street proper, but on the street's laneways. Zoe Roland, the designer, described these laneways as essential to understanding the "'secret' life of High Street" – the naughtier, less civil side of the street that kept gentrification from ever fully taking hold in the neighbourhood.

Participants were at their most engaged when the visceral imagery of the streetscape collided with atmospheric storytelling, especially around the laneways. The story of what was "SOL Square" – a small section of once-trendy alleyway along the street – as told by the charismatic former owner of the Cartel bar there, Johnny Moore, made up one corner of the map where even the most restless of users tended to linger. Moore's stories – of a drunk running off with a hefty 1950s pineapple lamp, for example – add character and life to the space in a way that resonated with the tourists I interviewed.

What helps enliven SOL Square as a locative story is that, although the site was fenced off from the rest of the street, there remains enough of what was once SOL Square for Moore's words to infuse the space. The SOL Square of late 2016 is overgrown with weeds and bombed out with graffiti, but the Cartel Bar's yellow cross still hangs there, albeit a bit worse for wear. A grand piano perches mysteriously on an adjacent building; equally baffling is the Mini Cooper that appears to be climbing its walls (see Figure 5.2). Even fenced off as it is, SOL Square is still clearly a living space – something that can hardly be said for many of the parking lots the app visits – and it has visual character in spades. SOL Square offers the tourist something to look at in both the past and present versions of itself, and – listening to its charismatic narrator describe the place it was against the muffled din of bar music within the app – it is easy to imagine the plush carpets and beanbag

Figure 5.2 Evidence of life and porous boundaries at Christchurch's SOL Square.

chairs that once spilled out into the laneways. After all, the SOL Square of 2016 already has the feel of a place where boundaries – between the public and the private, the natural and the built – are blurred, and so it is easy to imagine the more curated version of that already eclectic aesthetic. As a harbinger of gentrification and a symbol of High Street's erstwhile revival, SOL Square (even in its ruined form) fits right in with the brand image of the Transitional City. (Although, as Johnny Moore [2016] wrote in a more recent opinion piece, that shared eclectic aesthetic seems poised to be erased from the city's "monotone" vision of what comes next.)

What the example of SOL Square makes clear is that, although the city's vacant lots might seem to offer the best "blank slate" for augmentation, the app's conjuring of High Street's ghost was most effective when the narrative shroud had something to hang on to. Seeing the textures, the scale, and getting a sense for the feel of the place allowed users to activate their sensory imagination; unsurprisingly, a living space seemed easier to imagine as having once been lived in. Unfortunately, not all the sites in the story lent themselves so easily to the locative narrative.

Rhythms and (dis)orientation

The research on urban perceptions conducted by Lynch (1960) and his followers in Western cities lead them to conclude that "most individuals perceive a city predominantly as a set of built objects" – pathways, public squares, and landmarks to name a few of them (Hospers, 2011: 29–30). However, Lynch originally drew parallels between urban design and musical composition; the city was composed of "sequences" and followed a particular rhythm (Halpern, 2018: 90). The image or mental map of the city that people composed was, to him, always relational, its tenor modulated by a sequence of experiences and encounters (Halpern, 2018; Lynch, 1960). With this dual focus on built objects and rhythms in mind, let us explore why navigating Christchurch – with or without the app in hand – is such a disorienting experience.

You are (not) here

It is evening on High Street. A couple is walking down the street, their map splayed out before them, which I recognise as the same tourist map I claimed from my hostel upon arrival months before. The couple marches determinedly towards a large map board mounted midway down High Street. They have just come from Cathedral Square, so they know where they have been. They seem less certain of where they are going. Following some confused discussion and comparison of the maps, they wander uncertainly towards Manchester Street. Afterwards, I consult the map board myself, thinking it is a new addition to the corner. Instead, I find that it is the map board from the other side of Manchester Street, and as such it is not in the place so confidently marked "You are here." The construction workers have moved it up the street temporarily, which accounts for the confusion. The reader of the map is not "here" – although it is the map and not the person who has been displaced.

Although not directly tied to *High Street Stories*, this example illustrates a common element of both tourism and everyday life in Christchurch: disorientation. If the city is a narrative (to embrace for a moment the admittedly limited metaphor of space as something to be read) Christchurch's High Street is a book that has been torn up and only partially pieced back together, with a few new pages spliced in. Many of the landmarks around which one might orient oneself in this part of town are either gone or hidden from view. New developments have yet to gain considerable traction in the image of the city – they are not yet familiar enough to facilitate mental map making and are often disjointed from the surviving streetscape. High Street is not, therefore, an exceptionally "legible" place, to borrow from Lynch (1960). What is more, this lack of legibility is a problem not only for tourists, but for locals. Some Christchurch locals who were generous enough to share with me their own memories of the CBD describe the hugely disorienting experience of returning to the downtown core:

> Our whole skyline has changed, you know? We've lost all our landmarks. It's really strange when you grow up in a city and you come into central city and you don't even recognise it.
>
> (S., Christchurch local)

Landmarks are not just useful for tourists. While the intimate experience of a place may often be of little visual significance (Tuan, 2001), landmarks and the visible city can serve as anchors for lived experience. More than just a loss of the city's material heritage, then, the lost skyline represented a lost architecture of memory for locals. For tourists, while the disorientation of navigating High Street is nowhere near as profound, it is still thoroughly confounding.

Phantom landmarks and disorientation on High Street

As previously mentioned, one way to manage the perception of the city as a consistent narrative is through the creation of landmarks, which serve as points of reference around which a traveller in the city can orient him- or herself (Lynch, 1960). This conceptualisation of the city jives well with Urry's (1990) concept of a tourist gaze – points of photographic interest that are signposts for the consumable city. For Lynch, an imageable city "facilitates the making of a vividly identified, powerfully structured, highly useful mental images of the city" (Lynch, 1960: 9). The legible city tells a particular story; it is organised in such a way so as to make sense even without a map (Lynch, 1960). As such, the creation of landmarks is not only important for the touristic endeavour because of the extent to which it makes the city photographable, but also because it helps make the city sensible for the tourist. But what happens when those landmarks all but disappear?

One of the most novel capacities of the locative app is to replace landmarks that are destroyed or no longer accessible, thus rendering post-disaster landscapes legible during the road to recovery. AR apps have been suggested as a way to facilitate continuing tourism in areas of Japan that were hard hit by that country's 2011 Tohoku earthquake and subsequent tsunami (Ide, 2014). The AR game *Pokémon GO* was also seen as a viable option for getting people back into tsunami-affected prefectures in Japan ("Japan Quake Regions Use Pokémon Go," 2016) – and, in fact, authorities had to warn people not to venture into the Fukushima exclusion zone in search of Pokémon after at least one such creature was "spotted" in the red zone (Gibbs, 2016). Augmented-reality apps were also floated as a possibility for maintaining tourist presence in Nepal after the 2015 earthquake there destroyed many ancient and UNESCO-listed sites ("Nepal Is Open to All Visitors," 2015) and apps as well as open-sourced mapping tools were used to crowd-source information about various disaster sites to assist in the rebuild (Sinha, 2015). *High Street Stories* is another such post-disaster app, but this section will discuss how the lack of landmarks in Christchurch's CBD makes mapping the locative narrative on foot an especially disorienting experience for tourists.

Reorienting oneself within Christchurch's rapidly shifting environment absolutely requires a closer attunement to the environment. Take, for example, the disorientation invoked by looking for an alleyway in what is now a parking lot. I am at first convinced that the laneway to what was once SOL Square is hidden behind a containment wall, until I realise that it is no longer a laneway at all: paving stones line the back of the lot, but one whole side is now exposed. It is a stark reminder of just how much the space has changed – a reorientation that serves to make the content of *High Street Stories* even more poignant. There might be a careful balance to be struck between reorienting users and confounding them, however. Tourists – operating on a limited timeframe – are unlikely to tolerate a great deal of disorientation, to the extent that it detracts from the usability of the app or the accessibility of the content.

Since the app deals almost exclusively with stories of the street before the quake, *High Street Stories* manages to avoid most of the slippage that can plague locative apps; as with apps like Melbourne's *Lost! 100*, the difference between the streetscape as it is and the one described in the app is entirely the point. However, since the app does tend to mention which buildings along the street survived the quake, most ruptures that do occur here come courtesy of the redevelopment. For example, the app details the distinctive Moorish architecture of the Majestic Theatre, a building it describes as "having survived the earthquake quite well" (*High Street Stories*). After multiple days of hunting for the site, thinking I had my orientation wrong, a quick googling reveals that the Majestic Theatre had been torn down some months before to make way for redevelopment (in spite of public pushback to the decision). What does tend to "slip" when using the app is the user's grasp of the alignment between the city around them and the map they are walking.

Ironically, the same features of High Street which seemingly call out for augmentation – that is, the gaps in the streetscape – make Christchurch a less-than-ideal staging ground for a self-guided walking tour (especially one that is as dense in content as *High Street Stories*). GPS issues have commonly plagued locative tours and confounded users (Nisi et al., 2018) and *High Street Stories* is no different in that respect. The combination of the density of the content with a spotty GPS signal made it difficult to get one's bearings on the map. Because GPS technology does not always function accurately enough to differentiate between buildings that are right beside each other (Lee et al., 2012), in order to help users orient themselves and position themselves in such a way that the augmentation works most effectively, many locative apps often have other orientation cues built in – for example, street numbers. However, Christchurch's absent buildings have taken their street numbers with them, and even the buildings that remain are no longer clearly marked. Users typically had difficulty conceptualising the buildings within the space itself; the ghosts they were hunting needed real-world referents to put them in their place (see Figure 5.3).

Figure 5.3 Disorientation on High Street – an app user attempts to navigate the rapidly changing streetscape of the transitional city.

For locals, the app is an aid to memory – a way to recognise a fundamentally changed streetscape and anchor their feeling of loss in a landscape where evidence of that loss is either fading or already erased. For tourists walking the streets "as they were," however, the narrative of the app is not so entangled with their personal experiences of the space. (There are some exceptions: one of my participants, coming off a year on the ice in Antarctica, mourns the loss of a bar in the demolished Warner's Hotel where "winter-overs" would congregate to trade stories). On the whole, however, tourists do not have a memory of the space to merge with the map, making the experience much more disorienting.

The idea that GPS takes all the guesswork out of navigating a space is contradicted by the uneven process of trying to conjure up Christchurch's past. Tracing the ghost of a city in the present requires a much finer awareness of the ground beneath one's feet than it does of one's position on a map, and data points on a map lose considerable meaning when their real-world context dissolves. The map is a representation with its own encoded values and interpretations of space (Jackson, 1989) – and reading a map requires summoning an imagination of place regardless of whether the site that is mapped is in front of you – but in order for the map to facilitate orientation, it needs to have anchor points in the "real." Lacking these correspondences, the map – even one designed to be normative and somewhat utilitarian rather than revolutionary – becomes an agent of disorientation, and the locative tour slides (quite unintentionally) into the realm of "dislocative media" (Pinder, 2013).

Locative rhythms on High Street

As a storytelling app designed to re-establish the social bonds of a place, and particularly a place now defined as one for moving through rather than living in, *High Street Stories* has a particular rhythm. The app is "not a quick fix," its designer notes. "We haven't edited out the little nuances in the way people talk, I really like that and I think it's really important, especially in an introspective like this" (Roland, 2013). Combined with the overlapping content – where multiple histories are often traced in a single spot – it is easy to understand why tourists often found the sheer density of stories mapped on High Street somewhat overwhelming. (For example, looking at a zoomed-out image of the app's map, a user would find coloured destination points jumbled together and layered on top of one another; only upon zooming in or filtering out some topics could they get a better sense of the location of each story).

Here, sensory studies of the museum can shed some light. As Classen (2017) notes, the potential for visitors to experience visual fatigue is a real concern with the museum; visitors can become overwhelmed when confronted with a succession of artefacts and exhibits that are constructed as equally worthy of the gaze. As such, negative space is important for framing the exhibits and breaking up the continuity of looking.

In the case of Christchurch's High Street – reconstituted in the style of 'the city as museum' in *High Street Stories* – when everything becomes something worth looking at (or listening to), the experience becomes untenable, and users began to self-select. *High Street Stories* does allow users to organise content by theme. Users would often begin with the map settings open and then filter by theme once they realised that accessing all the stories would involve spending hours on a single street (one that is, to boot, often a bustling construction zone). For example, one of my participants was an architect, so, for her, the category about the city's lost Gothic revival and other heritage architecture was particularly interesting. Others found the architectural descriptions far less appealing – preferring, instead, the more intimate human stories that the app had to offer. In either case, filtering allowed the creation of some "negative space" in the app content, bringing its rhythm somewhat back in line with a more conventional tour.

Nevertheless, walking along with each participant furthered my understanding of how varied the rhythms of the locative tour can be, particularly when they meet contrasting rhythms in the environment. D. (a Canadian tourist) seems almost sheepish in the way he uses the app. Our rhythm clashes with the site of the tour, which, at the time of fieldwork, was in the thick of its ongoing transformation. Workers are carefully transporting large sheets of glass for one of the new shopping buildings along the strip. We have to weave our paths in and out of theirs as we traverse the street. As D. notes, "I feel like I'm in the way. I'd rather just look through them at home, where I can take my time." For him, the broken rhythm of the tour outweighs any added value from the site specificity.

Even when things go smoothly, however, the rhythm of the tour changes. M. (a Dutch tourist) opens nearly every story on the map, but likes to start a story and walk with it, rather than stand in any one place. She holds the tablet at eye level so she can get an impression of where the buildings belong, even on the move. B. (a British tourist) is considerably more deliberate, even stopping to read street placards that seem relevant to the architectural theme she is exploring. Several participants drew parallels between the experience of the app and that of a museum. T (an American tourist), for example, enjoyed the fact that the app allowed him to set the pace of his own tour, and connected the rhythm of the tour to the way he generally moved through museums – that is, moving quickly between exhibits in order to absorb as much content as possible.

The stories in the app itself also give some sense of what the rhythms of High Street were once like. One narrator describes the street in its heyday as an excellent place for people watching, with plenty of nooks to duck into to observe the bustling crowd flowing by. The High Street of 2016 has neither bustling crowds nor much by way of nooks to tuck into, given the fenced-off streetscape. Still, the contrast in rhythms adds considerable poignancy to the story.

Henri Lefebvre (2004) argues in his book *Rhythmanalysis* that "Disruptions and crises always have origins in and effects on rhythms" (44).

This statement seems especially salient for Christchurch, given the violent undulations that fundamentally altered its sensory rhythms, tremors of which remain to this day. From day to day, the pathways and rhythms of the city would change, to the point where even locals could not be sure of their routes through the city. The impossibility of freeze-framing the city was laid bare in this constant, rapid change – the tour was never the same because the city was never the same. In that respect, *High Street Stories* exposes the contingency of taking the museum to the streets. Because it relies on both the street and the user to animate it, locative tourism is always performed on a shifting stage.

The writing on the wall: encountering layered urban inscriptions

If we consider locative applications as one type of urban inscription, it is inevitable that these inscriptions will run up against other types of urban inscription – what McCullough (2006b) calls "urban markup." As part of Christchurch's transitional placemaking efforts, High Street and its environs now play host to an array of street art and public sculpture, much of it landing squarely in the frame of *High Street Stories*. Since both public art and locative media demand to be read in context (Stevens & Lossau, 2015), the app and the various public artworks – alongside other, less sanctioned forms of urban inscription – necessarily inform one another.

Owing to the violent rupture of the quakes, the story of Christchurch gets split into two parts: "Before" and "After." Not only the city's architecture but its sight lines have been fundamentally altered. (As one of the locals tells me, gesturing off towards the view of the Port Hills from the intersection of High Street and Manchester, "You never used to be able to see that.") In this context, surviving elements of the streetscape gain new significance as anchor points, but are reframed by the ruin around them.

Take, for example, Phil Price's (2006) kinetic sculpture *Nucleus* (see Figure 5.4) which, although it looks precarious, actually predates the earthquake. *Nucleus* is clearly visible in eyewitness video from High Street on the day of the second quake – rising between plumes of dust at the streetscape crumbles around it (Smyth, 2011). The sculpture takes on added poignancy when you read its artist's statement– the piece is a commentary both on the centrality of the city in the artist's own life story, as well as on its "well-planned and laid-out built environment" (Price, 2006), the latter now in disarray. While the sculpture's dynamic orange topper pivots gracefully in the gentlest of breezes, the world around *Nucleus* has spun off its axis.

As previously discussed, the city's streets tell a sanitised version of their own stories. Heritage organisations play a part in shaping this narrative, helping to determine what stays in our stories of the city and what gets edited out in the name of progress (Deutsche, 1998; Zukin, 1995). However, this process is not without contestation, and heritage organisations are just one of many social forces that shape the streetscape. The following section will look at how other forms of urban inscription – some sanctioned, some

Figure 5.4 Phil Price's sculpture *Nucleus* (2006) on post-earthquake High Street.

not – intersect with the heritage narratives of *High Street Stories* to tell their other stories of the city and its habitual use. We will also examine how place-embedded urban artforms may challenge the dominant meanings of city space.

When considering the state of aesthetic flux and contestation along High Street, the notion of "urban wildscape" is a useful concept to think through, particularly when framing High Street as in a state of transition rather than having been left entirely to decay. Dougal Sheridan (2012) defines urban wildscapes as "any area, space, or building where the city's normal forces of control have not shaped how we perceive, use, and occupy them" (201). While some open sites along the street have been bulldozed into oblivion to make way for redevelopment – and, in the interim, serve as central city parking – many others offer pockets of urban wildscape. The loosening of aesthetic controls in these wildscapes are also evidenced by the sheer volume of urban inscription that now peppers the (remaining) walls. Graffiti writers have certainly made their mark on the transitional city: "Since there is no sanction for composing works on neglected, often crumbling walls, certain sites are saturated with the work of such artists" (Edensor et al., 2012: 70). However, this made for zones of contention when, while the city's gallery remained closed over a period of years for repairs, fine art also started migrating into the streets.

While we have frequently touched on the concept of "taking the museum to the streets," Christchurch has put a novel spin on that idea during the transitional period by turning the city into an open-air gallery of sorts. High Street has two things in abundance: open sightlines and blank walls. Large, windowless facades that used to abut other buildings are now laid bare, primed to be used as canvases. As such, High Street offers the possibility of transposing images onto what might be the closest thing to the visuality of the White Cube that the urban street can offer. RISE, the street art festival that was brought to the city as a regeneration measure in 2014, has left walls throughout Christchurch decked in street art murals, and the city has only added to its open-air collection in the years since. These street art pieces have become part of the touristic landscape in the city, and a means of drawing more people into the downtown core as the city attempts to regenerate (Woods, 2016). They have also become useful for anchoring the vision of the transitional city in people's minds, serving as new visual nodes around which to orient one's travels. As one of the locals informed me, "They've become the new landmarks. ... You'll be trying to give someone directions and you'll ask, 'Have you passed the elephants? Have you passed the ice cream cones?'" (A., a Christchurch local). Indeed, these landmarks have persisted for so long – along with a slew of other "temporary" interventions in the space – that questions have arisen as to what will be lost when these placeholder (and place-making) landmarks are replaced by the end-goal architecture of the space, and the city becomes nearly unrecognisable once more.

However, the notion that the gaps left by the earthquake along High Street are entirely empty – and thus a perfect "gallery space" where the aesthetics of a piece can be appreciated from a distance but will not be touched – is challenged by the case of *No!* (see Figure 5.5). Based on an oil-on-canvas painting by notable New Zealand artist Tony Fomison, *No!* attempts to transplant a gallery work into the street, and its presence in the High Street landscape reflects the Christchurch Art Gallery's recovery efforts in the aftermath of the quakes. The city's gallery was closed for nearly four years for repairs, and – as a temporary measure to keep the city's art accessible to the public – it began moving some pieces into the streetscape. Yet, this move into the city-as-gallery, though driven by necessity, was far from uncontested. The staging of *No!* brought the piece into conflict with local graffiti writers, who had been using the wall for their own (unsanctioned) urban interventions (Woods, 2016). This collision of sanctioned and unsanctioned public art is visible on the wall today – where graffiti writers have "bombed out" the lower third of the piece as a sign of their displeasure. The site makes visible the battle over "legitimate" uses of street art in the city – particularly when they occupy spaces traditionally seen as illegitimate venues for artistic expression.

No! is an evocative piece. The central figure poses defiant – one hand up, in a sign that seems to refute the gaze, even as it invites it. As such, it is also an interesting piece to think through as an urban inscription which the app content bumps up against. When using *High Street Stories*, *No!* is an unavoidable part of the sightlines of augmenting the old site of the Excelsior

Figure 5.5 A street print of Tony Fomison's (1971) *No!* in the context of High Street's urban inscription.

Hotel, and yet the piece seems to resist the mobile-wielding user, as if to say "Please, no photographs." While many other street art pieces around the city are deliberately cheerful or at least colourful – drawing the tourist gaze – the muted colour palette and defensive subject of *No!* seems to suggest that the tourist is intruding. The tags around the piece, meanwhile, mark the graffiti writers along High Street – each tag functioning as a kind of "I was here" (Halsey & Young, 2006) – and thus refute the image of the site as empty or untouchable. Halsey and Young (2006) argue that graffiti "connects bodies known and unknown through the proliferation of images" (278), enabling encounters between writers and audiences across time that disrupt the alienating effects of the urban spectacle. Whether this encounter provokes aversion or appreciation, graffiti makes visible certain limits and possibilities for freedom of expression in hybridised public–private spaces.

The popularity of street art as an object of the gaze is part of a contested history of urban markup. Smith (1992), for example, discusses how ostensibly countercultural forms of representation were assimilated into "aestheticization of culture and politics" in the 1980s, a period which brought graffiti into galleries and punk fashion into glossy magazine spreads (77). Street art tours have developed as a way of endorsing "proper urban creative practice" and are "integrated into a longer lineage of endorsements for the cultural field of street art, and interpreted as branding strategies for the city" (Andron, 2018: 1036). Street art is thus an accepted way of creating an urban brand for a city, and has been heavily involved in the branding of the "Transitional City" in Christchurch. The street art tours visit the large-scale, sanctioned murals throughout the town, sometimes intertwined with the various public art sculptures (some permanent, some more temporary) that are woven through the streets by the SCAPE public art program. They do not visit the smaller, less-sanctioned interventions or generally take in the work of graffiti writers who paved the way for these broader-scale public artworks, neither of which have the same stability in the narrative structure of the space; they are busy with the business of turning these "independent, often anonymous surface markings into a marketable artistic commodity" (Andron, 2018: 1040), which the tours then reinforce.

As the city rebuilds, street art serves as a transitional commodity designed to bridge the gap between ruined spaces and the smooth city – an accelerated version of the gentrification and regeneration process that happens elsewhere (Ferrell, 2016; Hayward, 2004; McAuliffe, 2012; Zukin, 1995). While street art and graffiti are both engaged in a complex seduction of the public gaze – and the sheer saturation of these works in modern urban spaces can in turn render them invisible (Ferrell, 2016) – the altered sightlines of the Christchurch CBD serve to make (especially the larger pieces) highly visible parts of the city skyline. Tours further entrench street art as "something worth seeing" in the downtown – a direct counter to the perception of the downtown core as a touristic non-place.

When the app content in *High Street Stories* meets the street art that has proliferated across Christchurch's sightlines, the effect is of two in situ imaginings of space colliding: the city as archive meets the city as art gallery. High Street is adorned with an assortment of pieces that speak to both the city's trauma and its rebuild. Many of the city's large-scale murals date to the Street Art Festival (RISE 2014) that was brought to the city to aid in its revitalisation (Woods, 2016). These pieces serve their intended purposes of adding liveliness and visual interest back into the space, making Christchurch photographable once more. While tour participants rarely photographed the buildings in states of disrepair and reconstruction – or, for that matter, empty parking lots – the street art was one thing they did photograph. It was also one feature of a site that had made a definite impact when I asked users to reflect on whether their impression of Christchurch had changed after the tour. Although the site is not wanting for "bombed out buildings," tour participants saw the street art as a more acceptable object to train their lenses on. More than that, they describe it as something which gave them genuine enjoyment – the street art makes High Street a pleasure to consume.

However, just because the city's murals were openly designed to help revitalise the space – and to give locals and tourists "something to see" in the downtown – does not mean that they have been imposed on the city in a purely top-down process. Some speak more directly to the city's trauma and rebuild than others – most notably, the pieces across town that are phrases writ large are usually the result of public initiatives that asked

Christchurch locals to weigh in on what they would like their streets to say. Some, like the groovy, techni-coloured "WE GOT THE SUNSHINE" are unabashedly optimistic (though they take on a bittersweet tinge when one realises that the building in question is bathed in sunshine at least in part because the building which used to be opposite has been demolished). Others, like the insistent "I ALWAYS KNEW YOU WOULD COME BACK," are poignant reminders of the population (both local and tourist) who left the city in the wake of the earthquakes, and reads as much as an expression of hope for the city's future as a commentary on its current revitalisation.

Nature as urban inscription

Nature is also part of Christchurch's post-quake urban inscription, in both curated and more spontaneous forms. A wall of small planters is used to disguise part of the unsightly hole left behind at a cleared construction site – a particularly lonely spot where concrete pillars become submerged in water after a rain and twisted rebar tendrils snake their way skywards. The planters are accompanied by a sign marking these as plants that thrive under adversity – with little to no water or soil to speak of. Beyond them, the empty site and another soaring mural are both visible through gaps in the fencing. The plant becomes a metaphor for the Garden City, and particularly for its resilience in the face of natural disaster. Farther down High Street, a grove of artificial rimu trees are constructed from the salvaged ruins of houses (Regan Gentry's [2014] *Woods from the Trees*). They stand like dandelions gone to seed, looking like the whole of them could take off on a stiff breeze. Yet, here they remain. Christchurch's public art is actively involved in mediating the city's newfound sense of precarity with nature. Elsewhere, the overgrowth of plants – along with sprawling graffiti – are the clearest markers of the passage of time in sites that otherwise seem to resist the city's rapid rate of change. As Catherine Heatherington (2012) notes in describing natural narratives in urban wildscapes, "There is often a layer of plants writing a new history in the dereliction of the site" (173; see Figure 5.6).

While the notion of nature as something lost – or at least transformed – does not feature prominently in the app, it does appear in the Ngāi Tahu descriptions of the area as a mahinga kai (a Ngāi Tahu phrase referring to an area of natural resources, especially around waterways). It also features in the form of future imaginaries of the city's relationship with nature. At the street level, one patch of weeds and wildflowers has been fenced off by the "plant gang," marked as an essential pocket of green space for the city's endangered bee population. The app notes that a bee colony has been established on the nearby Alice's Video House, one of the first heritage buildings to be reopened on High Street after the earthquake. There is an established twinning here – the precarity (and resilience) of nature and of humans, the two inescapably entangled.

Figure 5.6 A wall of resilient plant life conceals a building site on High Street.

The city tells its own stories. As Tuan (2001) puts it:

> The city is a place, a centre of meaning, par excellence. It has many highly visible symbols. More importantly, the city itself is a symbol. The traditional city symbolized, first, transcendental and man-made order against the chaotic forces of terrestrial and infernal nature.
>
> (173)

The earthquake has, of course, unsettled that symbolism, upending buildings and scrambling the "ordered" environment of the city. Time, in the interim, has further eroded the concept of humans' mastery of nature in the city, instead allowing the relationship between the two to unfurl within the space. The new city is being designed to act in concert with the unsettled ground – to bend with the ground as it rolls, rather than break.

Future imaginaries: engaging with the rebuild

Before moving on to discuss how *High Street Stories* engages with future imaginaries, I want to briefly touch on encounters with two urban inscriptions along the tour route that prime the user to think about Christchurch's rebuild as a contested rather than inevitable process.

The first piece is a public installation by Mark Catley (2016) called *Sign o' the Times* (see Figure 5.7). The artwork, which in 2016 was on full display in the Re:START mall near the beginning of the tour, uses the familiar iconography of urban road signs – an especially prolific medium in the transitional city – to give voice to the local population's hopes and frustrations in the midst of recovery. The signs variously aim to stop bureaucratic constipation and warn against the flexing of egos. Although not designed to complement the app, the piece offers a mindful frame for encounters with the heavily signified rebuild farther down the path.

The second piece is a far more temporary – and likely unsanctioned – bit of urban inscription that appeared along the tour route in late 2016, and disappeared just as quickly. A small sign on a public bench outside C1 Café, the kind of brass plaque that usually dedicates a park bench to a dead loved one (see Figure 5.8), reads: "IN MEMORIAM: This plaque commemorates Christchurch that once graced this site for over 150 years. It was bulldozed by bureaucracy in 2015 to make way for vanity projects" (Unknown, 2016).

Within days, the plaque had been removed, a lone brass bolt the only trace of it. Blink and you would have missed it – and most probably did – but the plaque further exposed the role of urban inscription in contesting the dominant meanings surrounding the redevelopment of the city.

Figure 5.7 Mark Catley's (2016) installation *Sign o' the Times*.

Figure 5.8 A temporary inscription comments on the politics of the rebuild. (On a bench outside High Street's C1 Café).

Since Christchurch is a city in transition, it is a city of possibilities. Among locals and tourists alike, talk of Christchurch tends to centre not on what it is, but on what it will be. The boundaries and identities of many sites in the central city have yet to be fully redefined, and a variety of actors – including *High Street Stories* – are involved in negotiating the future imaginary of the city. This section will consider how *High Street Stories* engages users in this contested process of meaning-making.

One reason *High Street Stories* manages to escape the worst of the slippage that tends to plague locative media – in spite of its rapidly changing streetscape – is that the app rarely engages directly with the cityscape as it is in the present (or as it was in 2016). Rather, the designers saw it as a complete project that would not be troubled by the shifting streetscape – one focused on social bonds and human stories that could be re-animated in place, regardless of what the buildings looked like. For that reason, however, it is largely left to the users of the app to draw connections between the app content and the streetscapes they see unfolding around them.

This is not to say that *High Street Stories* never prompts users to reflect on the aesthetics of a heritage district. Tension remains in the app content between heritage organisations' desire for new buildings to pattern themselves after the character of the remaining heritage buildings (like the one that houses C1 Café and Alice's Cinema, described in the app as a shining beacon for how redevelopment should proceed) and the apparent appetite for reinvention that is written all over the rebuild. One narrator contrasts the aesthetics of modern buildings with heritage landscapes, seemingly as a reprobation of the heritage buildings that have been bulldozed to make way for redevelopment:

> Today modern architecture is these large flat expanses. The closer and closer you get to an old building, the more and more detail comes out, until you're down there looking at the pockmarks in the brick … also they embody the work that's gone into them … There are all kinds of human feelings and values that are embodied in these bits of concrete and mortar and stone.
>
> (Dr. Cliff Mason, "Human Buildings Embodied in Concrete, Mortar and Stone." In *High Street Stories* [Roland & HIT Lab NZ, 2013].)

In this way, Dr. Mason frames the ongoing erasure of the city's heritage landscape – and replacement with a modern, expansive skyline – as the sanitisation of the city's texture and of its human history.

These stories, combined with the rapid progression of the city's rebuild, do sometimes prompt users to reflect on the future of the city. One of my participants expresses dismay at the modern character of the rebuild. She thinks that the city should have tried to recapture what was there before, or at least to have tried to retain the spirit of the older buildings: "It's going to be such a strange mix," she says, holding the tablet up at eye level to see the old architecture transposed against the new. "I think I really would have loved this city before. I don't like all this modern stuff" (N., a Dutch tourist). She notes that her city in the Netherlands had undergone a similar transformation when rebuilding after World War II and that – in her mind – much of the character and history of the space had been erased. Even for participants who did not comment on the character of the rebuild while walking, though, many described feeling a new sense of connection to the city by the end of the tour, and with it an investment in what would come next for Christchurch.

The politics of Christchurch's glass box rebuild are hotly contested; some have argued that it proceeds under the guise of transparency and sociability, but that many of its ground-level qualities appear to rebut that ethos (Moore, 2016; Sargent, 2016). Reflections can obscure and even mirror, "giving both passersby and occupants a feeling they are watched," and tinted glass can downright glare at you in certain lights (Sargent, 2016). Since glass buildings also maximise the usable or leasable space of a building – and, therefore, maximise profit – some locals have argued that the aesthetics of the rebuild discard historical context and character in favour of catering to corporate interest (Moore, 2016; Sargent; 2016).

The glass box rebuild also has important implications for the inscription of urban space. High Street's current main tourist attraction – the large-scale street art and smaller accompanying public artworks, graffiti, and creative interventions – frequently rely upon the porous surfaces of the city's stone and brick architecture for their sticking power in the urban vernacular. As architect Nick Sargent (2016) argues,

> Importantly, glass also resists culture; it doesn't accept the dirt, marks or refurbishments that allow other materials, like brick or concrete or wood, to record history and take on local character. Glass, with an amply and aptly neurotic investment in cleaning, stays young forever.

The rebuilt High Street is likely to be more resistant to all but the most sanctioned forms of urban inscription. Absent any trace of the character or history which – for good or ill – marked the buildings they replaced, the transparent rebuild manages to obscure the scale of displacement occurring along the street. Furthermore, unlike the ornate architectural detail for which many buildings on High Street were renowned, or even the transitional spaces of the ruin that draw users in, the scale and lines of glass buildings make it such that one must stand back to appreciate them (Miodownik, 2018: 162). The monotone peaks and ripples of glass along the street risk making the place at once less knowable and less habitable; after all, as de Certeau put it, it is not the urban's "utilitarian" transparency, but rather the "opaque ambivalence of its oddities that makes the city liveable" (de Certeau and Mayol, 1998: 134).

Of course, *High Street Stories* as a tourist app – rather than a moment for local recollection and remembering – can run the risk of enabling the "have it both ways" approach to controlled urban grit as the calling card of "authentic" urban experience (Zukin, 2009). The app allows users to wander between sanitised glass boxes of familiar chain stores and "recall" the grittier, smellier side of the city at a moment's notice, and then shut out that authenticity at the push of a button.

Processes of regeneration have a fundamental impact on the sensory qualities of a neighbourhood. As Mónica Degen (2012) notes,

> Regeneration strategies entail the dismembering and re-assembling of the built environment. In such processes, buildings get white-washed or demolished, streets repaved and widened, new shops and attractions etched into a re-signified urban environment...An inevitable consequence is that the activity and sensory rhythms of a place change and are reorganized.
>
> (22–23)

Widened boulevards, for example – one characteristic of Christchurch's rebuild – serve the practical purpose of giving people more room to escape falling buildings but also fundamentally shift the rhythm of movement through the space in the interim towards one that values mobility over connection (Sheller & Urry, 2006).

While the app seeks to restore the lived-in character of the space that has been bulldozed along with so much of its material relations, what *High Street Stories* cannot do is shed light on the social relations that have developed in the interim as a result of this fundamental re-ordering of space. For example, the stories of High Street's role as the city's Red Light District were some of the highlights of the app for both its creator and tour participants, humanising the city's sex workers through personal narratives. What is less clear from the app is that the levelling of the CBD has also resulted in increased precarity for sex workers in Christchurch since the quakes, with street-based workers displaced into residential neighbourhoods, increasing the stigma they face. This displacement has made Christchurch the most dangerous city in New Zealand for sex workers (Abel & Sweetman, 2018).

What is more, the app's focus on the heritage streetscape – and particularly on narrating what was lost through gaps in the skyline – can at times limit understandings of whose heritage the rebuild should be protecting. This is often the result of users self-selecting what counts as "lost" in Christchurch. For example, the app's creator took care to include several stories of the Ngāi Tahu foundations of the city, particularly along the Otakaro (Avon) River. These stories ground the "garden city" brand of the city in its precolonial history as an important food source site for the Ngāi Tahu. However, given that most users seemed to find the primary allure of the app to be its comparison of the city pre- and post-earthquake, the lack of photographic representation of the Ngāi Tahu site in its "before" stage, combined with the sheer amount of time between the "before" and "after" meant that some users found these stories "out of place." (It is worth noting that the Ngāi Tahu stories attempt to combat this perception up front by stating that High Street was, first and foremost, a colonial construct). As such, the site's precolonial histories are erased from the landscape itself and filtered out of the vision of what has been lost.

A note on the latter point, however: Christchurch has taken the opportunity offered by the untimely reimagining of its CBD to write the history of the Maori back into the built history of the city. Although *High Street Stories* mourns the erasure of the architectural history of the central city, the distinctive Georgian and Edwardian styles of felled buildings had borne little trace of the precolonial configurations of space which those buildings had, themselves, blotted out. However, incorporating Maori elements into the redesign has become a priority of the rebuild. Stonework art pieces in the style of Nga Whariki (Maori welcome mats) are woven into the once-fractured pavement at the foot of the Bridge of Remembrance (Otakaro Limited, 2017), and the city's new central library building, Tūranga, heavily features Maori design elements that were intended to make the city's Ngāi Tahu past visible (Matapopore, 2020). The Ngāi Tahu history of the space is increasingly legible in the rebuilt streets and skyline of the city (though the brutality of Maori absences from Christchurch's "before" remains somewhat opaque). This acts as a caution against romanticising heritage streetscapes, a reminder that their distinctive local character and "old world charm" relies upon the selective exclusion of some narratives for the sake of "continuity."

As for the city's transitional projects, it seems unwise to get attached to these temporary fixtures of the High Street landscape. Street art, for example, has a history of being permitted in urban space as a temporary mechanism of regeneration (Andron, 2018; Jien, 2016). Gillian Jien (2016) uses the example of street art in an abandoned depot of a gentrifying Parisian suburb to demonstrate the transitional status of these urban interruptions:

> That interruption is only a momentary gesture in spaces undergoing renewal... Destined to re-enter the normative semiotic regime of governmental visuality, in early 2014 the wildstyle playground of the ruined depot was covered in scaffolding and netting as it was prepared to be wiped clean of its disorderly murals, tamed and returned to the smoothed-out landscapes of the canal's new marina complex.
>
> (99)

In late 2016, similar processes were already happening in the portion of High Street that was being rapidly redeveloped, with pieces of street art being dismantled to make way for the looming Crossing – an incoming shopping mall. The transitional projects – of which *High Street Stories* is one – can be interpreted as smoothing the transition back into the productive circuit of the city, but they also offer a form of future imaginary for the kinds of life the city can offer.

On the possibility that new builds will push out the temporary interventions in Christchurch, one local tells me: "I don't think it will all go. I think people have seen the possibilities now, of all this creativity in the city. I hope it won't all go" (S., Christchurch local).

Haunted imaginaries

I was told before arriving in Christchurch that the downtown was a "bit of a ghost town." The CBD is indeed haunted by the traces of what once was, by future imaginaries of what it can be, and by the urban inscriptions that seek to define the space in the meantime. The sensory reorganisation of place which any process of regeneration entails also re-encodes who and what is included or excluded from that space (Degen, 2012: 22–23; Zukin, 1995). Watching the rebuild progress through the lens of *High Street Stories*, one gets the impression that the new streetscape will have little room for the kind of sensory and social variety that marked the city before – or even for the traces of past lives that mark it in the interim.

Tourist experiences draw connections across both time and space and are entangled with histories (both personal and public) and future imaginaries (Bærenholdt et al., 2008: 199). The haunting of High Street by spectres of its former self produces, as hauntings are want to do, a "something-to-be-done" (Gordon, 2008: xvi). The present absence of High Street's lively former selves prompt users to reflect on the trajectory of the streetscape as it remains – to imagine not only what it once was, but what it could be.

The Christchurch which I left in December 2016 was not the same Christchurch I had encountered some three months earlier. It bore even less resemblance to the Christchurch I had encountered the previous May, on a preliminary fieldwork trip. The ghostly 3-D augmentations of *CityViewAR* had vanished, for one thing (shortly after I departed, the app was officially declared offline on the project website, making sense of its spectral presence in the *High Street Stories* app). New, shining meccas of commerce had arrived in their place. They seem almost alien amongst the stone rubble – yet, to many, their arrival brings a return to the familiar. Still, many of Christchurch's creative placemaking interventions remain for the time being, reminders of the possibilities of performing the city otherwise, even as the world around them begins to solidify.

Notes

1 This is not true for everyone or everyplace. Some ruins, bound up in red tape, funding problems or uncertain futures, become static nodes and sore spots for the locals, as is the case of the Christchurch Cathedral.

2 This obsolescence shifted the methods I used in this case study by necessity. Since the app generally would not download on newer devices, I lent users a tablet (preloaded with *High Street Stories* from previous fieldwork in the city) and walked along with them.

6 A city of screens

Augmenting the branded cityscape in Montreal

Locative encounters in Old Montreal

The app *Montréal en Histoires* (Montréal en Histoires, 2017) alongside its companion installation *Cité Mémoire* – a series of large-scale night-time projections designed to work with the app – has undergone a number of changes since the version I first encountered. The initial version of the app – launched as *Montréal en Histoires* in 2015 – was "a techno-historic circuit" that toured points of interest in the historic part of the city, inserting itself into the tourism scene of Old Montreal quite unobtrusively. However, as the project gained more brand sponsorship – and, notably, with the large cash infusion from the city that came with the development of *Cité Mémoire* as part of the city's 375th anniversary celebrations in 2017 ("Cité Mémoire," Ville Montreal) – the app became a much more established part of the touristic landscape of Old Montreal.

Although packaged together, there are fundamentally two different experiences of *Montréal en Histoires* – one for Montreal by day, and one for the city by night. The first version, the original "techno-historic circuits," looks more like the kind of time-travelling heritage app we have previously discussed, complete with old photos of the city that are layered over the new at various points of interest. However, even this version of the app has an added twist in the form of dramatic AR re-enactments that hazily burn through the present view, adding an element of movement and playfulness as they re-enact significant moments in the city's history. The techno-historic circuits work all day long – and, unlike the projected tableaux, they do not run the risk of you arriving at the site mid-projection – but they are most effective in the daytime, when the black-and-white tableaux can work with the streetscape, rather than the glare of the screen blocking out the user's surroundings.

Using *Montréal en Histoires* by night takes on a whole different character, however. The visual augmentation of the streetscape, for one thing, is offloaded onto the buildings themselves – the city becomes the screen. For another, while the user still has to press play to tune into the audio component of the installation, they can use trigger points (painted footprints on the sidewalk) to help start the projection, turning the city street into a

DOI: 10.4324/9781003142386-10

large-scale user interface. Finally, while the techno-historic circuits are generally designed as a private experience of space for the solo "time traveller," the projections – by virtue of being firmly, and indeed spectacularly, in public view – entangle the user in a collective experience. On its website, *Montréal en Histoires* describes the intended effect of the projections as follows:

> The tableaux presented in Cité Mémoire cover a range of milestones in Montréal's history, well-known (or not so well-known) characters, or sometimes a local slice of life. Narrative or impressionist, touching or amusing, they express our values of coexistence, innovation, tolerance and generosity that are the foundation of our city.
>
> ("Cité Mémoire," *Montréal en Histoires*)

The addition of the projections took recognition and public visibility of the app to the next level. Reviews for *Montréal en Histoires* now implore users to stick around for the night-time projections ("Cité Mémoire," TripAdvisor, 2018), and periodic info boards (what Michel Lemieux charmingly describes as "urban furniture"; in Vermont PBS, 2017), overhead projection signage, sidewalk markings, integrated advertisements on parking meters and billboards, and finally – especially – the projections themselves, all draw considerable attention to the app in both its daytime and night-time forms. The sheer investment in the visibility of this app as part of the Montreal 375 celebrations dwarfs that of any other project I encountered.[1] At a hostel, I receive a tourist map of the city that includes an advertisement for *Cité Mémoire*; the project may not have made it into the actual cartography, but it is map-adjacent. While many locative tourism apps act more like add-ons to the main show – browser extensions that let those who are so inclined peer into the informational layer of a given city or attraction – *Montréal en Histoires* and especially *Cité Mémoire* have become embedded in Montreal's analog format. They are part of the attraction – whether you go looking for them or not.

While reviews of a pre-*Cité Mémoire* iteration of the app tout *Montréal en Histoires* as an interesting – if at times glitchy and disorienting ("Montréal en Histoires," Google Play, 2015)– way to learn more about the city's history, reviews in the *Cité Mémoire* era champion the experience and the atmosphere that it creates. ("Cité Mémoire," Trip Advisor, 2018). The artists behind *Cité Mémoire*, Michel Lemieux and Victor Pilon, describe the app as "loosely inspired" by the history of Montreal, a "dreamy" and "poetic" dramatization of the city's past as told through its cast of top-billed characters (from Huron leader Kondiaronk, to the city's first executioner, to local philanthropist Joe Beef, to sports stars from Jackie Robinson to Maurice "Rocket" Richard) (Lemieux & Pilon, 2016). The artists describe their story of the city as follows:

> 375 faces of Montreal come to life among the trees, borne on the words of the city's poets. Cité Mémoire pays tribute to Montreal – receptive,

> perceptive, sensitive, progressive – and, above all, to the human beings peopling it in the present, who founded it in the past, and who will dream it into existence tomorrow.
>
> (Lemieux & Pilon, 2016)

The fact that the project is more "spectacular" and dramatic than strictly historical was a sore spot for some historical enterprises who had been fighting for Montreal 375 funding (Everett-Green, 2016). Journalist Robert Everett-Green noted that proposals by historical societies were widely rejected by the Montreal 375 planning committee, which ruffled some feathers amongst the city's historical organizations, who were competing against the "party crowd" bent on making the celebrations into an event (Everett-Green, 2016). Rather than rigidly adhere to historical fact, *Cité Mémoire* takes an openly "poetic, humanistic" approach (Lemieux & Pilon, 2016) designed to be "deeply moving" and to inspire an emotional – rather than a purely intellectual – connection (Lemieux & Pilon, 2017). *Cité Mémoire* leans into the experience economy not only through its spectacular scale, but through the intimacy of both the audio and the use of gaze. This intimacy allows these projections of the past to connect to the present – not only do viewers look into the past, but the past looks back out at them.

Montréal en Histoires, like many of the applications in this study, brands itself as an experience of history, less a tour than an "encounter." (The app's description invites users to "roam the streets of Montreal with this application to immerse yourself in the city's history, with more than 60 unique items to discover.") Users can either choose from a selection of pre-determined circuits in different areas of the Old Port, ranging from 30 to 60 minutes depending on the length of time they are willing to commit to the tour, or they can choose to "Walk Around Freely." The notion that the app can be "explored freely" plays into its branding as an almost serendipitous encounter with history – a story of Montreal that is discovered by rather than presented to the user. The navigation component of the app allows users to view the map in either 2-D (the view from above) or 3-D (the view from below).

Montréal en Histoires offers an assortment of "items" that the user can discover, ranging from points of interest (which are generally historical photos with accompanying narration), represented by blue dots, to the white eye icons, which are augmented reality experiences that stage interpretive re-enactments on site, to the little yellow houses that represent the tableaux (projections) of *Cité Mémoire*. While the sites of the tableaux were more beholden to the demands of a projection (such as a blank wall) than actually "placing" history – and are thus generally spread further apart – the blue dots and white eyes that mark the waypoints of the techno-historic circuit are much more frequent, and generally site-specific. While the novelty of the AR projections does tend to mark them as the de facto signposts of any given circuit, the density of mediated points of interest – particularly in the tourist hot zone along St Paul Street – means that *Montréal en*

Histoires weaves a pretty continuous narrative through the streetscape of Old Montreal. As such, the app has many opportunities to shape the atmosphere of Old Montreal that users encounter, and to inspire the emotional connection to the city which it openly courts.

Shaping urban atmospheres

Locative tours do not only add to the spectacle of the street. As Sandvik (2010) argues, "Augmentation of reality implies an enhancement of the emotional character of the places: a certain mood, atmosphere, or narrative surplus of meaning has been implemented" (138). This mood is not just a "layer" over the streetscape – it is co-produced and exists in the relationship between the user, the media, and the augmented environment. Since they frame the experience of place, these atmospheres can also alter the mental souvenirs of the city which users take with them, making them especially effective media for urban branding. In the increasingly designed sensescapes of the experience economy (Pine & Gilmore, 1999; Thibaud, 2015), an ambiance which strikes the "proper" tone is something to be courted and maintained (Thibaud, 2015: 40-43), and the "practice of purposefully staging and manipulating atmospheres is pervasive" in urban destination space (Buser, 2017: 8).

The "poetic" vision of space and memory that Pilon and Lemieux have created is arguably shaped more by an artistic sensibility than an archival one, which accounts for the way historical events and figures were re-enacted and re-animated for the projections (rather than projecting archival footage across the city's architecture, for example). This artistic approach might lose some of the perceived "reliability" of historical narrative, but it does create "sensual arrangements that seem to offer better access to an experiential realm" (Highmore, 2013b: 75). Not only does this re-animation allow the work to maintain a cohesive aesthetic across multiple time periods – many of them pre-photographic – it allows for the creation of dynamic, charged atmospheres in otherwise mundane spaces.

This mood management is especially effective in situations where the gaze is used to connect more than one projection across a street. A spectator watching in horror from a window while protesters raze parliament ("The Burning of the Parliament in Montreal"), a colonial settler and an Indigenous warrior staring each other down across a parking lot ("Jean Mance"), or a couple of sailors on leave visibly delighting in the peep show of burlesque performer Lily St Cyr ("Babylon of the North") – each of these moments feature characters reacting to each other across multiple "screens," and so they instruct us on the atmosphere that hangs between them (see Figure 6.1). These atmospheric relationships are enhanced by the app's audio, where both foreground narration and background sounds (like the wind whistling across the plain between the settler and native, or the music, catcalls, and clink of ice into lowball glasses that add texture to the burlesque show) set the scene.

Figure 6.1 Gazing between screens at *Cité Mémoire*'s "Babylon of the North."

(Image credit: the author; *Cité Mémoire* a creation of Michel Lemieux and Victor Pilon, in collaboration with Michel

Another tableau which particularly speaks to the "poetic" and intimate approach that the designers took in constructing these stories is "The First Executioner." The tableau tells the 17th-century story of a military drummer in the city who was exposed as gay and forced to choose between being put to death or becoming the colony's first executioner. The story plays over a stylized dance between the drummer and his lover, with both intimacy and tragedy conveyed through their touch – the camera lingers on the intertwining of hands, the ritualistic removal of clothing (see Figure 6.2). What is at first the sensuality of a love story turns to the grim practicality of removing the drummer's regimental garb so that he can take up the robe of the executioner.

While the large-scale projections certainly make an impact, absent the context of the app, their "meaning" within the broader narrative of the city is somewhat illusory, their presence more spectral and ephemeral than concrete. Rather, it is the intimacy of the audio that lends the events and people in the projections their "'feel' of reality" (Bull, 2014: 240) by weaving the ghostly images into a historical narrative. Both the designers behind *High Street Stories* and *Cité Mémoire* describe a connection between aurality and intimacy. The spectacular projections of *Cité Mémoire* are monumental – scaled to have the impact of a building, with some added dynamism – and designed to awe. Meanwhile, bringing the phone to one's

Figure 6.2 Spectacular intimacy at *Cité Mémoire*'s "The First Executioner."
(Image credit: the author; *Cité Mémoire* a creation of Michel Lemieux and Victor Pilon, in collaboration with Michel Marc Bouchard).

ear (as Michel Lemieux depicts it)[2] is an intimate act – tied to the technological extension of the self; listening to the phone is conceived of as an intimate way of perceiving the environment, rather than a distancing one.

Smooth operators: rhythms, tour guides, and the 'smoothing out' of experience

As we have touched on at multiple points over the course of this study, augmented reality and locative tours rely upon users' "alignment work" to bring the app content in line with the urban environment and actualise the tour (Licoppe, 2016; see also Hansen, 2004). As we have also seen, that process rarely proceeds smoothly, exposing gaps and seams in the augmentation. Locative tours usually offer the perceived benefit – from a place-branding perspective – of offloading the performative labour of tour guides (tasked with maintaining a certain mood in themed spaces; Bryman, 2004: 2) onto the arguably more consistent app framework. However, just because the app content maintains a certain mood does not mean that that mood will translate to the tourist's performance of locative narrative.

A variety of factors can intervene to make, break, or alter the mood of the tour, and without a tour guide's smoothing influence or capacity to improvise, and in the hands of a tourist who is already navigating unfamiliar terrain, the story can quickly jump the tracks.

Montréal en Histoires (and specifically the night-time *Cité Mémoire* circuit) is unique amongst the apps included in this study in that the organizers have employed guides onsite to help users troubleshoot the application and answer questions about the projections, thus smoothing out the experience. Even when leading their own tours using the app, often these guides will stop along the way to help solo users with any issues. They also smooth over glitches in the technological fabric of the tour, reporting problems to on-the-ground technicians so that any visible "seams" in the tour can be effectively erased. Over the course of one tour that I observed, for example, the guide called in both a broken projection and an errant cursor (see Figure 6.3) to technical support crew members.

Tour operators manage the rhythm of the tour; depending on a guide's gait, their improvisation, and their interaction with the tourists or with the place, the cadence of the tour will shift, and these shifts can impact tourists'

Figure 6.3 Seams in the tour – a wild cursor appears at *Cité Mémoire's* "The Creation of the World."

sense of the city (Cox, 2018: 371). In addition, *Cité Mémoire*'s tour guides also curate what parts of the circuits of projections they show tourists. Some of these decisions are driven by practicality – not showing a French poem to an English tour, for example, or avoiding projections that are not working on the night. In other cases, tour guides draw together a succession of sites into micro-narratives within the tour – combining the projections on the women's movement, the criminalization of homosexuality, and history of racism in the city into a small tour of the city's history of oppressive practices.

The human guide fulfils an essential role in the app – that of smoothing out the experience of the tour. A tour guide facilitates the improvisation that is often required to weave the city into a cohesive narrative (Cox, 2018), and a human guide can shift course around obstacles and fill unexpected detours or gaps with additional context, in a way that the apps themselves cannot. As one tour guide notes, many people are required on the ground to keep *Cité Mémoire*'s projections running: "If we left it alone for two days, it would fall apart." Technological achievement in automation though it may be, *Cité Mémoire*'s success relies on continual human intervention in the environment (both in the front stage – people using the app, and those who sometimes guide them – and the backstage of engineers and onsite technicians) for much of its magic.

However, even tour guides are not immune to falling out of sync with the rhythm of the tour. Having opted to compare the solo experience of the app to the guided one, I sign up for a guided tour. I find myself alone on the tour – the last of the season before winter chases away the tourist crowd – and so we start a few minutes early. Because of this, we skip the BMO projection – "Builders of the City" – which has already started, although the guide explains that the projection gives an overview of the development of Montreal and how the city has changed over time. We begin, instead, with the tableau "The Jewish Children's Transport Train," about the refugee children who were resettled in the city after the Second World War. We have timed it a little wrong, so the projection has not yet started. The next projection we visit ("The Ouimetoscope"/"Babylon of the North") has the same issue – the Ouimetoscope portion of it is nearly over, and we tune in to the tableau halfway through. The guide remarks on his bad luck with the timing.

While the guide is good-natured about it, the propensity for falling out of sync with the tour is a bit of a sore spot for some users of the tour. After all, tourists are generally subject to time constraints in their touring. As one disgruntled reviewer puts it:

> We tried to do the tour of Old Montreal with the app describing the history of the city with projections on different parts of the city … NEVER SAW A SINGLE PROJECTION! There is an over abundance of construction along the suggested route which finally made us abandon this tour.
>
> ("Cité Mémoire," TripAdvisor, 2018)

In the absence of the tableaux, the projection sites are, after all, mostly parking lots facing blank walls and thus – without augmentation – make rather poor stand-ins for a tourist destination. (Unlike the gaps in Christchurch's streetscape, these walls are primarily scrubbed clean of any street art, save the odd ghost of an old advertisement likely left in place for its heritage allure). What is more, road works to restore Old Montreal's characteristic cobblestones have disrupted many of the more common routes followed by the tour, turning what is meant to be a pleasant stroll through historic streets into an obstacle course between projections. However, *Cité Mémoire* uses a number of narrative and technological interventions to re-sync the bodies of users with the timing of the tour and to reorganise its timeline.

The Grand Tableau: getting the "big picture" in Old Montreal

What is worth noting about *Montréal en Histoires* is that, although it is akin to Christchurch's *High Street Stories* in that it embeds a large amount of historical content over a relatively contained geographic area, the two apps differ in the way that they present the history of any given site or building. *High Street Stories* foregrounded personal narratives, leading to the sedimentation of stories around any given area and breaking up the authorship of High Street's story, albeit within the curated context of the app. *Montréal en Histories* takes a more authoritative perspective, tracing the lifecycle of a building from above. The effect of these different viewpoints is that *Montréal en Histoires* offers its users *the* history of a place (delivered in the same soothing tones as an airplane safety video), while *High Street Stories* offers a (curated) selection of histor*ies* in different voices. As we will discuss in greater detail shortly, *Montréal en Histoires* tries to counteract this de-personalised tone in a variety of ways, particularly by breaking the fourth wall in both its augmented reality offerings and in its *Cité Mémoire* projections.

While the pre-determined circuits have suggested starting points (chief amongst them the BMO building at Place des Armes, BMO being the chief sponsor of the application), they can ultimately be consumed in any direction and from any starting point. This is one of the defining features of the locative narratives that historical apps generally present – because the stories are organised around the paths that users take, they almost never follow a linear progression through time. The effect can be that of a collapsed timeline, where users encounter a mélange of historical time periods mashed into one. This variation is especially evident in the projections, where the characters dancing on the city walls swap colonial garb for swinging-sixties hemlines over the course of a short walk. Because the on-site projections are presented anachronistically (unless a user were to take the considerable time needed to weave them back into chronological order by foot), the user finds him- or herself navigating a jumbled version of history where points in the city's past are compressed and reassembled in the now.

Cité Mémoire has a unique trick up its sleeve to reorganise that timeline, however. During scheduled projection days, *Cité Mémoire* stages what is called the "Grand Tableau" every half hour at the city's Champs de Mars. The Grand Tableau effectively acts as the app's "big picture" – both literally and figuratively (see Figure 6.4). Snippets of the various projections are assembled (in chronological order) in a roughly 30-minute screening, projected 18 storeys high on a building against a background of the city skyline. The Grand Tableau does away with the lauded intimacy of the app's audio, opting instead for spectacle on a grand scale with an evocative selection of music (one which also conveys the passage of time, shifting from colonial-era dirges to a poppy modern dance number over the screening's run time). Having situated all of its characters in time, the Grand Tableau then proceeds to combine them all into an exercise in pastiche – a closing dance number that features characters from each of the tableaux as well as various icons of the city. Montreal-style bagels, a shower of brightly coloured balls culled from over the streets of the gay village, and a parade of penguins from the city's popular BioDome attraction are interspersed

Figure 6.4 The various projections of *Cité Mémoire* are collected into one narrative at the "Grand Tableau."

(Image credit: the author; *Cité Mémoire* a creation of Michel Lemieux and Victor Pilon, in collaboration with Michel Marc Bouchard).

with characters from all over the city's projections, bopping together to an upbeat song. At the projection's end, the simple, stark image "MONTREAL" flashes across the screen – this is Brand Montreal.

Augmenting the branded cityscape

As we previously discussed when looking at the Derry-Londonderry's *Walk the Walls* app, branding has become a pervasive element of the urban environment, expanding from localised sites and themed spaces to infiltrate both the public spaces of the city and its urban imaginaries (Klingmann, 2007). As Klingmann (2007) notes, while the abstract notion of branding took spatial shape in flagship stores and shopping malls, in recent decades it has "reached another level as a ubiquitous formula of market culture that permeates urban centres, the edges of cities and residential communities alike" (81). Urban tourist destinations become focal points for the interplay of both corporate and city branding initiatives (Dinnie, 2011). Place branding also plays a role in negotiating the meanings and cultural memories of sites, and performing the branded tour helps further entrench those dominant (or dominating) understandings of place (Bird et al., 2018: 651). The urban brand not only refashions the city's present, it refashions its past (Sturken, 1997).

Part of the visceral impact of branding (and branded experience) lies in its power to envelop us within the urban environment (Taussig, 2009: 271). "'What in the end makes advertising so superior to criticism?' asks [Walter] Benjamin (1979: 86). 'Not what the moving red neon sign says – but the fiery pool reflecting it in the asphalt'" (qtd. In Taussig, 2009: 271). This type of envelopment is on full display in the application, and especially in the night-time circuits, where the city-turned-screen is mirrored in the screen in your hand while its story is pumped directly into your ears.

While cities generally build their brand around "material characteristics of the place such as buildings or events, or its immaterial aspects, for example, stories, slogans and logos" (Hospers, 2011: 27), *Cité Mémoire* manages to take the stories of the city and turn them into events in and of themselves. It also manages to combine the three most common "image carriers" involved in successfully branding a city as worthy of the tourist gaze – "the built environment, hallmark events, and famous personalities" (Hospers, 2011: 34) – into one attraction. *Cité Mémoire* is engaged in constructing a highly imageable city out of Old Montreal's nightscapes – both in the more conventional touristic sense of a city which demands to be photographed, but also in Lynch's (1960) sense of a city that sticks in the visitor's mind, and which leaves an impression. This process makes it an effective carrier not just for "Brand Montreal," but for other branded images and stories that are woven into its map.

Mapping brand values in Montreal

Having watched *Montréal en Histoires* evolve from its smaller beta version into the much larger version currently on offer, it is worth noting that brand partnerships were seemingly part of its development from the start. Both the *Montréal en Histoires* app and *Cité Mémoire* installation embed branded content into the streetscape of the old city, starting with the Bank of Montreal (BMO). The "natural" starting point of the application is the old site of the Bank of Montreal (which still bears the name of the company carved into its stately facade). Here, users are informed of the central role of the Bank of Montreal – one of the sponsors of the application in the evolution of the city. Even during the day, the saturation of branded imagery here is intense – from the logos and brand names on the bank buildings, to the bank logo on the app's loading screen, to the brand-friendly content embedded in the site. The bank is depicted as a driver of progress, a starting point and a cornerstone for the tour. Guided tours of *Cité Mémoire* also depart from here, and the tableau "Builders of the City," a story of urban development in Montreal (courtesy in part of the Bank of Montreal) is projected onto the bank's walls, serving as a frame for all of the buildings to come.

This brand integration of BMO works its way into the map of *Montréal en Histoires* as well. In addition to various points of interest and AR vignettes, the map handily notes the location of every BMO ATM in the vicinity. With the arrival of *Cité Mémoire*, these BMO markers move from the map onto the physical geography of the Old Port. The brand logo is featured on the *Cité Mémoire* "loading screen" – the small projection that marks out the (otherwise blank) walls where a projection will soon begin. This has the effect of stamping the BMO logo on buildings across the city for captive audiences who are waiting for the rhythm of their tour to sync up with the projection.

Moving through Old Montreal, other brand content unfurls itself. Among the most obvious are the stops dedicated to the Molson family, where brand-friendly descriptions of the company as a paragon of family values and major contributors to the city are scattered amongst non-partner content. Similarly, CN Rail's content becomes intermingled with the regular circuits through the Old Port. While *Montréal en Histoires* positions branded content as separate tours that it offers – accessible in a section called "Partner Circuits" – the points on the map that make up those tours often become indistinguishable from the rest of the app and can be freely encountered while wandering.

Some of these Partner Circuits are especially relevant to the infrastructure and mobility of the city, such as the CN Railway's "Birth of the Railway" tour, and the "Stories and Bridges" tour sponsored by Jacques Cartier and Champlain Bridges Incorporated. The effect of such tours is that the "invisible" architecture of the city (its informational network) and its flows (pedestrian use) make visible the more solid but often taken-for-granted elements of the city's construction – making the utilitarian into something worthy of consumption and folding it into the celebration of the city's 375th anniversary.

Second to the front-and-centre Bank of Montreal content, the brand narrative a user is most likely to encounter while simply walking the streets of Old Montreal is the John Molson circuit. This circuit discusses the evolution of the Molson Company with emphasis on the "family values" and philanthropic character of the company. Positive brand imagery in this circuit is even on display in the unique capitalisation in the walk's description, which invites users to delve into the history of "One of Canada's Most Prestigious Family Businesses" – a description which might as well be followed by a trademark. The company is given gravitas through an exploration of its rich heritage, and is highlighted – much like the Bank of Montreal – as a cornerstone of the development of Montreal. The significance of the company's role is said to be encapsulated in the Molson sign and clock, described as an enduring and beloved part of the city's skyline.

The Molson stops on the tour also indicate the continuity between branding efforts in the techno-historic circuits and in the tableaux. While the tableaux generally speak to Brand Montreal more than they promote any specific brand (with the previously mentioned nods to BMO serving as an exception), consuming the tableaux in connection with the points of interest in the techno-historic circuits does strengthen certain brand associations. The tableau "Moving with the Rocket" – which features famous Montreal Canadiens hockey player Maurice "Rocket" Richard – is presented just steps from a point of interest about seven generations of the Molson family, including several generations who have invested in the Canadiens franchise.

The 2017 introduction of new tableaux and AR experiences set in the Queen Elizabeth Hotel's agora further blurred the lines between the wider urban brand and partner branding (in this case, the hotel). The AR projections inside the metro tunnel leading from Place Ville Marie draw users and passers-by alike along an enchanted, interactive corridor towards the hotel's agora. Once inside, projections inspired by John Lennon and Yoko Ono's 1969 bed-in at the hotel add star power to the brand experience of the hotel. As the hotel chain's president of investments, Sylvain Fortier, notes: "These installations perfectly illustrate our vision of enhancing the urban hotel experience, in collaborations with local artists, while contributing to Québec's cultural heritage" (in Lemieux & Pilon, 2017).

The tableaux are designed to highlight the hotel's cultural significance through its association with high-profile guests – from members of the Beatles to its titular monarch – while also conveying positive brand associations for the hotel (its "landmark" historical status and hospitality standards worthy of a queen, for example). Furthermore, the indoor projections make it possible for users to experience *Cité Mémoire* in a more constant and controlled environment – one that is not dependent on nightfall or hampered by the cold or the rain. The tunnel to the hotel also features fewer of the "unruly" sensory elements of the tour that break through in the alleyway projections, such as the smell of urine or the sometimes raucous atmosphere.

Carnivalesque brandscapes and branded multiculturalism

While carnivals and theme parks were said to offer "sensory refreshment" to urbanites (Mack, 2015: 103), the powerful sensations of the fair and carnival have increasingly been subjected to control, either shifted to the margins of modern life or watered down and sprinkled over the spectacular city (Edensor, 2016). The theme park frames the experience of the city as a whole, particularly in tourist hot zones; "popular desires for the carnivalesque ... have often been coopted by advertising and marketing strategists, who produce spaces which appear to promise a cornucopia of sensations and 'uncontrolled social differences,' but only ever deliver a 'controlled diversity'" (Edensor, 2016: 43; drawing from Mitchell, 1995).

Commercial historical tours – and historical re-enactments, especially – tend to sanitise the past for public consumption, a process "often derided as Disneyfication of history, the creation of a cute cartoon version of life that simplifies highly complex social and political environments" (Gordon, 2016: 6). By telling the story of Montreal in the style of on-site "heritage moments,"[3] *Cité Mémoire*'s storytelling style is familiar, even for users who marvel at its scale and unique delivery. The format also speaks to the city's tourism development strategy, which puts a heavy focus on cultural experiences and the creation of "moments" – rather than simply sites – in the lead-up to the Montreal 375 celebrations (Tourisme Montreal, 2014). This familiar format safely confines some of the more troubling aspects of the city's identity to the past.

As with most exercises in branding, the "City of Memories" requires a certain amount of oversimplification of its stories and characters to render the brandscape sensible to users (Dinnie, 2011). Some of the most overt Indigenous representation in the app, for example, borders on what Gordon calls the "Indian stereotype" (2016: 293) – that is, Indigenous people in recognisable dress, seemingly frozen in the colonial past, who resemble the images of native people which tend to circulate in the popular imaginary (280–293). This follows a pattern which defined much of the native representation in Canadian museums throughout the 20th century, which, Gordon argues, "continued the colonization of Aboriginal culture" in the museum space by drawing on Euro-Canadian perceptions of accommodation through pluralism. The addition of Aboriginal stories simply inserted one more culture into the narrative of the national march toward the modern incarnation of multicultural Canada" (293). This notion of the progressive march towards multiculturalism is embodied in the closing musical number of the projection at Champs-de-Mars, where the app's cast of characters dance together like one big happy family, erasing much of the nuance expressed in the tour (for example, the discussion of the erasure of Indigenous culture which app users are privy to in their experience of *Cité Mémoire's* "The Creation of the World," as we will discuss later in this chapter).

The skyline of the city has long played host to branded images. Speaking of the power of urban advertising at the turn of the 20th century, and particularly its role in the city skyline, Ewen (2018) notes: "A seductive, imagistic panorama had been installed above the American landscape" (44). The horizon was populated not only by the city's buildings but by the many delights it had to offer the consumer – from automobiles to underwear (Ewen, 2018: 44). By turning assorted walls in Old Montreal into a series of urban screens, *Cité Mémoire* gives Montreal the opportunity to project Brand Montreal onto that skyline – alongside an assortment of other brand logos for consumption.

The city as screen

Struppek (2006), examining the role of urban screens in shaping public space, notes that the proliferation of urban screens realises Debord's (1970) Society of the Spectacle, but also argues that these screens have the potential to generate joint experiences, whether it is taking part in a public cultural screening or cheering on a sports team together (174–175). Urban screens can also trouble notions of public and private space – interiority and exteriority – by, for example, allowing art galleries and museums to offer a sampling of what is inside to be consumed on the outside, or screening intimate portraits representing the diversity of local inhabitants (176–178). The arrival of the internet and mobile technology have also allowed these screens to become increasingly interactive (Struppek, 2006: 183) and locative media is part of this more interactive iteration of screening the city (186).

Based on the amount of user feedback online, *Montréal en Histoires* was the probably the most widely used of the apps studied here. Arguably, this success is in some part attributable to the fact that the large-scale projections of *Cité Mémoire* offer a considerable hook – many play scenes with obvious dialogue or scenes (such as "The Beaver Rebellion," which uses animated beavers to tell the story of the French and Iroquois Wars) that beg for contextualisation which only the application can offer. Some users describe initially seeing a projection from their hotel window and being lured out into the street to explore more. If users want to get the "whole story," they have to download the app. *Cité Mémoire*'s projections thus contribute prominently to urban spectacle – and particularly to the spectacle of Montreal's urban night, which is increasingly marked by large-scale projects of selective illumination – while at once reframing the city as a screen.

It is worth noting that the artists behind *Cité Mémoire* do not primarily aim to remake the city as a series of screens. As Michel Lemieux notes (in a documentary of the project called *Into the Light with Cité Mémoire*), the idea is, rather, "to make appear a giant in the city" – to have the history of the city emerge from the walls in such spectacular fashion that it forces passers-by to slow, to stop, and to turn their faces to the sky. Their aim, Lemieux suggests, is to create a moment of pause – and of wonderment – amidst the frantic pace of the city. (As we will discuss later in this chapter, the projections often succeed in doing just that). However, it is still worth considering the implications of "screening" Montreal through the lens of

Cité Mémoire – including how the "giants" summoned by Lemieux and Pilon relate to broader practices of urban spectacle and illumination.

Although the projection of the Grand Tableau at Champs de Mars is the most stationary from a user perspective – in that users can experience it in its totality without leaving the square – the unfolding of the city's history here is the most provocatively soaring. Part of this is the sheer height of the "screen," which itself soars some 18 storeys into the air, projected on the side of the city's imposing modernist Palais de Justice. But this soaring quality is also related to the way so many of the projections move across the screen – moving vertically, before vanishing into the night sky. This lends a sense of almost linear progress to the narrative, with Montreal's history ever reaching upwards – a city in perpetual motion. This type of screening also acts on the body of the spectator. The soaring projections draw the gaze upwards, away from the square – as Naim June Paik notes, "Cinema isn't I see, it's I fly," and Diana Vertov further claims that "I fall and I fly at one with the bodies falling or rising through the air" (both qtd. in Taussig, 2009: 271).

Screening the story of Montreal this way complements the existing skyline by continuously drawing the gaze upwards, away from the parts of the streetscape that are less primed for consumption. As Howes (2016) notes:

> while "close up there are things that are not very comforting: littered streets, corner drug deals, broken down tenements" (Douglas, 1996: 2), by keeping eyes looking upward, skyscrapers diverted the senses from the often far less attractive scenario of the ground environment.
>
> (28)

The scale of the projections thus also provokes the user to stand back. While the app is site-specific (should a user attempt to access *Cité Mémoire*'s projection narratives from a far-off place, the app will prompt you to go to Vieux Montréal), users have to navigate the app's demand – get close – and the "screen's" inherent warning: but not too close. Nevertheless, the projections cannot help but also foreground elements of the Old Montreal streetscape that might otherwise be unremarkable (or at least unremarked upon).

These screenings also have the effect of turning what is often the non-consumable "back stage" of the tourist space – parking lots, alleyways, and the sides of museums, to name a few – into sites worthy of the tourist gaze. Notably, at least in the case of parking lots, this effect cuts both ways, making the parking lot both less and more visible in turns. As the lights go out and the projection begins, it draws the user's eye upwards, away from the parking lot. The combination of illumination and darkness does the tour's work of obscuring less desirable aspects of the place (Gordon, 2016: 308). When the lights come back on, however, the parking lot is suddenly in stark relief. In some cases, *Cité Mémoire* even gains some unexpected characters during screening – a parking lot attendant guiding someone out of a tight spot, or a local restaurant worker, still wearing his apron, running to grab something from his car. All of these mundane elements and everyday performances of the space come into sharper focus with the projection screen behind them. As we previously discussed, the specific way that apps like *Montréal en Histoires* position users means that these "backstage" parts of the tourist environment cannot be framed out, and are brought to the foreground.

Montreal by night: a highlight reel

Screening the city involves a judgement about what belongs on the city's walls – what narratives of the space are worthy of being projected onto its streetscape while others are buffed away – that works in concert with the enhanced visibility of particular spaces and landmarks. This highlighting process is especially perceptible in the urban night, when Montreal (often literally) puts a spotlight on places it considers culturally valuable.

Artificial lighting has a long history in the (re)organization and mediation of spatial relations in urban public spaces (Edensor, 2017; Krajina, 2009). Lighting is a key mechanism of setting the mood of a given place (Highmore, 2013). As Edensor (2017) argues that, "Light possesses a particularly rich capacity to defamiliarize familiar places, transforming what is well known into an uncanny realm and thereby suggesting that place may be apprehended otherwise" (115). This transformative quality accounts for its popularity in reshaping urban space to set the scene for things like festivals and art installations. The atmosphere of the urban night differs from that of the city by day – it is more broken up, less evenly constituted (Anderson, 2009: 93). Illumination can attempt to rectify that discontinuity. On the other hand, atmospheres also "bathe everything in a certain light," serving to "unify a diversity of impressions" (Böhme, 2013: para. 4).

Montreal's nightscape offers the tourist an illuminated highlight reel of what Old Montreal has to offer as a destination space. Landmarks like the Notre Dame Basilica and the Bonsecours Market are bathed in evocative uplighting, usually in shades of blue or violet, a complement to the warm lighting that blankets the streets, bouncing off the old city's cobblestones. Across the St. Lawrence River, an illuminated Biosphere – a remnant of Expo 67 – seems positively subtle compared to the vibrant swirls of colour that trace the contours of roller coasters and other rides in LaRonde (a nearby theme park). The recently illuminated Jacques Cartier Bridge connects that carnival to its branded dupe in the Old Port's Natrel Basin, which recently added a multi-coloured Ferris wheel to its buffet of attractions, making the delicate yellow of the Old Port's illuminated clock tower seem subtle by comparison. If you time it right, you might even find one of Cirque du Soleil's big top tents here, completing the carnivalesque atmosphere.

Many of these illuminated landmarks also make it onto the highlight reel of *Montréal en Histoires*, with points of interest, augmented reality segments, and tableaux working together to add further interest to many of the above sites. The clocktower, for example, gets an inky cloak of (simulated) dark sky thrown over its yellow skin every half hour, becoming the stage for a ghostly dance number set to Leonard Cohen's "Suzanne." The illuminated Ferris wheel – seemingly a poster child for the desire to gain a panoramic view of the city from within a protective bubble – gets a more personal touch in the form of various faces projected onto the trees at its feet, accompanied by overlapping personal stories in the app ("The Face of Montreal"). Stringing together the illuminated landmarks of the city, *Cité Mémoire*'s tableaux give the urban night a knowable, almost intimate quality.

When the artists declare that the city's memories "come to life among the trees" (Lemieux & Pilon, 2016), they are being quite literal. The projections onto the trees at the foot of the Ferris wheel are among the project's most uncanny, because they embody the city as at once a screen and a living, changing entity. The branches grow, the surface of the trees gets more uneven as time passes, and the faces that snap in and out of view get somewhat distorted (see Figure 6.5). The narration which accompanies this projection is also the app's least linear – with an assortment of stories and poems highlighting the diversity of experience in the city fading in and out on each other's heels, weaving together. "The Face of Montreal" is the piece which perhaps most exemplifies the notion of Montreal as a city of stories – rather than just presenting *the* story of Montreal. Here, the stories of Montreal are diffused through multiple voices, spoken in a multitude of tongues, offered in prose and snippets of poetry, and layered over each other. Even the

Figure 6.5 "Faces of Montreal" personalise the Old Port's carnivalesque atmosphere.

("Image credit: the author; *Cité Mémoire* a creation of Michel Lemieux and Victor Pilon, in collaboration with Michel Marc Bouchard")

faces – diverse in age and ethnicity – take on an uncertain quality, projected as they are against the broken, tremulous, and uneven surfaces of the trees. As the seasons change, these faces become even more ephemeral; the face of Montreal is harder to trace in the tourist offseason.

The tableaux can also take on an air of atemporality, depending on the time of year when you view the projections. In "Soir d'hiver" ("A Winter's Night"), snow blows across a mournful wall as the titular poem is read aloud, and the winter wind of "Jeanne Mance" – whistling through the audio and tousling screens on either side of a parking lot – seems to fill the space between opposed projections of colonists and natives even in the thick of summer. Conversely, real snowfall turns the interactive tableau "Creation of the World" into a soft-focus, impressionistic canvas – a soft frozen blanket which plays host to images of sun-bathed grass and flowing water. Intertwined as it is with the natural world, the city makes for an uneven, shifting screen.

Haunted Montreal

According to one of *Cité Mémoire*'s (human) guides, the "Peace of Montreal" tableau is the only projection that is staged in the exact place where the historic event that it narrates happened. The tableau, which centres on the historic peace treaty brokered on the site and features the iconic marks of 39 First Nations leaders that signed that treaty, is projected on the broad side of the Point aux Callieres Museum,[4] nestled between two trees. The projection of a third tree naturalises the tableau – between the other two, it seems to "fit," anchoring the narrative in the space of present-day Montreal. Elsewhere, the project faced the considerable challenge of finding blank, and ideally windowless, walls in Old Montreal. The projection sites were, in fact, secured before any of the tableaux went into production, and architectural details of these uneven "screens" are used to anchor the projections. In "The Jewish Children's Transport Train," the chimney seam of an old building is transfigured into a post for the tableau's railway platform. Another, "From Marie-Josephe to Jackie Robinson," which includes images of a burning Montreal, uses the outline of peaked roofs – relics of long-since-vanished buildings – to its advantage in tracing the city skyline (see Figures 6.6 and 6.7). In the fenced-off lot in front of "Joe Beef's Funeral," the old crumbling foundations of a building – long gone, if the overgrowth that blankets the lot is any indication – form a perfect bench for a group of travellers taking in the app. Each of these projection sites are gaps in the skyline – places where another building used to be. Not unlike in Christchurch, this process of tracing the city's past lives through these gaps makes Montreal's ghosts more visible in the daytime.

The tableaux are similarly haunted by old advertisements that bleed through the projection. A projected burlesque number (in "Babylon of the North") is haunted by an ad for wholesale hardware lurking just backstage (see Figure 6.1). While the effect of *Cité Mémoire*'s projections is novel,

Figure 6.6 Ghosts of Montreal past by day.

these ghosts of advertisements past draw attention to the fact that these hollowed-out nooks of the Old Port have long been used to project narratives over the city – some more transparently branded than others. While the notion of turning buildings into projection screens is somewhat novel – and a technical feat – the concept of using the urban façade as a staging ground for brand narratives has a long history (Ewen, 2018: 44).

The city looks back: intimate gaze and surveillance in Montréal en Histoires

As we have discussed, many of *Montréal en Histoires*' points of interest take an authoritative perspective on the city's history, and the tableaux are of such grand scale that they force the user to stand at a distance to take it all in. Combined, these factors threaten to make the app's stories feel impersonal, and thus endanger the emotional connection which the designers were aiming to inspire. *Cité Mémoire* counters some of this depersonalisation through its use of the gaze. Many of the tableaux engage with an active breaking of the fourth wall – their characters stare back at the viewer. Sometimes this is seduction, as in the case of burlesque performer Lily St Cyr ("Babylon of the

Figure 6.7 Ghosts of Montreal past by night, in *Cité Mémoire*'s "From Marie-Josephe to Jackie Robinson."

(Image credit: the author; *Cité Mémoire* a creation of Michel Lemieux and Victor Pilon, in collaboration with Michel Marc Bouchard).

North"). Sometimes it is more plaintiff, as when Marie-Josephe Angelique – a slave accused of starting a huge fire in the city, and who shortly thereafter is put to death – looks out at the user while Montreal burns behind her ("From Marie-Josephe to Jackie Robinson") (see Figure 6.7). It can also be confrontational, as when suffragettes and women's rights activists march defiantly toward the screen ("Eva Circe-Cote"). At other times the storytelling function of this gaze is less obvious, as when every other person in the procession at local philanthropist Joe Beef's funeral turns to look at the viewer while they walk, as though the app user was being invited to join the procession ("Joe Beef's Funeral") – or, as the artists suggest, being asked to give an accounting of what *they* have done for their fellow man (Zolf, 2020). By breaking the fourth wall of the projections, *Cité Mémoire* invites the user to engage, and to see themselves as part of the story of Montreal.

This feature of creating intimacy through the gaze extends beyond the *Cité Mémoire* tableaux and into the AR re-enactments of the daytime techno-historic circuits. Take, for example, the old Dalhousie rail station, the tracks of which – curving off towards shiny new condo buildings – suddenly become visible once the app tells you where you are. The narrator asks if you hear a distant whistle, and the augmented view before you becomes occluded by smoke, and people mill around the platform. One woman looks back, locking eyes with the user as the people from the past mill around them (see Figure 6.8). There is an intensity about the experience that cannot be denied.

This intense gaze is mirrored by the CCTV cameras that decorate the outside of what is now a circus, pointing into the square. Since *Montréal en Histoires*' AR effects require lining up the app view with the contours of the building – here, the old rail station; these cameras are brought squarely into frame. The city looks back here in more ways than one. One tour guide also notes that the standing spots – the yellow *Cité Mémoire* footprints that decorate the pavement in front of each projection site, which I had previously taken to be simple "ideal viewing spots" (see Figure 6.9) – are actually designed to re-sync the projection with the user's extended body. A user standing in these spots is made viewable to overhead sensors – the guide points out the light of one sensor on a rooftop above us – which can start the projection, minimising the lag between the tourist's arrival and the delivery of the content. The fact that the user must stand in a particular spot in order to activate the application (by making the user knowable to both the sensors overhead and the sensor in his or her hand) adds a layer to Hansen's (2004) notion that the movement of his or her body is what makes new media real for the user (41): the "spectator" must perform for a watchful city before (s)he is given access to the secrets hidden in its walls.

This monitoring is not an exclusive element of *Montréal en Histoires*. Any app which uses geolocational technology is tied – by virtue of the origin of

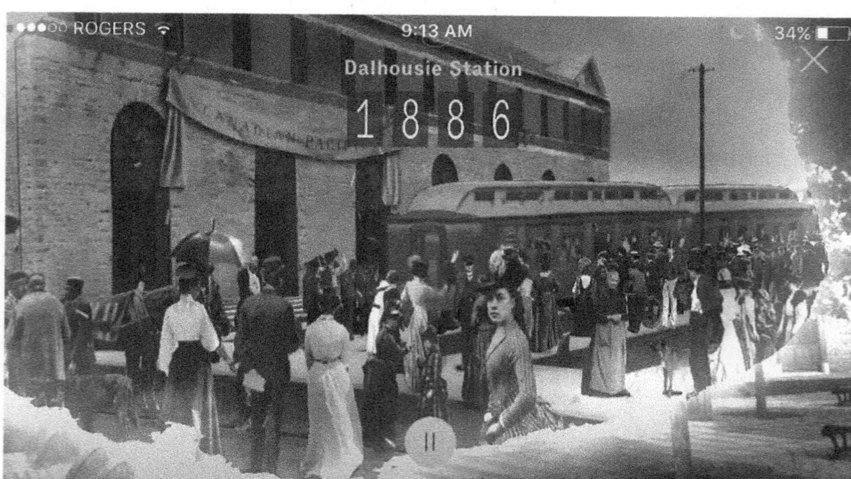

Figure 6.8 Intimate gaze in an AR tableau at Dalhousie station.
(Image credit: Montréal en Histoires).

Figure 6.9 Enabling the city to sense you in *Cité Mémoire*.
(Image credit: the author, *Cité Mémoire* branding by *Montréal en Histoires*).

GPS technology – to surveillance (Cosgrove, 2005; Farman, 2010; Tuters & Varnelis, 2006). A tourism practice that enables the expansion of tracking in public space is a subject worthy of at least attention if not concern, coming as it does under the guise of offering users a more seamless experience. We routinely sacrifice privacy for ease of use and trade personal information as the entrance fee for information and connection (Bennett et al., 2014; Murakami Wood & Ball, 2013). (Try to erase your search history on any given platform, for example, and you might be prompted to reconsider – knowing your search history allows that platform to customize your results.) From a user experience perspective, this tracking is perhaps most interesting when it becomes a visible function (rather than a utilitarian or background function).

Sensing the tourist

While, as Crang and Graham (2007) noted, electronic media has not substituted the physical encounters of everyday life, it has permeated and often reconfigured those encounters, and become embedded in the background of urban life (790). For de Certeau (1984), the city made perfectly knowable and transparent was a nightmare city, and the opacity of practices like walking were a counter to that dystopic vision (see Crang & Graham, 2007: 791). However, in the "sentient city," "the transience of practices, the opacities of mobility and the hidden geographies of memory are now being rendered visible" (Crang & Graham, 2007: 791). In as much as this study has attempted to think between the concept city and the experience of everyday urban life, it cannot ignore the extent to which experiences below are increasingly being used to construct the totalising "view from above."

For example, one of the noted side-benefits of the app *Guidekick* developed for the de Young Museum in San Francisco was its ability to track the metadata of where particular museum-goers spend their time in museums – where they stop and how they move through the space – generating heat maps that were meant to help the museum enhance their collections space through better design (Robson et al., 2016). To achieve this in the context of the museum required considerable technological innovation in order to allow users to be effectively tracked indoors. Alongside the Museum of London's use of the *Streetmuseum* app to ostensibly drive users to visit the collections – to embed data in virtual public space in order to move users into brick-and-mortar private space – the design of these apps is not simply to move users through streets, but to move them off of those streets and into buildings – and then prompt them to move through buildings as desired.

Technological surveillance has become a commonplace part of urban architecture, and the rise of satellite imagery and geolocation technologies has taken the gaze to a global scale (Howes, 2016: 13). CCTV cameras can be spotted throughout Old Montreal for those keen to look for them, but their presence has become so commonplace that they fade into the background (see Crang & Graham, 2007). Surveillance is one part of the regulatory regimes that "constrain or enable" mobilities in the city (Edensor, 2016). Within these regulatory regimes, the pedestrian, given his or her inherent potential to disrupt the forward-moving, planned mobilities of the city (Fan, 2017: 9) is subject to increasing surveillance (Edensor, 2016; Fyfe, 2004; Murakami Wood & Ball, 2013).

Processes of urban branding are inextricably linked with practices of surveillance, and brandscapes are often typified – though to varying degrees – by exercises of aesthetic and social control (Klingmann, 2007; Murakami Wood & Ball, 2013; Parrika, 2015). As Murakami Wood and Ball (2013) argue, "Brandscapes also become securityscapes, as their boundaries and interiors are heavily policed to protect the dreams of safety and riskless living they offer." The more specific the brand image of a place becomes, the more mood management and brand-policing it requires to maintain (Parrika, 2015: 2005). In particular, regulatory practices in the themed spaces of the city are often aimed at removing obstacles – human or otherwise – to consumption in and of the city (Bryman, 2004).

Brand policing also involves limiting the kinds of urban inscriptions that are allowed to proliferate in the streetscape. Old Montreal is already a relatively controlled aesthetic space; restrictions on historical redevelopment attempt to maintain a consistent character in the neighbourhood, and a combination of buffing and surveillance seems to keep graffiti at bay, although the latter thrives in neighbouring warehouses on the edges of the old port, and street art has become a defining feature of nearby St. Laurent Boulevard (Murray, 2010). The staging of the projection for Leonard Cohen's "Suzanne" on the Old Port Clocktower mirrors two similar large scale murals depicting the poet-songwriter that were erected on buildings across the city in the wake of his 2016 death, drawing a common vernacular across spaces where writing on the walls is more or – in the case of the Old Port – less allowed. Staging these sanctioned portraits of Montreal on a grand scale across the streetscape also has the effect of precluding – or at least dwarfing – other forms of urban inscription in these places.

Our mobile phones and other technological devices act as sensors in the sensor society (Andrejevic & Burdon, 2015), and the consumer-subject is increasing seduced to offer up their data in exchange for smooth experiences and to "perform work in their own surveillance" (Murakami Wood & Ball, 2013: 51; see also Andrejevic, 2002; Mathiesen, 1997). The makers of augmented reality technologies like Google Glass tend to downplay the potential invasiveness of the technology by emphasizing notions of emancipation, exploration, and experience; they stress that value of making "everything" knowable outweighs that of privacy (Tuters, 2015: 246–247). Giving *Montréal en Histoires* access to your location (while the app is in use) not only unlocks the content and allows you to access the experience, it seemingly frees you up to wander the city. Geolocation is an essential part of what allows apps like *Montréal en Histoires* to brand their experiences as "encounters" with history, rather than just tours.

This process of extending the gaze is a double-edged sword, cutting both ways; it expands what users can visualize whilst also expanding what is visible about the user. After the widespread civilian adoption of GPS technology in the 2000s, the tracking of cell-phone movements has been rebranded as a social good, as a technology to be embraced for safety and ease of navigation (Bennett et al., 2014). Our lives have become increasingly transparent; "Almost everything we do generates an electronic record: we cannot go online, walk downtown, attend a university class, pay with a credit card, hop on an airplane, or make a phone call without data being captured" (Bennett et al., 2014: 3). Using a locative app necessarily involves consenting to having the app track your location, but what about the built-in monitoring infrastructure apps that use urban sensors to smooth out the locative experience? Those who do not consent are just as subject to that surveillance simply by opting to participate in public life and by walking through city streets.

The notion of the sentient city also further counters the imaginary of public space as a neutral container for social action (Crang & Graham, 2007: 811). The city is not merely something to be observed, it observes. Of course, it is not only the technology that watches users. The interactive quality of the projection also makes users into performers who become part of the spectacle – watching each other. This is never more obvious than in the project's interactive projection, "The Creation of the World."

Re-enchanting the city

"*The Creation of the World*"

While the intended significance of each tableau within the overarching history of Montreal is generally made quite clear by *Cité Mémoire*'s audio, the decontextualised projections can take on a life of their own, and never is this more obvious than in the case of "The Creation of the World." Tucked away in a cobblestoned but otherwise unremarkable alleyway, "The Creation of the World" is an interactive installation that tracks users' movements through the alleyway and uses them to transform the projection. As users walk through the space, it transforms from a sky full of stars into a flowing river. The river becomes marked by pathways (carved out by pedestrians) which then give way to cobblestones. Eventually, the pathways walkers leave in their wake become streaks of blood along the cobblestones (see Figure 6.10). The projections along the cobblestone street are ephemeral, entrancing. They seem to almost universally inspire a sense of awe in visitors as they walk through the alley.

Figure 6.10 Co-producing the projection with others in *Cité Mémoire*'s "The Creation of the World."

(Image credit: the author; *Cité Mémoire* a creation of Michel Lemieux and Victor Pilon, in collaboration with Michel Marc Bouchard).

Walking "The Creation of the World" with the app in hand allows you to contextualise what you are seeing in the alleyway in terms of a history of colonialism and the erasure of Indigenous histories within the built environment. The narrator begins by relating an Anishinaabe creation story that complements the tableau, while the latter portion of the projection – where the street is marked with blood – represents the erasure of Indigenous cultures and the suppression of their oral histories in Canadian culture. As one of the project's creators, Michel Lemieux, notes, this interactive experience is meant to draw attention to the fact that Montreal is built on the unceded lands of Indigenous peoples. Combined with the audio, the projection conveys a collective responsibility for the brutalisation of both nature and first peoples alike.

The presencing of Indigenous history through animation and storytelling addresses a clear problem with "time travel" apps that rely upon the contrast between photographic representations of "then" and "now" that necessarily invisibilise pre-photographic organisations of the landscape. When the user's understanding of what has changed depends on comparing old photographs to the street view, versions of a place that predate these photographs – or just never made it into the archives, as Hetherington (2013) notes – are absent not only from the physical streetscape but also from the augmented vision of what is lost. *Cité Mémoire* – in dramatically restaging colonial encounters with Indigenous peoples as well as highlighting Anishinaabe oral history and the violence of colonialism in "The Creation of the World" – at least acknowledges the Indigenous history of the space.

However, owing to the spectacular augmentation of the physical environment involved in "The Creation of the World," tourists are not necessarily confronted with the deeper intended meaning of the spectacle unless they choose to download the app – something that was rarely observed over extended observations at the site. (Though it is possible that the visceral nature of the experience prompted some passers-by to seek out the app after the fact.)

This is not to say that interacting with the projection without the app is an experience devoid of meaning. Many participants seemed utterly enchanted by the projection, and swept up in the playful mood that it engenders (at least, for the first part of its run). Some pass through unaware that they leave trails of aurora borealis behind them – or else blasé, having seen it too many times. But many more gape in awe as they realise the projection changes as they move through it – that people make the dirt pathways that meander through the "grass" – and they stop to watch others. They stick a toe in the flowing river to experiment. Because the projection changes when the user moves, this also involves a reflexive gaze – of observing one's own trace on the environment (both within the narrative and more literally in the projection). They walk in circles, or they snake down the alley in elaborate configurations, and turn to look at their paths.

The intimacy of the alleyway is also magnified by "The Creation of the World." One becomes aware of the presence of strangers – not in a threatening way, but in a way that reinserts a sense of communal experience of space. Tourists and travellers become objects of the gaze, not just spectators. They must be aware of their own position, and they become acutely aware of the progress of others. They are collectively performing the experience of the space. They also become more aware of the technology which facilitates that experience, particularly those who stay for more than one round of the projection. They begin to play with it, but also to look for its source. This is especially true when the tableau does not meld with the environment seamlessly. On one evening in the alleyway, for example, there is some speculation that a blank square in the projection is blocked by one of the old hanging lanterns that dot the walls above. As walkers progress through the alleyway, they speculate as to the mechanics of the experience, pointing at the smaller lights that rim the top of buildings over the alleyway, attempting to unveil the magic. They are aware that something is tracking them in order to make the projection work. "That's a bit creepy," one participant notes. Most, however, make little of the tracking other than to wonder at its source.

The moment of encounter with the projection can bewilder, as well. Most notably, dogs seem to find the projection utterly confounding, pawing at the river as it changes beneath them but resists being caught. On another occasion, a tour guide describes the shock of spectators when a child fell at the exact moment that the pavement becomes bathed in blood. He notes that he found it funny, but many of the people there at the time did not. Stripped of its context, the blood can still disturb, but it is lacking the connection to colonialism that the app provides.

The disconnect between the experiences of "The Creation of the World" with and without the app narration can create some jarring displays as the public interacts with the projection. Especially for someone who does not know how the story ends (spoiler: it ends in blood), playing with the projection is a purely light-hearted affair. Children delight in jumping into the river of light to see if they can make it splash, adults laugh as they realize the fish will follow them. Erasing the green of the alleyway to cover it with dirt and then with stone becomes a challenge – a game. So, too, does coating the alleyway in what is meant to be a river of blood (a visual much more firmly connected with the practices of colonialism and environmental exploitation when one experiences the projection through the app). This seems to get more elaborate later in the evenings, when strangers and groups in various states of inebriation weave haphazard streaks down the alley, narrowly avoiding collision. One particularly ambitious group bands together, determined to write something. The projection begins before they can decide on the word, and they all choose a different letter, scrawling bloody gibberish across the cobblestones.

"The Creation of the World" is an interesting example of the possibility for these apps not just to account for other people but to capitalize on their flow through the tour site in order to bring their narratives to life, thus animating the app content just as a locative app seeks to animate the world around it (Didur, 2014). On a quiet night, the projection will eventually cycle through its stages – from an aurora landscape in a field of stars, to water, to grass, then dirt, cobblestones, and blood – without any human intervention (beyond the observer's), but it lacks the punch that watching people carve these trails can have. In contrast to the various locative tours that I note "don't play well with people,"[5] without people, "The Creation of the World" is only half a story.

The app creates a divergent experience of the alleyway as at once a commons and "uncommons" (Parrika, 2015) – a space constructed as at once shared and not shared by the layering of the extended space of the tour over the coproduction of the projection with other tourists. Rather than simply "aesthetically drawing in the urban world" (like the flaneur) or "solipsistically transcending it" (like the personal stereo user) (Bull, 2008, p. 143), the locative tourist must do both for the app to work its magic. This interactive projection also emphasises the extent to which the creation of narrative ambience in the locative tour is a contingent (Fan, 2017) and co-produced (Adey et al., 2013; Thibaud, 2015) performance. Depending on the people animating the projection alongside you, the experience can be solemn, awe-ful, chaotic, or invigorating. By creating these spectacular interludes in Old Montreal, *Cité Mémoire* mediates the social relations of those who are otherwise just passing through – offering instead, moments of connection with the stones beneath their feet and the people with whom they are now walking (and making) the city.

A tale of two cities

Examining the proliferation of urban screens in everyday life, Anna McCarthy (2001) calls on us to "explore what screens 'do'" to engage mobile subjects (see Krajina, 2009: 415). In the case of *Montréal en Histoires* and *Cité Mémoire*, these screens both direct and arrest urban movement, draw people into the streets, convey intimacy while setting users at a distance, amplify the branded imagery of the skyline and create mood through the gaze. They allow for an encounter with history – or, at least, *histoires* – that feels at once strikingly novel and comfortably familiar.

The authoritative narration of the app does at times obscure the extent to which the history of Montreal is layered and contested, and by extension the way its format necessarily excludes certain spatial narratives (Heatherington, 2012). Although the app openly claims to be "inspired" by the history of Montreal, the choice to use an objective voice in the narration of the daytime tour does give the app something of the "institutional authority" of the museum – the authorship of its interpretations are obscured, and it presents the history of the city, as opposed to histories. The tableaux, on the other hand, more often give voice to their various characters – perhaps in recognition of the artists' desire to "let the walls speak." ("Cité Mémoire, with Michel Lemieux," Vermont PBS, 2017).

By suggesting that *Montréal en Histories at times* often offers a comfortable brand experience of the space, I am not suggesting that the app never engenders uncomfortable moments or gives critical purchase on the city's multicultural brand identity. The projections and the app content variously reflect on racism, cultural erasure, sexism, homophobia, and social inequality– all part of the story of Montreal. However, the context required to fully understand these issues are available only to those who go looking for them, and the problems of the past are seemingly swept aside in a triumphant final dance number.

Both *High Street Stories* and *Cité Mémoire* situate users in seemingly "ideal" sites for urban augmentation – namely empty parking lots and gaps in the skyline left by demolished buildings – and both bring the "background" of these spaces into the touristic foreground as a result. Between *Montréal en Histories* and *High Street Stories*, then, we can see a variety of uses for the "spectacular" and for the city as a site of projection. In Christchurch, the use of colour and of large-scale artworks as well as smaller-scale interventions (like the app) allows the city to re-mediate the ruin while it waits to rebuild. In Montreal, leaning into the spectacle is seen as a way of courting the new – of nodding to history primarily by way of charging forward. At the same time, it manages to shape the history of Montreal around the people who lived in it – bringing the large empty facades to life and personalising the architecture. Whereas in Christchurch, the murals and augmentations give users something to look at besides empty streets and parking lots, in Old Montreal, the projections and daytime augmentation have the effect of turning what would ordinarily be "through space" into something worth looking at, suffusing the city with spectacle. At the same time, because the projections offer something new to look at, they curate the space in a different way – breaking up the parade of old stone architecture and highlighting some ghosts of buildings past.

These case studies are a tale of two cities: a city of gaps, and a city of screens. The locative app in Christchurch is at once a mourning of what has been lost and an attempted reclamation of the social character of the space. It patches together a fractured cityscape. In some ways, *Montréal en Histoires* and its attendant installation *Cité Mémoire* act as gap fillers of their own – taking some of the "unremarkable" spaces of Old Montreal and turning them into sites of spectacle – carving human interest out of seemingly impersonal brick and mortar. Both strive to connect the architectural heritage of the city to the stories that linger in its walls, but above all to connect users to the city. Given the unevenness of the way these connections are forged, however, both case studies also make evident the role of users and the living (and sensing) cityscape in animating the locative experience.

Notes

1 By way of comparison, *High Street Stories*' creator Zoe Roland mentioned having postcards printed up and left in various places around High Street as her on-site marketing campaign.

2 While Michel Lemieux describes users bringing a phone to their ear (Vermont PBS, 2017), users were more often observed either using headphones – for themselves or shared between touring partners – or holding the phone out with the volume up. This suggests that the phone as an audio device invites a different posture from that of the phone as a communication device, although, in the case of split headphones, there is a certain shared intimacy in users' experience of the tour.

3 "Heritage moments" are historical vignettes that used to play (in place of commercials) on Canadian television. These short clips dramatised the history of Canada, particularly through notable figures.

4 Inside the museum, a similar projection of these iconic marks is available to the tourist – a station where the signatures of the First Nations and their French treaty partners is projected, more intimately, onto one's skin.

5 See, for example, the augmented holograms from the space spots in Seattle's *Space Needle* app that I discussed in Chapter 3, which shimmer and dissipate when people walk through them.

Conclusion

I began this book by situating locative tourism at the juncture of two trains of thought in tourism studies – the influential concept of the tourist gaze, and the more thoroughly embodied notion of touristic performance. These are not distinct schools of thought to begin with – notions of touristic performance acknowledge the gaze as part of the multisensory experience of tourism, and the concept of the tourist gaze has been modified to better account for its embodied interactions (within the broader field of mobility studies) by its author in recent years (see Urry & Larsen, 2011). Nevertheless, locative tourism apps are an interesting object to both examine with and reflect upon these two lines of inquiry. The locative app, by multiplying the touristic signposts of the city, setting the user at a particular distance from sights/sites, contributing to the sedimentation of photographs around certain nodes in the city, and laying a branded image over the city, could be interpreted as technological extension of the tourist gaze par excellence. These apps can even turn Urry's (1990) movement between the destination's photographic high points into a game, rewarding users for uploading photos of the city's signposts. At the same time, using these applications exposes the sensory entanglements of tourism and the unevenness of practices of augmentation. In reflecting on these latter elements of locative tourism, the performance metaphor gives us greater purchase on contrasting rhythms of the tour and the extent to which elements of the "backstage" of the tour meld with, break through, and come squarely in the frame of the locative tour.

If, as Edensor (2007) suggests, there is something of the everyday in tourism practices, the study of mobile tourism applications also provides an entrée into much broader questions. In particular, this book has explored how mobile tourism applications fit with the processes of mediation and sense-making at work in our everyday lives. It offers a particularly important contribution to the sociology of tourism by rethinking the theory of the tourist gaze to account for the new avenues of way-finding and sense-making opened up by ubiquitous computing and "miniaturised mobilities." Crucially, this study opens up a timely (and sorely needed) dialogue on emergent technologies in tourism, and the potentials and pitfalls of locative and augmented reality technologies in particular.

DOI: 10.4324/9781003142386-11

Our "maps of meaning" (Jackson, 1989) are value laden, and those offered by locative tours are no different. They are often imbued with particular understandings of what is culturally valuable in the city – what sites are worthy of the tourist's gaze, whose stories are worth listening to, how best to taste, touch, and even smell the city, and whose imagining of the city counts when observing the evolving streetscape. These tours frequently extend the senses in normative ways. Many offer users the chance to "step through time" or "see the streets as they were," primarily by contrasting old visions of the street with the new. Still others offer the promise of technologically extended sensory superpowers, augmenting the panorama and letting users (appear) to look through walls and concrete floors. However, a number of apps in this study provoke the user to sense the city in unexpected ways, whether that means feeling for the chill of a passing ghost or trying to imagine the rancid smell of a butchery seeping out of a vanished building's walls.

Locative tourism apps can often mediate a branded experience of the city. In places like Hong Kong, where cosmopolitanism and a buffet of multisensory delights are part of the brand image, users can expect to be fully engaged in the experience economy. At other times, the branded frame offered by the locative app can take on a spectacular scale, with famous personalities and on-brand imagery written large across the cityscape (as in Brand Montreal).

Locative tourism apps – particularly the "time-travelling" genre of apps that trade on the allure of being in two places at once by embedding historical photographs in the landscape – can also tend to solidify the history of a space around a particular image of the past. Billed as turning the present into something transparent, these apps instead often occlude visions of the space that pre-date photography, or which cannot be neatly attached to a (still-standing) heritage building. In other cases – like that of Derry-Londonderry – 3-D reconstructions allow the user to glaze over more recent (and more recently imaged) histories of the city, searching for a past that can be comfortably digested. These apps are often funded by heritage organisations and "city of culture" initiatives, and so they offer us insight into whose heritage – and whose culture – counts when it comes to the branded or "official" story of the city.

However, grand narratives aside, locative apps also create intimate experiences of space. App in hand, the locative tourist explores a semi-private layer of touristic experience that can conflict with the broader flows of public space, or – more poignantly – bump up against other private zones and moments in the city. An app that takes you "off the beaten track" makes these other ways of being in the urban abundantly clear – and casts the notion of consuming these private moments and spaces in an uncomfortable light.

Because so many of these apps "take the museum to the streets," they can bring some of the museum's more limiting aesthetic regimes with them – setting the user at a distance from the object of their gaze, putting everything in its place. While they might outwardly aim to turn the streetscape into an exhibit, as we have seen throughout this book, the more rigidly these apps attempt to freeze the urban into a still-life, the more rapidly it all comes undone. This happens even in relatively aesthetically controlled spaces.

For one thing, these apps are not the only maps of meaning that tourists encounter when walking a given site. Tours can be disrupted by the contrasting flows of other tours, or by the more pedestrian or everyday mechanics of urban life. They can encounter contrasting narratives in the environment around them, and the branded mirage of the city can dissipate upon encountering off-brand sensations, or even just other people (who seem rarely to "fit" the branded image).

Some apps seem to forget that people are part of the spaces they animate (and, depending on the destination, quite a lot of them). Some apps remember but prompt the user to forget. For example, the app at France's historic Palace of Versailles (*Versailles 3D*; Chateau de Versailles, n.d.) is designed to show users how the palace looked at the time of its construction, but, given how faithfully the palace has been restored to that original condition, its chief value seems to be erasing the churning crowds of tourists that surrounded the user. However, not all apps have "people problems" – some rely on the flow of pedestrians in the city to complete their stories (and are often much the better for it).

Extending the screen onto the walls of the city created moments of truly collective experience and conscious co-production of the city in *Cité Mémoire's*' "Creation of the World." This offloading of the screen also unsettled the position of the user in relation to city – the urban became something to be engaged with rather than simply something to look at. However, it also enhanced the parallel experiences of urban space offered by the tour, wherein the more critical meaning of the installation was fully available only to those who experienced it through the app.

Cynically, one could suggest that these apps gain traction on city tourism websites because showing some of this "texture" adds to the cosmopolitan appeal of a city – there is something for everyone, given the right filter. Realistically, one seems unlikely to devote a lot of time to a tour Queering the map of Toronto without already being open to hearing the stories of the LGBTQ+ community. Similarly, how likely is a person to devote a tour to Melbourne's lost heritage buildings without some appreciation for the perceived value of built heritage? There is self-selection involved in choosing what "layer" of the city you opt to tour. In this respect, many locative apps share a quality with themed experiences of the city (food tours, literary tours, ghost tours) – they are most likely to find their audience amongst those with whom those themes already resonate. However, that quality can make the experiences they offer particularly impactful (and, thus, the character of these theming exercises important to examine).

While the critical potential of locative art projects has been lauded (and also questioned), its more commercial counterpart in the locative tour has been derided as too mundane to be worthy of mention. After all, what is to distinguish the experience of the locative tour from any other guided tour, save its branded focus on "exploration" and "encounter"? However, the "self-guided" nature of the tour does, in fact, shift the experience of the city in meaningful ways – although, admittedly, not always in ways that were intended. Lacking the smooth operators of the traditional guided tour, these apps expose their own narration, and trouble the objectivity of the map.

Both urban development and its mediation are far from even processes (Logan & Molotch, 2007; Zukin, 1989). Conflicting urban imaginaries are at work, and locative apps in some respect make that conflict even more visible to the user. They contest the development of the streetscape, and they can even contest the process of mapping the city. They can also engender moments of serendipity – where the app sings with the environment and the user's "material premises" – adding depth to the experience. While this capacity has been acknowledged in media about locative narrative (Greenspan, 2011), it was interesting to observe how the narrative instability of these apps – and, thus, their inherent potential for both rupture and serendipity – could create moments of critical purchase on the environment in the locative tour.

However, it isn't only chance encounter that fills in the gaps in the locative narrative. Users also layer the city with their own personal memories and experiences – any narrative of the city can tend to provoke stories from closer to home – and they draw on shared frames of reference to make sense of the city alongside the application. Sometimes this means that users can transform the experience of the tour into something more normative than it was designed to be. Because users often perform the tour according to broader understandings of what touring *means*, they sometimes filter meaning-saturated spaces into more easily digestible parts, or approach the city as a museum even when the app never proposes taking the museum to the streets. However, this experiential baggage also means that users fill the place of the tour with their own reflections, pauses, moments of solemnity, or laughter. They direct others in the city to look at empty walls and parking lots, just by virtue of training their device on these places. They expose the ghosts of the city which the app cannot animate alone.

Locative tourism apps– and locative media more generally – rely upon the body of the user to give life to the stories they tell. As we have seen throughout this book, locative narratives become cohesive stories only when they are (literally) "fleshed out" and set in motion by the user. An app cannot smell for the ghostly hint of pipe tobacco outside an author's favourite haunt – but it can attune the user to do just that. The study of locative tourism must similarly attend to the bodily experience of users, and cultivate an awareness of locative tourism as a sensory practice. Sensory ethnography offers us the tools to do just that – to share in the sensible of the locative tour, to follow its rhythms and trace its patterns, and to locate the embodied experiences it offers within the broader sensory history and meaning-making practices of the city. Perhaps more than anything, *Locative*

Tourism Applications is a story of sensing the city with others (be they corporeal or technological).

Locative tourism involves the co-creation, or at least the co-evocation, of place. This is always true when we consider the intersection of the app, the body, and the space – but the sensory relations of a place become especially thick when we use locative technology with others, and when their stories become layered with the stories of the app. The sociality of sensation – and the permeability of urban atmospheres – is part of what makes this act of co-creation so potentially rich. Done right, it can invite not just shared consumption, but shared experience.

It is people – their embodied interactions, their traces, their stories – that truly make the magic happen. Users conjure the layered places of the locative tour into being through alignment work, tuning their body to the streetscape, orienting the map and reorienting themselves – and shifting the world around them in the process. As such, it is to people that creators must attend if they want to mediate the experience of the city in meaningful ways.

Apps that are looking to avoid obsolescence might find that allowing user-created content can re-align their narratives with the streetscape as it changes. However, this requires a willingness to unsettle the authoritative meanings of spaces and allow their multiple histories to shine through – and for new imaginings of the city to proliferate. Users will likely encounter multiple narratives of the city in any case; providing the opportunity to openly share in the meaning-making of the space might enhance a user's experience by allowing them to leave a "trace" even in a place that is not broadly photographable – and enabling them to encounter the traces of others.

The locative apps in this study frequently expose how "being" in two places at once has to do with more than just seeing two places at once. Narration that evoked the multi-sensory memory of a city allowed the user to put themselves in another's shoes while walking, to resonate with past rhythms and understand that these were lived stories. By contrast, apps that primarily relied on positioning the user in a specific spot to line up past and present images of the city were often the first to have their meaning "slip" – the city rarely holds still long enough to easily achieve that kind of alignment. If the magic is in "being there," it requires the whole body of the user, entangled with living and dynamic elements of the city, to summon that magic.

As much as this book has traced a series of narrative ruptures and explored the trouble of "alignment work," it has also been a study in the way that locative apps can create moments of real connection between tourists and the world around them. Furthermore, as we saw in the case of *High Street Stories*, re-establishing those connections can have real consequences, not just for the tourist, but also for the city. We can acknowledge that these apps disable certain types of connection to the urban environment while also recognising that they enable others.

As they endeavour to re-enchant the urban – to layer the city with a veil of the extraordinary, and thus render it fit for touristic consumption – locative tourism apps are often haunted by the spectre of the everyday. Because they rely on the city, its inhabitants and tourists to animate them, locative tourism apps must take on board some of the living city's mess, its splendour, its dynamism and resistance, and its histories and cultures, seen and unseen. In doing so, they illuminate the uneven process of mediating the urban as destination space, and they tease out the threads of alternative narratives and ways of sensing the city with which they are so thoroughly entangled.

In the end, perhaps we ought not to think only of locative apps as the extension of the self, but of people as extensions of locative apps – as living, breathing, sensing dynamic elements who add richness to what might otherwise be a rather two-dimensional portrait of urban life (time travelling though it may be).

Appendix

Twelve-city tour of applications

City	*Locative application(s)*	*Context*
London	• *Streetmuseum* • *Streetmuseum Londinium*	The Museum of London's *Streetmuseum* app – a pioneering app when it comes to the practice of "taking the museum to the streets" (as befits the name) allowed users to overlay historical photos with modern day London streetscapes. A later spinoff app – *Streetmuseum Londinium* – allowed users to peer even deeper into the past of the city (to the time of the Roman Empire) by, for example, embedding virtual artefacts for travellers to uncover throughout the city (just by "digging" on their screen with their finger).
Edinburgh	• *World Heritage City*	Edinburgh's *World Heritage City* app turned the practice of exploring heritage highlights of that city into a game, allowing users to accumulate points for visiting various sites along certain tours, and to score additional points for uploading photos for fellow app users to peruse.
Dublin	• *Dublin Storymap* • *Dublin Walls*	*Storymap* geolocates videos of people relating historical stories, folklore, and personal tales throughout the city. The designers particularly wanted to lure people to less-visited corners of the city, although funding concerns ultimately determined much of their map. *Dublin Walls* offers animated 3-D reconstructions along the contours of a now-demolished old city wall.

(*Continued*)

City	*Locative application(s)*	*Context*
New Orleans	• *Wicked Walks* • *Historic NOLA*	*Historic NOLA* offers users the chance to capture a ghostly snapshot of photo overlays between the present and the past, while *Wicked Walks* takes users on a haunted pub crawl, invoking multiple senses in its hunt for the supernatural.
Seattle	• *Space Needle + Space Needle 360* • *STQRY Public Art tour*	The *Space Needle* app solves the dilemma of landmark towers everywhere by re-injecting itself into the views of Seattle that it provides. *STQRY* is a multi-tour platform that, among other routes, takes users on a public art tour through a bustling market and urban park.
Hong Kong	• *Discover Hong Kong: Heritage Walks* • *Discover Hong Kong: City Walks*	*Discover Hong Kong: Heritage Walks* and *City Walks* were produced by the Hong Kong tourism board and generally mediate the same dense tourist areas, but according to different themes (from historical sites to a celebration of bustling modern urbanity). This density and theming offers interesting points of cross comparison, as well as highlighting Hong Kong's cosmopolitan "World City" urban brand.
Derry-Londonderry	• *Walk the Walls*	Designed as part of the push to market the cultural attractions of Derry-Londonderry after the city was named the 2013 UK City of Culture, *Walk the Walls* mediates the city's historic walled centre with an eye towards the 17th-century siege of the city, and notably avoids engaging with the more recent conflicts that mark the city's architecture and identity.
Toronto	• *Queerstory* • *Toronto in Time*	*Toronto in Time* aims to offer app users the chance to time travel by re-embedding archival photographs in the streetscape, while *Queerstory* offers a tour of the city that aims to put the history of the city's queer population on its map (beyond the confines of the Gay Village).

(*Continued*)

City	*Locative application(s)*	*Context*
San Francisco	• *Detour* • *Golden Gate Park Field Guide (Guidekick)*	*Detour* is among the most sophisticated apps surveyed in its use of geolocational technology, and many of the tours it offers use famous San Francisco landmarks or districts as jumping-off points for alternative narratives about the city's history and development. *The Guidekick Golden Gate Park Field Guide* explores the artificial construction of the park and its role in marking San Francisco as a "civilised" city.
Melbourne	• *Museum Victoria Tours: Walk Through History* • *Melbourne's Lost! 100* • *Along the Yarra (previously titled: Transforming the Yarra)* • *Heritage Vic* • *Our City*	Melbourne has a wide variety of locative apps, which made for an interesting survey of overlapping and divergent spatial narratives around the city. *Walk Through History* is a classic heritage app (one that takes the museum to the streets) with user authorship features; *Melbourne's Lost! 100* and *Along the Yarra* offer users somewhat opposing standpoints on urban redevelopment; *Our City* is a personal narrative app that offers a local perspective on the city's landmarks.
Montreal	• *Montréal en Histoires + Cité Mémoire (CASE STUDY #1)*	*Montréal en Histoires'* "techno-historic circuits" embed photos, audio narration, and augmented reality re-enactments at points of interest around Old Montreal, and are currently accompanied by a multi-sited projection/sound installation designed to work with the app (called *Cité Mémoire*). The app thus combines a more intimate audio experience with highly spectacular projections.
Christchurch	• *High Street Stories (CASE STUDY #2)*	*High Street Stories* attempts to deal with the impact of the 2010–2011 earthquakes on the city's historic central business district by restoring the city's heritage buildings and old street scenes through a combination of 3-D imagery, photo overlay, and (chiefly) through layered personal narratives. As an exercise in post-disaster placemaking via locative app, *High Street Stories* was a particularly rich field of inquiry for examining how the locative tour interacts with the rapidly shifting stage of a city in transition.

Bibliography

Abel, G., & Sweetman, B. (2018). *Street-based sex work in Christchurch*. Dunedin: Otago University Press.

Acoustiguide, Ltd. (2013). *Dunluce Castle*. [Mobile app]. Retrieved from play.google.com/store/apps/details?id=com.espro.android.mediaplayer.Dunluce&hl=en_CA

Adey, P., Brayer, L., Masson, D., Murphy, P., Simpson, P., & Tixier, N. (2013). "Pour votre tranquillité": Ambiance, atmosphere, and surveillance. *Geoforum*, *49*(1), 299–309.

Adler, S., & Brenner, J. (1992). Gender and space: Lesbians and gay men in the city. *International Journal of Urban and Regional Research*, *16*(1), 24–34.

Allen, E. (1996). "Money and little red books": Romanticism, tourism, and the rise of the guidebook. *LIT: Literature Interpretation Theory*, *7*(2–3), 213–226.

Allen, P. (2008). Framing, locality and the body in augmented public space. In A. Aurigi & F. De Cindio (Eds.), *Augmented urban spaces: Articulating the physical and electronic city*. Burlington, VT: Ashgate Publishing, 49–62.

Alper, M. (2018). Inclusive sensory ethnography: Studying new media and neurodiversity in everyday life. *New Media & Society*, *20*(10), 3560–3579.

AlSayyad, N. (2006). *Cinematic urbanism: A history of the modern from reel to real*. New York: Routledge.

Anderson, B. (2009). Affective atmospheres. *Emotion, Space and Society*, *2*(1), 77–78.

Anderson, J. (2010). *Understanding cultural geography: Places and traces*. New York: Routledge.

Andrejevic, M. (2002). The kinder, gentler gaze of Big Brother. *New Media & Society*, *4*(1), 251–270.

Andrejevic, M., & Burdon, M. (2015). Defining the sensor society. *Television & New Media*, *16*(1), 19–36.

Andron, S. (2018). Selling streetness as experience: The role of street art tours in branding the creative city. *The Sociological Review*, *66*(5), 1036–1057.

Auerbach, A. (2006). Interpreting urban screens. *First Monday*. Special Issue 4. Accessed online: https://uncommonculture.org/ojs/index.php/fm/article/view/1546/1461

Augé, M. (2008). *Non-places: An introduction to the anthropology of super-modernity*. Translation by John Howe. New York: Verso.

Bærenholdt, J. O., Haldrup, M., & Larsen, J. (2008). Performing cultural attractions. In J. Sundbo & P. Darmer (Eds.), *Creating experiences in the experience economy*. Northhampton, MA: Edward Elgar Publishing, 176–202.

Bærenholdt, J. O., Haldrup, M., Larsen, J., & Urry, J. (2004). *Performing tourist places*. Burlington, VT: Ashgate Publishing.

Barber, J. F. (2014). Walking-talking: Soundscapes, flaneurs, and the creation of mobile media narratives. In J. Farman (Ed.), *The mobile story: Narrative practices with locative technologies*. New York: Routledge, 95–110.

Bekele, M. K., Pierdicca, R., Frontoni, E., Malinvern, E. S., Gain, J. (2018). A survey of augmented, virtual, and mixed reality for cultural heritage. *ACM Journal on Computing and Cultural Heritage*, *1*(2), 1–36.

Bennett, C. J., Haggerty, K. D., Lyon, D., & Steeves, V. (Eds.). (2014). *Transparent lives: Surveillance in Canada*. Athabasca, AB: Athabasca University Press.

Berg, B. L. (1998). *Qualitative methods for the social sciences*. London: Ally and Bacon.

Berg, B. L. (2007). *Qualitative research methods for the social sciences*. Toronto: Pearson.

Bernard, H. R. (2011). *Research methods in anthropology: Qualitative and quantitative approaches*. Lanham, MD: Rowman Altamira.

Binter, J. T. (2014). Unruly voices in the museum: Multisensory engagement with disquieting histories. *The Senses and Society*, *9*(3), 342–360.

Bird, G., Westcott, M., & Thiesen, N. (2018). Marketing dark heritage: Building brands, myth- making and social marketing. In P. R. Stone et al. (Eds.), *The Palgrave handbook of dark tourism studies*. London: Palgrave Macmillan, 645–665.

Boddy, T. (1992). Underground and overhead: Building the analogous city. In M. Sorkin (Ed.), *Variations on a theme park: The new American city and the end of public space*. New York: Macmillan, 123–153.

Böhme, G. (2013). The art of the stage set as a paradigm for an aesthetics of atmospheres. Ambiances: Environnement sensible, architecture et espace urbain. Retrieved from https://journals.openedition.org/ambiances/315

Boyer, M. C. (1992). Cities for sale: Merchandising history at South Street Seaport. In M. Sorkin (Ed.), *Variations on a theme park: The new American city and the end of public space*. New York: Macmillan, 181–204.

Branter, C. (2018). New visualities of space and place: Mapping theories, concepts and methodology of visual communication research on locative media and geomedia. *Westminster Papers in Communication and Culture*, *13*(2), 14–30.

Brighenti, A. M. (2012). New media and urban motilities: A territoriologic point of view. *Urban Studies*, *49*(2), 399–414.

Bryman, A. (2004). *The Disneyization of society*. London: Sage.

Buccitelli, A. B. (2017). Locative gaming, folk geographies, and the experience of cultural heritage. *Cultural Analysis*, *16*(1), 7–29.

Bull, M. (2004). Sound connections: An aural epistemology of proximity and distance in urban culture. *Environment and Planning D*, *22*(1), 103–116.

Bull, M. (2005). No dead air! The iPod and the culture of mobile listening. *Leisure Studies*, *24*(4), 343–355.

Bull, M. (2006). Investigating the culture of mobile listening: From Walkman to iPod. In K. O'Hara & B. Brown (Eds.), *Consuming music together: Social and collaborative aspects of music consumption technologies*. New York: Springer, 131–149.

Bull, M. (2016). Sensory media: virtual worlds and the training of perception. In D. Howes (Ed.), *A cultural history of the senses in the Modern Age, 1920–2000* (Vol. 6). London: Bloomsbury, 219–241.

Burgess, J. A., & Gold, J. R. (1985). *Geography, the media and popular culture*. New York: St. Martin's Press.

Buser, M. (2017). The time is out of joint: Atmosphere and hauntology at Bodiam Castle. *Emotion, Space and Society*, *25*(1), 5–13.

Calvino, I. (2005). "Under the jaguar sun." In D. Howes (Ed.), *Empire of the senses: The sensual culture reader*. Oxford: Berg, 304–317.

Candlin, F. (2010). *Art, museums and touch*. New York: Manchester University Press.

Carpiano, R. M. (2009). Come take a walk with me: The "Go-Along" interview as a novel method for studying the implications of place for health and well-being. *Health & Place*, *15*(1), 263–272.

Carter, S. M., & Little, M. (2007). Justifying knowledge, justifying method, taking action: Epistemologies, methodologies, and methods in qualitative research. *Qualitative Health Research*, *17*(10), 1316–1328.

Castells, M. (1976). *City, class and power*. New York: St. Martin's Press.

Castells, M., Fernandez-Ardevol, M., & Qie, J. (2007). *Mobile communication and society: A global perspective*. Cambridge, MA: MIT Press.

Catley, M. (2016). *Sign o' the times* [Public sculpture]. New Zealand: Christchurch.

CBD Christchurch. (n.d.). *Trip Advisor*. Last accessed online, July 2019: https://www.tripadvisor.ca/Attraction_Review-g255118-d4341818-Reviews-CBD_Christchurch-Christchurch_Canterbury_Region_South_Island.html

Chang, M., & Goodman, E. (2006). Asphalt games: Enacting place through locative media. *Leonardo Electronic Almanac*, *14*(3). 4.

Chang, Y. L., Hou, H. T., Pan, C. Y., Sung, Y. T., & Chang, K. E. (2015). Apply an augmented reality in a mobile guidance to increase sense of place for heritage places. *Educational Technology & Society*, *18*(2), 166–178.

Chateau de Versailles (n.d.). *Versailles 3D* [Mobile app]. Retrieved from https://apps.apple.com/us/app/versailles-3d/id786153506

Christchurch & Canterbury Tourism. (2014). *Five year strategic plan 2014–2019*. Christchurch, New Zealand: Christchurch & Canterbury Tourism.

Christopherson, S. (2008). The fortress city: Privatized spaces, consumer citizenship. In A. Amin (Ed.), *Post-Fordism: A reader*. Indianapolis, IN: John Wiley & Sons.

"Cité Mémoire." (n.d.). *Montréal en Histoires*. Retrieved from: https://www.montrealenhistoires.com/en/cite_memoire/#citememoire

Cité Mémoire. (n.d.). TripAdvisor. Retrieved from https://www.tripadvisor.ca/Attraction_Review-g155032-d11980466-Reviews-Cite_Memoire-Montreal_Quebec.html

Classen, C. (2005). The deodorized city: Battling urban stench in the nineteenth century. In M. Zardini (Ed.), *Sense of the city: An alternate approach to urbanism*. Montréal: Lars Müller Publishers, 292–322.

Classen, C. (2017). *The museum of the senses: Experiencing art and collections*. London: Bloomsbury Publishing.

Classen, C., & Howes, D. (2006). The museum as sensescape: Western sensibilities and indigenous artefacts. In E. Edwards, C. Gosden, & R. Phillips (Eds.), *Sensible objects: Colonialism, museums and material culture*. London: Bloomsbury, 199–222.

Clintberg, M. (2014). Where publics may touch: Stimulating sensory access at the National Gallery of Canada. *The Senses and Society*, *9*(3), 310–322.

Coats, A., & Ferguson, S. (2013). Rubbernecking or rejuvenation: Post earthquake perceptions and the implications for business practice in a dark tourism context. *Journal of Research for Consumers*, *23*(1), 32–65.

Cohen, E., & Cohen, S. A. (2012). Current sociological theories and issues in tourism. *Annals of Tourism Research*, *39*(4), 2177–2202.

Coleman, S., & Crang, M. (2002). Grounded tourists, travelling theory. In S. Coleman & M. Crang (Eds.), *Tourism: Between place and performance*. Oxford: Berghahn Books, 1–20.

Cosgrove, D. (1984). *Social formation and symbolic landscape*. London: Croom Helm.

Cosgrove, D. (2005). Maps, mapping, modernity: Art and cartography in the twentieth century. *Imago Mundi*, *57*(1), 35–54.

Cosgrove, D., & Jackson, P. (1987). New directions in cultural geography. *Area*, *19*(2), 95–101.

Cosgrove, D. E. (2008). *Geography and vision: Seeing, imagining and representing the world*. London: I. B. Tauris.

Cox, R. (2018). Walking without purpose. In D. Howes (Ed.), *Senses and sensation: Critical and primary sources* (Vol. 1). London: Bloomsbury, 363–375.

Crang, M., & Graham, S. (2007). Sentient cities ambient intelligence and the politics of urban space. *Information, Communication & Society*, *10*(6), 789–817.

Crawford, A., & Goggin, G. (2009). Geomobile web: Locative technologies and mobile media. *Australian Journal of Communication*, *36*(1), 97–109.

Crawford, M. (1992). The world in a shopping mall. In M. Sorkin (Ed.), *Variations on a theme park: The new American city and the end of public space*. New York: Macmillan, 3–30.

Cresswell, T. (1996). *In place/out of place: Geography, ideology, and transgression*. Minneapolis: University of Minnesota Press.

Cresswell, T. (2010). Towards a politics of mobility. *Environment and Planning D: Society and Space*, *28*(1), 17–31.

Creswell, J. W., & Miller, D. L. (2000). Determining validity in qualitative inquiry. *Theory into Practice*, *39*(3), 124–130.

Crouch, D. (2000). Places around us: Embodied lay geographies in leisure and tourism. *Leisure Studies*, *19*(2), 63–76.

Crouch, D., & Desforges, L. (2003). The sensuous in the tourist encounter – Introduction: The power of the body in tourist studies. *Tourist Studies*, *3*(1), 5–22.

Culhane, D. (2017a). Imagining: An introduction. In D. Elliott & D. Culhane, (Eds.), *A different kind of ethnography: Imaginative practices and creative methodologies*. Toronto: University of Toronto Press, 1–21.

Culhane, D. (2017b). Sensing. In D. Elliott & D. Culhane (Eds.), *A different kind of ethnography: Imaginative practices and creative methodologies*. Toronto: University of Toronto Press, 45–67.

Dann, G., & Jacobsen, J. K. S. (2003). Tourism smellscapes. *Tourism Geographies*, *5*(1), 3–25.

Davis, M. (1992). Fortress Los Angeles: The militarization of urban space. In M. Sorkin (Ed.), *Variations on a theme park: The new American city and the end of public space*. New York: Macmillan, 154–180.

de Certeau, M. (1984). *The practice of everyday life*. Los Angeles: University of California Press.

de Certeau, M., & Mayol, P. (1998). *The practice of everyday life: Living and cooking* (Volume 2). Minneapolis: University of Minnesota Press.

de Freitas, C. A. (2010). Changing spaces: Locating public space at the intersection of the physical and digital. *Geography Compass*, *4*(6), 630–643.

de Lange, M. (2009). From always-on to always-there: Locative media as playful technologies. In A. de Souza e Silva & D. M. Sutko (Eds.), *Digital cityscapes: Merging digital and urban playspaces* (Digital Formations, Volume 57). New York: Peter Lang Publishing, 55–70.

de Souza e Silva, A. (2006). From cyber to hybrid: Mobile technologies as interfaces of hybrid spaces. *Space and Culture*, *9*(3), 261–278.

de Souza e Silva, A. (2016). Creative appropriations: Mobile interfaces in art, games, and education [Conference presentation]. *Aesthesis and the Common: Reconfiguring the Public Sphere*. McGill University, March 9.

de Souza e Silva, A., & Frith, J. (2012). *Mobile interfaces in public spaces: Locational privacy, control, and urban sociability*. New York: Routledge.

de Souza e Silva, A., & Frith, J. (2014). Re-narrating the city through the presentation of location. In J. Farman (Ed.), *The mobile story: Narrative practices with locative technologies*. New York: Routledge, 34–50.

de Souza e Silva, A., & Sutko, D. M. (2008). Playing life and living play: How hybrid reality games reframe space, play, and the ordinary. *Critical Studies in Media Communication*, *25*(5), 447–465.

Debord, G. (1970). *The society of the spectacle* (Translated by F. Perlman & J. Supak). Detroit, MI: Black & Red.

Degen, M. (2012). Consuming urban rhythms: Let's Ravalejar. In T. Edensor (Ed.), *Geographies of rhythm: Nature, place, mobilities and bodies*. London: Ashgate, 21–31.

Degen, M. M. (2008). *Sensing cities: Regenerating public life in Barcelona and Manchester*. New York: Routledge.

DeLyser, D. (2003). 'A walk through Old Bodie': Presenting a ghost town in a tourism map. In S.P. Hanna & V. Del Casino Jr. (Eds.), *Mapping Tourism*. Minneapolis: University of Minnesota Press, 79–107.

Department of Environment, Land, Water, and Planning. (2016). *Heritage Vic* (now Vic-Heritage) [Mobile app]. Retrieved from https://apps.apple.com/au/app/vic-heritage/id481956934

Detour. (2016a). *Detour: Beyond the Painted Ladies* [Mobile app: inactive].

Detour. (2016b). *Detour Haight-Ashbury: Summer of Love* [Mobile app: inactive]. Narrated by Peter Coyote.

Deutsche, R. (1998). *Evictions: Art and spatial politics*. Cambridge, MA: MIT Press.

Deutsche, R. (2014). The National September 11 Memorial Museum. *Artforum*, September 2014. Retrieved from https://www.artforum.com/print/201407/the-national-september-11-memorial-museum-47864

Diaconu, M. (2011). Mapping urban smellscapes. In M. Diaconu, E. Hueberger, R. Mateus-Berr, & L. M. Vosicky (Eds.), *Senses and the city: An interdisciplinary approach to urban sensescapes*. London: Transaction Publishers, 223–238.

Didur, J. (2014). Walk this way: Curating botanical gardens with mobile media [Conference presentation]. *Leaders in Conservation: Botanic Gardens and Biodiversity in the 21st Century*. Concordia University, Montreal, October 23.

Didur, J., & Fan, L.-T. (2018). Between landscape and the screen: Locative media, transitive reading, and environmental storytelling. *Media Theory*, *2*(1). Retrieved May 2019 from http://mediatheoryjournal.org/jill-didur-lai-tze-fan-between-landscape-and-the-screen/#_edn5

Dieter, M. (2015). Dark patterns: Interface design, augmentation and crisis. In D. M. Berry et al. (Eds.), *Postdigital aesthetics*. London: Palgrave MacMillan, 163–178.

Dinnie, K. (2004). Place branding: Overview of an emerging literature. *Place Branding*, *1*(1), 106–110.

Dinnie, K. (2011). Introduction to the theory of city branding. In K. Dinnie (Ed.), *City branding: Theory and cases*. London: Palgrave Macmillan, 3–7.

Doak, P. (2014). Beyond Derry or Londonderry: Towards a framework for understanding the emerging spatial contradictions of Derry–Londonderry—UK City of Culture 2013. *City*, *18*(4–5), 488–496.

Dodds, R., & Joppe, M. (2001). Promoting urban green tourism: The development of the other map of Toronto. *Journal of Vacation Marketing*, *7*(3), 261–267.

Dodge, M., Kitchin, R., & Perkins, C. (2011). *The map reader: Theories of mapping practice and cartographic representation*. New York: John Wiley & Sons.

Donald, J. (1999). *Imagining the modern city*. London: The Althone Press.

Donald, S., & Gammack, J. G. (2007). *Tourism and the branded city: Film and identity on the Pacific Rim*. Burlington, VT: Ashgate Publishing.

Douglas, G. H. (1996). *Skyscrapers: A social history of the very tall building in America*. Jefferson, NC: McFarland & Company.

Edensor, T. (1998). *Tourists at the Taj: Performance and meaning at a symbolic site*. London: Routledge.

Edensor, T. (2001). Performing tourism, staging tourism: (Re)producing tourist space and practice. *Tourist Studies*, *1*(1), 59–81.

Edensor, T. (2005a). *Industrial ruins: Space, aesthetics, and materiality*. Oxford: Berg Publishers.

Edensor, T. (2005b). The ghosts of industrial ruins: Ordering and disordering memory in excessive space. *Environment and Planning D: Society and Space*, *23*(1), 829–849.

Edensor, T. (2005c). Waste matter: the debris of industrial ruins and the disordering of the material world. *Journal of Material Culture*, *10*(3), 311–332.

Edensor, T. (2007). Mundane mobilities, performances and spaces of tourism. *Social & Cultural Geography*, *8*(2), 199–215.

Edensor, T. (2011). Illuminated atmospheres: Anticipating and reproducing the flow of affective experience in Blackpool. *Environment and Planning D: Society and Space*, *30*(1), 1103–1122.

Edensor, T. (2016). Walking through ruins. In J. L. Vergunst, & T. Ingold (Eds.), *Ways of walking*. New York: Routledge, 135–154.

Edensor, T. (2017). *From light to dark: Daylight, illumination, and gloom*. Minneapolis: University of Minnesota Press.

Edensor, T. (2018a). Sensing the ruin. In D. Howes (Ed.), *Senses and sensation: Critical and primary sources* (Vol. 1). London: Bloomsbury, 159–168.

Edensor, T. (2018b). The more-than-visual experiences of tourism. *Tourism Geographies*, *20*(5), 913–915.

Edensor, T., & Holloway, J. (2008). Rhythmanalysing the coach tour: The Ring of Kerry, Ireland. *Transactions of the Institute of British Geographers*, *33*(4), 483–501.

Edensor, T. et al. (2012). Playing in industrial ruins. In A. Jorgensen, & R. Keenan (Eds.), *Urban wildscapes*. London: Routledge, 65–79.

Ellis, M. (2010). Streetmuseum: Q&A with Museum of London. *Electronic museum*, June 1, 2010. Retrieved from https://blog.variousbits.net/2010/06/01/streetmuseum-qa-with-vicky-lee-museum-of-london/

Elo, S., & Kyngas, H. (2007). The qualitative content analysis process. *Journal of Advanced Nursing*, *62*(1), 107–115.

Esterberg, K. G. (2002). *Qualitative methods in social research*. Boston: McGraw-Hill.

Evans, L. (2014). Maps as deep: Reading the code of location-based social networks. *IEEE Technology and Society Magazine*, *33*(1), 73–80.

Everett, S. (2009). Beyond the visual gaze? The pursuit of an embodied experience through food tourism. *Tourist Studies*, *8*(3), 337–358.

Everett-Green, J. (2016). Bringing a history lesson to Montreal's anniversary party. *The Globe and Mail*, June 3, 2016. Retrieved September 2018 from https://www.theglobeandmail.com/arts/art-and-architecture/bringing-a-history-lesson-to-montreals-anniversary-party/article30268713/

Ewen, S. (2018). All-consuming images: The marriage between art and commerce. In D. Howes (Ed.), *Senses and sensation: Critical and primary sources* (Volume 4). London: Bloomsbury.

Fan, L. T. (2017). Writing while wandering: Material and spatial contingency in locative media narratives. *Convergence: The International Journal of Research into New Media Technologies*, *23*(1), 5–19.

Farías, I. (2010). Sightseeing buses: Cruising, timing and the montage of attractions. *Mobilities*, *5*(3), 387–407.

Farman, J. (2010). Mapping the digital empire: Google Earth and the process of postmodern cartography. *New Media & Society*, *12*(1), 1–19.

Farman, J. (2012). *Mobile interface theory: Embodied space and locative media*. New York: Routledge.

Farman, J. (2014). *The mobile story: Narrative practices with locative technologies*. New York: Routledge.

Farman, J. (2015). Map interfaces and the production of locative media space. In R. Wilken & G. Goggin (Eds.), *Locative media*. New York: Routledge, 83–93.

Ferrell, J. (2016). Graffiti, street art, and the dialectics of the city. In K. Avramidis & M. Tsilimpoundini (Eds.), *Graffiti and street art: Reading, writing and representing the city*. Abingdon, UK: Taylor & Francis Group, 27–38.

Flaherty, A., & Rowley, T. (2018). About Storymap. *Storymap*. Retrieved from http://storymap.ie/about

Flanagan, M. (2007). Locating play and politics: Real world games and activism. *Leonardo Electronic Almanac*, *16*(2–3), 1–13.

Fletcher, J., & Hayward, M. (2016). "Overkill" central Christchurch intersection has 19 lights. *Stuff*, October 13. Retrieved from https://www.stuff.co.nz/the-press/news/85268851/overkill-central-christchurch-intersection-has-18-lights

Foote, K. E. (1994). *Re-reading cultural geography*. Austin: University of Texas Press.

Forsyth, E. (2011). AR U feeling appy?: Augmented reality, apps and mobile access to local studies information. *Australasian Public Libraries and Information Services*, *24*(3), 125–132.

Foster, M. D. (2009). What time is this picture? Cameraphones, tourism, and the digital gaze in Japan. *Social Identities*, *15*(3), 351–372.

Franklin, A., & Crang, M. (2001). The trouble with tourism and travel theory? *Tourist Studies*, *1*(1), 5–22

Friedrich, M., Stone, P. R., & Rukesha, P. (2018). Dark tourism, difficult heritage, and memorialisation: A case of the Rwandan Genocide. In P. R. Stone et al. (Eds.), *The Palgrave handbook of dark tourism studies*. London: Palgrave Macmillan, 261–289.

Frith, J. (2015a). *Smartphones as locative media*. New York: Wiley.

Frith, J. (2015b). Writing space: Examining the potential of location-based composition. *Computers and Composition*, *37*(1), 44–54.

Frith, J., & Ahern, K. F. (2015). Make a sound garden grow: Exploring the new media potential of social soundscaping. *Convergence: The International Journal of Research into New Media Technologies*, *21*(4), 496–508.

Fyfe, N. (2004). Zero tolerance, maximum surveillance? Deviance, difference and crime control in the Late Modern city. In L. Lees (Ed.), *The emancipatory city?* London: Sage, 40–56.

Galloway, A., & Ward, M. (2006). Locative media as socialising and spatializing practice: Learning from archaeology. *Leonardo Electronic Almanac*, 14(3). Retrieved from https://www.leoalmanac.org/leonardo-electronic-almanac-volume-14-no-3-4-june-july-2006/

Galloway, A. R. (2012). *The interface effect*. Cambridge: Polity Press.

Gaye, L., & Holmquist, L. E. (2006). Performing Sonic City: Situated creativity in mobile music making. *Leonardo Electronic Almanac*, *14*(3). Retrieved from https://www.leoalmanac.org/leonardo-electronic-almanac-volume-14-no-3-4-june-july-2006/

Gemeinboeck, P., & Saunders, R. (2011). Urban fictions: a critical reflection on locative art and performative geographies. *Digital Creativity*, *22*(3), 160–173.

Gentry, R. (2014). *Woods from the trees* [Public sculpture]. Christchurch, New Zealand.

Germann Molz, J. (2007). Eating difference: The cosmopolitan mobilities of culinary tourism. *Space and Culture*, *10*(1), 77–93.

Germann Molz, J. (2012). *Travel connections: Tourism, technology and togetherness in a mobile world*. New York: Routledge.

Gibbs, S. (2016). Pokemon Go players urged not to venture into Fukushima disaster zone. *The Guardian*. July 26. Retrieved from https://www.theguardian.com/technology/2016/jul/26/pokemon-go-players-fukushima-disaster-zone-nuclear

Gibson, S. (2006). A seat with a view: Tourism, (im)mobility and the cinematic-travel glance. *Tourist Studies*, *6*(2), 157–178.

Goffman, E. (1959). *The presentation of self in everyday life*. New York: Anchor Books.

Goodwin, M. (2017). Screen dance: Interfacing culture and history in the urban space [Conference presentation]. *Spaces and Flows: Eighth International Conference on Urban and ExtraUrban Studies*. University of Hull, Hull, UK, October 12.

Gordon, A. (2016). *Time travel: Tourism and the rise of the living history museum in mid-twentieth-century Canada*. Vancouver: University of British Columbia Press.

Gordon, A. F. (2008). *Ghostly matters: Haunting and the sociological imagination*. Minneapolis: University of Minnesota Press.

Gordon, E. (2010). *The urban spectator: American Concept Cities from Kodak to Google*. Lebanon, NH: University Press of New England.

Gordon, E., & de Souza e Silva, A. (2011). *Net locality: Why location matters in a networked world*. Chichester, UK: Wiley-Blackwell.

Gotham, K. F. (2007). (Re)branding the Big Easy: Tourism rebuilding in post-Katrina New Orleans. *Urban Affairs Review*, *42*(6), 823–850.

Graham, M., Zook, M., & Boulton, A. (2013). Augmented reality in urban places: Contested content and the duplicity of code. *Transactions of the Institute of British Geographers*, *38*(3), 464–479.

Greenspan, B. (2011). The new place of reading: Locative media and the future of narrative. *Digital Humanities Quarterly*, *5*(3), 1–29.

Guba, E. G., & Lincoln, Y. S. (2003). Paradigmatic controversies, contradictions, and emerging confluences. In N. Denzin, & Y. S. Lincoln (Eds.), *The landscape of qualitative research* (2nd ed.). London: Sage Publications, 253–291.

Guidekick. (2016). *Golden Gate Park* [Mobile app]. Retrieved from https://play.google.com/store/apps/details?id=com.guidekickinc.android.goldengatepark&hl=en

Haldrup, M., & Larsen, J. (2010). *Tourism, performance and the everyday: Consuming the Orient*. London: Routledge.

Halpern, O. (2018). Visualizing: Design, communicative objectivity and the interface since 1945. In D. Howes (Ed.), *Senses and sensation: Critical and primary sources* (Volume 4). London: Bloomsbury, 89–110.

Halsey, M., & Young, A. (2006). "Our desires are ungovernable": Writing graffiti in urban space. *Theoretical Criminology*, *10*(3), 275–306.

Hanna, S. P., & Del Casino, V. J. (Eds.). (2003). *Mapping tourism*. Minneapolis: University of Minnesota Press.

Hannam, K., & Yankovska, G. (2018). Tourism mobilities, spectralities, and the hauntings of Chernobyl. In P. R. Stone et al. (Eds.), *The Palgrave handbook of dark tourism studies*. London: Palgrave Macmillan, 9–32.

Hansen, M. (2004). *New philosophy for new media*. Cambridge, MA: MIT Press.

Hansen, M. (2006). *Bodies in code: Interfaces with digital media*. New York: Routledge.

Hayward, K. (2004). *City limits: Crime, consumer culture and the urban experience*. Portland: Glasshouse Press.

Heatherington, C. (2012). Buried narratives. In A. Jorgensen, & R. Keenan (Eds.), *Urban wildscapes*. London: Routledge, 171–186.

Hebert, S. (2010). A taut rubber band: Theory and empirics in qualitative geographic research. In D. DeLyser, S. Hebert, S. Aitken, M. Crang, & L. McDowell (Eds.), *The Sage handbook of qualitative qeography*. London: Sage Publications, 69–81.

Hemment, D. (2006). Locative arts. *Leonardo*, *39*(4), 348–355.

Hess, A., & Herbig, A. (2013). Recalling the ghosts of 9/11: Convergent memorializing at the opening of the National 9/11 Memorial. *International Journal of Communication*, 7(1), 2207–2230.

Hetherington, K. (2013). Rhythm and noise: The city, memory, and the archive. *The Sociological Review*, *61*(1), 17–33.

High Street Stories. (2016). *High Street Stories*. Retrieved from http://www.highstreetstories.co.nz

High Street Stories. (n.d.). NV Interactive. Retrieved from https://www.nvinteractive.com/work/high-street-stories

Highmore, B. (2005). *Cityscapes: Cultural readings in the material and symbolic city*. London: Palgrave Macmillan.

Highmore, B. (2013a). Feeling our way: Mood and cultural studies. *Communication and Critical/Cultural Studies*, *10*(4), 427–438.

Highmore, B. (2013b). Memories of catastrophes yet to come: New Brutalism and thing- memory. In A. Smelik, & P. Liedeke (Eds.), *Performing memory in art and popular culture*. New York: Routledge, 75–92.

Hight, J. (2006). Views from above: Locative narrative and the landscape. *Leonardo Electronic Almanac*, 14(7–8), 1–9.

Hight, J. (2007). Immersive sight within the Third Space: Augmentation and spatial interface in exhibition space. *NeMe*. Retrieved from https://www.neme.org/texts/immersive-sight

Hinchliffe, S. (2007). *Geographies of nature: Societies, environments, ecologies*. Thousand Oaks, CA: Sage.

Hjorth, L. (2008). Being real in the mobile reel: A case study on convergent mobile media as domesticated new media in Seoul, South Korea. *Convergence*, *14*(1), 91–104.

Hjorth, L. (2009). Cartographies of the mobile: The personal as political. *Communication, Politics and Culture*, *42*(2), 24–44.

Hjorth, L. (2011). *Games and gaming: An introduction to new media*. Oxford: Berg.

Hong Kong Tourism Board. (2012). *Hong Kong City Walks* [Mobile app; inactive].

Hornsey, R. (2010). "He who thinks, in modern traffic, is lost": Automation and the pedestrian rhythms of interwar London. In T. Edensor (Ed.), *Geographies of rhythm: Nature, place, mobilities and bodies*. Burlington, VT: Ashgate Publishing, 99–112.

Hospers, G. J. (2011). City branding and the tourist gaze. In K. Dinnie (Ed.), *City branding: Theory and cases*. London: Palgrave Macmillan, 27–35.

Howes, D. (2003). *Sensual relations: Engaging the senses in culture and social theory*. Ann Arbor: University of Michigan Press.

Howes, D. (2005). Hyperaesthesia, or, the sensual logic of late capitalism. In D. Howes (Ed.), *The empire of the senses: The sensual culture reader*. Oxford: Berg, 265–303.

Howes, D. (2010). *Sensual relations: Engaging the senses in culture and social theory*. Ann Arbor: University of Michigan Press.

Howes, D. (2011). Vienna: Sensory capital. In M. Diaconu, E. Hueberger, R. Mateus-Berr, & L. M. Vosicky (Eds.), *Senses and the city: An interdisciplinary approach to urban sensescapes*. London: Transaction Publishers, 63–76.

Howes, D. (2014a). Introduction to sensory museology. *The Senses and Society*, *9*(3), 259–267.

Howes, D. (2014b). Introduction: "Make it new!" – Reforming the sensory world. In D. Howes (Ed.), *A cultural history of the senses in the Modern Age, 1920–2000* (Vol. 6). London: Bloomsbury, 1–30.

Howes, D. (2015). The science of sensory evaluation: An ethnographic critique. In S. Kuchler & M. Drazin (Eds.), *The social life of materials*. Abingdon: Routledge, 81–97.

Howes, D. (2018a). Introduction: On the geography and anthropology of the senses. In D. Howes (Ed.), *Senses and sensation: Critical and primary sources, Volume 1*. London: Bloomsbury, 1–22.

Howes, D. (Ed.). (2018b). *Senses and sensation: Critical and primary sources, Volume 2*. London: Bloomsbury.

Howes, D. (2019). Multisensory anthropology. *Annual Review of Anthropology*, *48*(1), 17–28.

Howes, D., & Classen, C. (2014). *Ways of sensing: Understanding the senses in society*. New York: Routledge.

Howes, D., & Salter, C. (2018). Mediations of sensation: Designing performative sensory environments. In D. Howes (Ed.), *Senses and sensation: Critical and primary sources, Volume 4*. London: Bloomsbury, 381–387.

Hudson, S., & Ritchie, J. B. (2009). Branding a memorable destination experience: The case of "Brand Canada". *International Journal of Tourism Research*, *11*(2), 217–228.

Ide, A. (2014). ICT and Dark Tourism. *IPSJ SIG Notes*, 4(1), 1–6.

Ingold, T. (2004). Culture on the ground: The world perceived through the feet. *Journal of Material Culture*, *9*(3), 315–340.

Ito, M., Okabe, D., & Anderson, K. (2010). Portable objects in three global cities: The personalization of urban places. In R. Ling, & S. Campbell (Eds.), *The Reconstruction of Space and Time: Mobile Communication Practices*. New Brunswick, NJ: Transaction Books, 67–88.

Jackson, P. (1989). *Maps of meaning: An introduction to cultural geography*. London: Unwin Hyman.

Jaguaribe, B. (2005). The shock of the real: Realist aesthetics in the media and the urban experience. *Space and Culture*, *8*(1), 66–82.

Japan quake regions use Pokemon Go to revive tourism. (2016). *BBC News*. August 11, 2016. Retrieved from https://www.bbc.com/news/blogs-news-from-elsewhere-37048250

Jeater, M. (2012). Smartphones and site interpretation: The Museum of London's Streetmuseum applications. In C. Bonacchi (Ed.), Archaeology and Digital Communication: Towards Strategies of Public Engagement. London: Archetype Publications, 66–82.

Jien, G. (2016). Suburbia, interrupted: Street art and the politics of place in the Paris Banlieues. In S. Jordan, & C. Linder (Eds.), *Cities interrupted: Visual culture and urban space*. London: Bloomsbury, 87–104.

Jones, C. A. (2018). The mediated sensorium. In D. Howes (Ed.), *Senses and sensation: Critical and primary sources, Volume 4*. London: Bloomsbury, 219–262.

Jones, P., Bunce, G., Evans, J., & Gibbs, H. (2008). Exploring space and place with walking interviews. *Journal of Research Practice*, *4*(2), Article D2.

Kassabian, A. (2016). Listening and digital technologies. In J. G. Papenburg, & S. Holger (Eds.), *Sound as popular culture*. Cambridge, MA: MIT Press, 197–203.

Kelly, C. (2009). *Cracked media: The sound of malfunction*. Cambridge, MA: MIT Press.

Kennedy, C., & Lukinbeal, C. (1997). Towards a holistic approach to geographic research on film. *Progress in Human Geography*, *21*(1), 33–50.

Kenny, N. (2014). *The feel of the city: Experiences of urban transformation*. Toronto: University of Toronto Press.

Kenyon, S. (2006). Reshaping patterns of mobility and exclusion? The impact of virtual mobility upon accessibility, mobility and social exclusion. In M. Sheller, & J. Urry (Eds.), *Mobile technologies of the city*. New York: Routledge, 177–191.

Khaled, R., Barr, P., Greenspan, B., Biddle, R., Vist, E. (2011). StoryTrek: Experiencing stories in the real world. In *Proceedings of the 15th International Academic MindTrek Conference: Envisioning Future Media Environments*, 125–132.

Klingmann, A. (2007). *Brandscapes: Architecture in the experience economy*. Cambridge, MA: MIT Press.

Knudsen, B. T., & Waade, A. M. (2010). Performative authenticity in tourism and spatial experience: Rethinking the relation between travel, place and emotion in the context of cultural economy and emotional geography. In B. T. Knudsen, & A. M. Waade (Eds.), *Re-investing authenticity: Tourism, place and emotions*. Bristol, UK: Channel View Publications, 1–19.

Koeck, R., & Warnaby, G. (2015). Digital chorographies: conceptualising experiential representation and marketing of urban/architectural geographies. *Arq*, *19*(2), 183–191.

Kohn, M. (2004). *Brave new neighborhoods*. London: Psychology Press.

Krajina, Z. (2009). Exploring urban screens. *Culture Unbound: Journal of Current Cultural Research*, *1*(1), 401–430.

Lagerkvist, A. (2007). Gazing at Pudong (with a drink in your hand): Time travel, mediation, and multisensuous immersion in the future city of Shanghai. *The Senses and Society*, *2*(2), 155–172.

Lagerkvist, A. (2008). Travels in thirdspace: Experiential suspense in mediaspace – the case of America (Un)known. *European Journal of Communication*, *23*(3), 343–363.

Laplantine, F. (2015). *The life of the senses: Introduction to a modal anthropology*. Abingdon: Routledge.

LaRochelle, L. (2018). *Queering the map*. Retrieved July 2019 from https://www.queeringthemap.com/

Larsen, J. (2001). Tourism mobilities and the travel glance: experiences of being on the move. *Scandinavian Journal of Hospitality and Tourism*, *1*(2), 80–98.

Larsen, J. (2008). Practices and flows of digital photography: An ethnographic framework. *Mobilities*, *3*(1), 141–160.

Larsen, J., & Urry, J. (2011). Gazing and performing. *Environment and Planning – Part D*, *29*(6), 1110–1125.

Larsen, J., Urry, J., & Axhausen, K. W. (2007). Networks and tourism: Mobile social life. *Annals of Tourism Research*, *34*(1), 244–262.

Lavery, C. (2009). Mourning walk and pedestrian performance: History, aesthetics and ethics. In R. Mock (Ed.), *Walking, writing, & performance: Autobiographical texts*. Bristol: Intellect Books, 25–56.

Law, L. (2001). Home cooking: Filipino women and geographies of the senses in Hong Kong. *Cultural Geographies*, *8*(3), 264–283.

Le Corbusier. (2010). The city of tomorrow and its planning. 1929 [Reprint]. In G. Bridge & S. Watson (Eds.), *The Blackwell city reader*. Hoboken, NJ: John Wiley and Sons, 345–354.

Leaver, T., & Lloyd, C. (2015). Seeking transparency in locative media. In R. Wilken & G. Goggin (Eds.), *Locative media*. New York: Routledge, 162–174.

Lee, G. A., Dünser, A., Kim, S., & Billinghurst, M. (2012, November). CityViewAR: A mobile outdoor AR application for city visualization. In *2012 IEEE International Symposium on Mixed and Augmented Reality-Arts, Media, and Humanities (ISMAR-AMH)* [Conference Proceedings], 57–64.

Lefebvre, H. (1991). *The production of space*. Oxford: Blackwell.

Lefebvre, H. (2004). Rhythmanalysis: Space, time and everyday life. London: A&C Black.

Lemieux, M., & Pilon, V. (2016). Cité Mémoire. http://4dart.com/en/creation/2016/cite-memoire/

Lemieux, M., & Pilon, V. (2017). Cité Mémoire: The adventure continues at the Fairmont the Queen Elizabeth Hotel. http://4dart.com/en/news/detail/2017/10/17/cite-memoire-the-adventure-continues-at-the-fairmont-the-queen-elizabeth-hotel/

Leszczynski, A. (2014). Spatial media/tion. *Progress in Human Geography*, *39*(6), 729–751.

Liao, T., & Humphreys, L. (2015). Layar-ed places: Using mobile augmented reality to tactically reengage, reproduce, and reappropriate public space. *New Media & Society*, *17*(9), 1418–1435.

Licoppe, C. (2016). Mobilities and urban encounters in public places in the age of locative media: Seams, folds, and encounters with "pseudonym strangers". *Mobilities*, *11*(1), 99–116.

Ling, R. (2004). *The mobile connection: The cell phone's impact on society*. San Francisco, CA: Morgan Kaufmann Publishers.

Little, K. (1991). On safari: The visual politics of a tourist representation. In D. Howes (Ed.), *The varieties of sensory experience: A sourcebook in the anthropology of the senses*. Toronto: University of Toronto Press, 148–163.

Logan, J. R., & Molotch, H. (2007). *Urban fortunes: The political economy of place* (2nd ed.). Oakland: University of California Press.

Loo, G., Sindhwani, S., Jing, C., & Loo, T. (2011). Brand Hong Kong. In K. Dinnie (Ed.), *City branding: Theory and cases*. London: Palgrave Macmillan, 157–161.

Lukas, S. A. (2007a). Introduction. In S. A. Lukas (Ed.), *The themed space: Locating culture, nation, and self*. Lanham, MD: Rowman & Littlefield, 1–22.

Lukas, S. A. (2007b). A politics of reverence and irreverence. In S. A. Lukas (Ed.), *The themed space: Locating culture, nation, and self*. Lanham, MD: Rowman & Littlefield, 271–293.

Lyden, J. (2006). A Visit to an Irish Rambling House. *NPR*. December 24, 2006. Retrieved from https://www.npr.org/templates/story/story.php?storyId=6671064

Lynch, E., Howes, D., & French, M. (2020). A touch of luck and a "real taste of Vegas": A sensory ethnography of the Montreal Casino. *The Senses and Society, 15*(2), 192–215.

Lynch, E. E. (2013). *'Scripting the street': Exploring geographies of crime in popular films* [MA Thesis]. University of Ottawa, Ottawa, Ontario, Canada.

Lynch, E. E. (2021). Laws of perpetual motion: the sensory regulation of mobility in public space. *The Senses and Society*, 16(1), 102–109.

Lynch, K. (1960). *The image of the city*. Cambridge, MA: MIT Press.

MacCannell, D. (1973). Staged authenticity: Arrangements of social space in tourist settings. *American Journal of Sociology, 79*(3), 589–603.

MacCannell, D. (2001). Tourist agency. *Tourist Studies, 1*(1), 23–37.

Mack, A. (2015). *Sensing Chicago: Noisemakers, strikebreakers, and muckrakers*. Chicago: University of Illinois Press.

Manovich, L. (2006). The poetics of augmented space. *Visual Communication, 5*(2), 219–240.

Marcus, E. G. 1995. Ethnography in/of the world system: The emergence of multi-sited ethnography. *Annual Review of Anthropology, 24*(1), 95–117.

Massey, D. B. (1994). *Space, place, and gender*. Minneapolis: University of Minnesota Press.

Masson, C. (2016). Design anthropology. *General Anthropology Bulletin, 23*(2), 8–11.

Matapopore. (2020). Tūranga: The new Christchurch Central Library [Project sheet]. Retrieved from https://matapopore.co.nz/wp-content/uploads/2020/11/Final-Turanga.pdf

Mathiesen, T. (1997). The viewer society: Michel Foucault's "Panopticon" revisited. *Theoretical Criminology, 1*(2), 215–234.

Maxwell, M. (1990). The authenticity of ethnographic research. *Communication Disorders Quarterly, 13*(1), 1–12.

McAuliffe, C. (2012). Graffiti or street art? Negotiating the moral geographies of the creative city. *Journal of Urban Affairs, 34*(2), 189–206.

McCarthy, A. (2001). *Ambient television: Visual culture and public space*. Durham, NC: Duke University Press.

McCotter, S. S. (2001). The journey of a beginning researcher. *The Qualitative Report, 6*(2), 1–22.

McCullough, M. (2006a). On the urbanism of locative media. *Places*, *18*(2), 26–29.

McCullough, M. (2006b). On urban markup: Frames of reference in location models for participatory urbanism. *Leonardo Electronic Almanac*, *14*(3), 1–5.

McCullough, M. (2008). Epigraphy and the public library. In A. Aurgi & F. De Cindio (Eds.), *Augmented urban spaces: Articulating the physical and electronic city*. Burlington, VT: Ashgate Publishing, 61–72.

McGarrigle, C. (2010). The construction of locative situations: Locative media and the Situationist International, recuperation or redux? *Digital Creativity*, *21*(1), 55–62.

McKay, I. (1988). Twilight at Peggy's Cove: Towards a genealogy of 'Maritimicity' in Nova Scotia. *Border/Lines*, *12*(1), 29–37.

McLuhan, M. (1964). *Understanding media: The extensions of man*. New York: McGraw-Hill.

Meinig, D. W. (1979). *The interpretation of ordinary landscapes: Geographical essays*. Oxford: Oxford University Press.

Merchant, S. (2011). Negotiating underwater space: The sensorium, the body and the practice of scuba-diving. *Tourist Studies*, *11*(3), 215–234.

Miodownik, M. (2018). Stuff matters: Glass. In D. Howes (Ed.), *Senses and sensation: Critical and primary sources, Volume 4*. London: Bloomsbury, 153–162.

Mitchell, D. (1995). The end of public space? People's Park, definitions of the public, and democracy. *Annals of the Association of American Geographers*, *85*(1), 108–133.

Miyazaki, S. (2015). Going beyond the visible: New aesthetic as an aesthetic of blindness? In D. M. Berry et al. (Eds.), *Postdigital aesthetics*. London: Palgrave MacMillan, 219–231.

Moles, K., & Saunders, A. (2014). Sound response: The public reception of audio walks. In J. Lossau & Q. Stevens (Eds.), *The uses of art in public space*. New York: Routledge, 110–124.

Molotch, H. (1976). The city as a growth machine: Toward a political economy of place. *American Journal of Sociology*, *82*(2), 309–332.

Montréal en Histoires. (2017). *Montréal en Histoires* [Mobile app]. Retrieved from: https://apps.apple.com/ca/app/montr%C3%A9al-en-histoires/id1001185556

Montreal en Histoires. (n.d.). Google Play Store. Last accessed online, July 2019: https://play.google.com/store/apps/details?id=com.SpaceAndDream.MontrealEnHistoires&hl=en_CA

Moore, J. (2016). Johnny Moore: Claims pre-quake central Christchurch dying exaggerated, replacement "monotone". *Stuff*, September 15. Retrieved from https://www.stuff.co.nz/the-press/business/the-rebuild/84288413/johnny-moore-reports-of-christchurchs-previous-death-greatly-exaggerated

Morais, A. R. (2016). Streetmuseum in screenspace: Exploring urban museums and cultural archives through augmented reality applications. *The Space and Place Project 6* [Conference proceedings]. InterDisciplinary.Net.

Morretti, C. (2017). Walking. In D. Elliot & D. Culhane (Eds.), *A different kind of ethnography: Imaginative practices and creative methodologies*. Toronto: University of Toronto Press, 91–112.

Morten, R., Stone, P. R., & Jarratt, D. (2018). Dark tourism as psychogeography: An initial exploration. In P. R. Stone et al. (Eds.), *The Palgrave handbook of dark tourism studies*. London: Palgrave Macmillan, 227–255.

Murakami Wood, D., & Ball, K. (2013). Brandscapes of control: Surveillance, marketing and the co-construction of subjectivity and space in neo-liberal capitalism. *Marketing Theory*, *13*(1), 47–67.

Murakami Wood, D., & Graham, S. (2006). Permeable boundaries in the software-sorted society: Surveillance and differentiations of mobility. In M. Sheller, & J. Urry (Eds.), *Mobile technologies of the city*. New York: Routledge, 177–191.

Murray, K. (2010). *The tools of engagement: Tactics and strategies employed for the creation of alternative places, spaces, and modes of citizenship within the Montreal graffiti subculture* [MA Thesis]. Concordia University, Montreal.

Museums Victoria. (2016). *Museum Victoria Tours: Walk Through History* [Mobile app]. Retrieved from https://apps.apple.com/au/app/mv-tours-walk-through-history/id696370101

Muzzio, D., & Halper, T. (2002). Pleasantville? The suburb and its representation in American movies. *Urban Affairs Review*, *37*(4), 543–574.

Nakamura, K. (2013). Making sense of sensory ethnography: The sensual and the multisensory. *American Anthropologist*, *115*(1), 132–135.

National Trust [Victoria]. (2012). *Lost! Melbourne's Lost 100* [Mobile app].

Nepal is open to all visitors. (2015). *Nepali Times*, June 26, 2015. Retrieved from http://archive.nepalitimes.com/article/Nepali-Times-Buzz/Nepal-is-open-to-all-visitors%20,2357

Neuman, W. L., Wiegand, B., & Winterdyk, J. A. (2004). *Criminal justice research methods: Qualitative and quantitative Approaches* (Canadian ed.). Toronto: Pearson.

Nisi, V. et al. (2018). A mixed reality neighbourhood tour: Understanding visitor experience and perceptions. *Entertainment Computing*, *27*(1), 89–100.

Nolte, C. (2016). Detour app offers guided "un-tours" of SF. *SF Gate*. Retrieved from https://www.sfgate.com/bayarea/article/Detour-app-offers-guided-un-tours-of-SF-7254311.php

Northern Ireland Environmental Agency. (2014). *Walk the Walls: The Historic Walls of Derry- Londonderry* [Mobile app; inactive].

Obrador-Pons, P. (2009). Building castles in the sand: Repositioning touch on the beach. *The Senses and Society*, *4*(2), 195–210.

Oppegaard, B., & Grigar, D. (2014). The interrelationships of mobile storytelling: Merging the physical and the digital at a national historic site. In J. Farman (Ed.), *The mobile story: Narrative practices with locative technologies*. New York: Routledge, 17–33.

Otakaro Limited. (2017). *Otakaro/Avon River Precinct: Lesson plan*. Retrieved from https://www.otakaroltd.co.nz/assets/Documents/GeneralDocuments/Avon-River-Precinct-Teaching-Resource.pdf

Otto, T., & Smith, R. C. (2013). Design anthropology: A distinct style of knowing. In W. Gunn, T. Otto, & R. C. Smith (Eds.), *Design anthropology: Theory and practice*. London: Bloomsbury, 14–39.

Ozkul, D. (2015). Mobile communication technologies and spatial perception: Mapping London. In R. Wilken & G. Goggin (Eds.), *Locative media*. New York: Routledge, 39–51.

Park, R.E. (1915). The city: Suggestions for the investigation of human behavior in the city. *American Journal of Sociology*, *20*(5), 577–612.

Parrika, J. (2015). The city and the city: London 2012 visual (un)commons. In D. M. Berry et al. (Eds.), *Postdigital aesthetics*. London: Palgrave Macmillan, 203–218.

Parrinello, G. L. (2001). The technological body in tourism research and praxis. *International Sociology*, *16*(2), 205–219.

Peacock, A. (2005). Being here: performative aspects of locative media. *International Journal of Performance Arts and Digital Media*, *1*(2), 127–146.

Penglase, B. (2007). Barbarians on the beach: Media narratives of violence in Rio de Janeiro, Brazil. *Crime Media Culture*, *3*(3), 305–325.

Perkins, C. (2009). Performative and embodied mapping. *International Encyclopedia of Human Geography*, *8*, 126–132.

Pesonen, J., & Horster, E. (2012). Near field communication technology in tourism. *Tourism Management Perspectives*, *4*(1), 11–18.

Pinder, D. (2013). Dis-locative arts: mobile media and the politics of global positioning. *Continuum*, *27*(4), 523–541.

Pinder, D. (2016). Sound, memory and interruption: Ghosts of London's M11 link road. In S. Jordan & C. Linder (Eds.), *Cities interrupted: Visual culture and urban space*. London: Bloomsbury, 65–86.

Pine, B. J., & Gilmore, J. H. (1999). *The experience economy: Work is theatre and every business a stage*. Cambridge, MA: Harvard Business Press.

Pink, S. (2009). *Doing sensory ethnography*. London: Sage.

Pink, S., & Hjorth, L. (2012). Emplaced cartographies: Reconceptualising camera phone practices in an age of locative media. *Media International Australia*, *145*(1), 145–155.

Price, P. (2006). *Nucleus* [Public sculpture]. Christchurch, New Zealand.

Reiser, M. (2009). Locative media and spatial narratives. *NeMe*. May 28. Retrieved from https://www.neme.org/texts/locative-media-and-spatial-narratives

Relph, E. (1976). *Place and placelessness*. London: Pion.

Richardson, I. (2007). Pocket technospaces: The bodily incorporation of mobile media. *Continuum*, *21*(2), 205–215.

Ritchie, J. (2014). The affordances and constraints of mobile locative narratives. In J. Farman (Ed.), *The mobile story: Narrative practices with locative technologies*. New York: Routledge, 53–67.

Robson, T., Castro, G., Paddon, M., & Beaman, A. (2016). The de Young Museum App by Guidekick as a model for collaborative development, technological innovation, and visitor behaviour insight. *Museums and the Web 2016* [Conference Proceedings]. Retrieved from https://mw2016.museumsandtheweb.com/paper/the-de-young-museum-app-by-guidekick-as-a-model-for-collaborative-development-technological-innovation-and-visitor-behavior-insight/

Roland, Z. (2013). There's nothing to see here! Experiencing Christchurch's High Street precinct through audio stories and augmented reality [Conference presentation]. *2013 National Digital Forum Conference*, Wellington, New Zealand, November 27. Retrieved from https://www.youtube.com/watch?v=i0QoDijkQ_c

Roland, Z, & HIT Lab NZ. (2013). *High Street Stories* [Mobile app; inactive].

Rossetto, T. (2012). Embodying the map: Tourism practices in Berlin. *Tourist Studies*, *12*(1), 28–51.

Rougeon, M. (2016). At the city's threshold: The caseira ambiance of Goiás' spaces of proximity. Translated by Samantha LeClair and Carmen Ruschiensky. *The Senses and Society*, *11*(3), 320–332.

Saker, M., & Evans, L. (2020). Personalising the urban: A critical account of locative media and the digital inscription of place. In P. R. Lakshmi, & N. D. Odeleye (Eds.), *Mediated identities in the futures of place: Emerging practices and spatial cultures*. New York: Springer, 39–55.

Salter, C. (2018). Resonances: Experimental encounters with sound art in the making. In D. Howes (Ed.), *Senses and sensation: Critical and primary sources, Volume 4*. London: Bloomsbury, 111–145.

Sample, M. (2014). Location is not compelling (until it is haunted). In J. Farman (Ed.), *The mobile story: Narrative practices with locative technologies*. New York: Routledge, 68–78.

Sandvik, K. (2010). Crime scenes as augmented reality: Models for enhancing places emotionally by means of narratives, fictions and virtual reality. In B. T. Knudsen & A. M. Waade (Eds.), *Re-investing authenticity: Tourism, place and emotions*. Bristol, UK: Channel View Publications, 138–153.

Sant, A. (2006). Trace: Mapping the emerging urban landscape. *Leonardo Electronic Almanac*, *14*(3), 1–7.

Sargent, N. (2016). The politics of Christchurch's glass box rebuild. *Stuff*, December 5. Retrieved from https://www.stuff.co.nz/the-press/business/the-rebuild/86168244/the-politics-of-christchurchs-glass-box-rebuild

Saunders, A., & Moles, K. (2015). Sound response: The public reception of audio walks. In J. Lossau, & Q. Stevens (Eds.), *The uses of art in public space*. London: Routledge, 98–114.

Schivelbusch, W. (1986). *The railway journey: The industrialization of space and time in the nineteenth century*. Oakland: University of California Press.

Scholl, S., Lahr-Kurten, M., & Redepenning, M. (2014). Considering the role of presence and absence in space constructions. Ethnography as methodology in human geography. *Historical Social Research/Historische Sozialforschung*, *39*(2), 51–67.

Schwandt, T. A. (2007). Judging interpretations. *New Directions for Evaluation*, *114*(1), 11–14.

Sears, J. T. (2001). *Rebels, rubyfruit, and rhinestones: Queering space in the Stonewall South*. New Brunswick, NJ: Rutgers University Press.

Seaton, T. (2018). Encountering engineered and orchestrated encountering engineered and orchestrated remembrance. In P. R. Stone et al. (Eds.), *The Palgrave handbook of dark tourism studies*. London: Palgrave Macmillan, 9–32.

Sennett, R. (1994). *Flesh and stone: The body and the city in western civilization*. New York: W. W. Norton.

Shaw, R. (2014). Beyond night-time economy: Affective atmospheres of the urban night. *Geoforum*, *51*(1), 87–95.

Sheller, M., & Urry, J. (2004). *Tourism mobilities: Places to play, places in play*. New York: Routledge.

Sheller, M., & Urry, J. (2006). Mobile cities, urban mobilities. In M. Sheller, & J. Urry (Eds.), *Mobile technologies of the city*. New York: Routledge, 1–19.

Sheridan, D. (2012). Disordering public space: Urban wildscape processes in practice. In A. Jorgensen, & R. Keenan (Eds.), *Urban wildscapes*. London: Routledge, 201–220.

Shields, R. (2003). Political tourism: Mapping memory and the future at Quebec City. In S. P. Hanna & V. Del Casino Jr. (Eds.), *Mapping tourism*. Minneapolis: University of Minnesota Press, 1–27.

Sibley, D. (1995). *Geographies of exclusion: Societies and difference in the West*. London: Psychology Press.

Simmel, G. (2010/1903). The metropolis and mental life. 1903 [Reprint]. In G. Bridge & S. Watson (Eds.), *The blackwell city reader*. Hoboken, NJ: John Wiley and Sons, 103–110.

Sinha, S. (2015). Three ways Nepalis are using crowdsourcing to aid in quake relief. *The New York Times*. May 1, 2015. Retrieved from https://www.nytimes.com/2015/05/02/world/asia/3-ways-nepalis-are-using-crowdsourcing-to-aid-in-quake-relief.html

Skinner, J. (2018). "The smoke of an eruption and the dust of an earthquake": Dark tourism, the sublime, and the re-animation of the disaster location. In P. R. Stone et al. (Eds.), *The Palgrave handbook of dark tourism studies*. London: Palgrave Macmillan, 125–150.

Smith, N. (1992). New city, new frontier: The Lower East Side as wild, wild west. In M. Sorkin (Ed.), *Variations on a theme park: The new American city and the end of public space*. New York: Macmillan, 60–93.

Smyth, G. (2011). *When a city falls* [Documentary]. New Zealand: Frank Film.

Sobchack, V. (2004). *Carnal thoughts: Embodiment and moving image culture*. Berkeley: University of California Press.

Soja, E. W. (1996). *Thirdspace: Journeys to Los Angeles and other real-and-imagined places*. Oxford: Blackwell.

Sontag, S. (1977). *On photography*. New York: Farrar, Strauss and Giroux.

Sorkin, M. (Ed.). (1992). *Variations on a theme park: The new American city and the end of public space*. London: Macmillan.

Soyini Madison, D. (2006). Staging fieldwork/performing human rights. In J. A. Hamera (Ed.), *The Sage handbook of performance studies*. London: Sage, 397–418.

Space Needle. (2016). Space Needle [Mobile app; inactive].

Spring, U. (2006). The linear city: Touring Vienna in the nineteenth century. In M. Sheller, & J. Urry (Eds.), *Mobile technologies of the city*. New York: Routledge, 21–43.

Springgay, S., & Truman, S.E. (2017). A transmaterial approach to walking methodologies: Embodiment, affect, and a sonic art performance. *Body & Society*, *23*(4), 27–58.

Stevens, Q., & Lossau, J. (2015). Framing art and its uses in public space. In J. Lossau & Q. Stevens (Eds.), *The uses of art in public space*. London: Routledge, 1–18.

Steward, J., & Cowan, A. (2007). Introduction. In A. Cowan, & J. Steward (Eds.), *The city and the senses: Urban culture since 1500*. Farnham, UK: Ashgate Publishing, 1–21.

Stinson, J. (2016). Re-creating wilderness 2.0: Or getting back to work in a virtual nature. *Geoforum*, *79*(1), 174–187.

STQRY. (2016). *Pike Place Market – Steinbrueck Park Public Art Tour*. [Mobile app]. retrieved from https://discover.stqry.com/v/pike-place-market%e2%80%93steinbrueck-park-public-art-tour/o/b724be1b7ebc058e005916ce005229be

Strain, E. (2003). *Public places, private journeys: Ethnography, entertainment and the tourist gaze*. New Brunswick, NJ: Rutgers University Press.

Struppek, M. (2006). The social potential of urban screens. *Visual Communication*, *5*(2), 173–188.

Sturken, M. (1997). *Tangled memories: The Vietnam war, the AIDS epidemic, and the politics of remembering*. Berkeley: University of California Press.

Suominen, J., Silvast, A., & Harviainen, T. (2018). Smelling machine history: Olfactory experiences of information technology. *Technology and Culture*, *59*(2), 313–337.

Tang, Y. (2018). Dark tourism to seismic memorial sites. In P. R. Stone et al. (Eds.), *The Palgrave handbook of dark tourism studies*. London: Palgrave Macmillan, 423–442.

Taussig, M. (2009). Tactility and distraction. In D. Howes (Ed.), *The sixth sense reader*. London: Bloomsbury, 267–276.

Thibaud, J. P. (2015). The backstage of urban ambiances: When atmospheres pervade everyday experience. *Emotion, Space and Society*, *15*(1), 39–46.

Thielmann, T. (2010). Locative media and mediated localities. *Aether: The Journal of Media Geography*, *5*(1), 1–17.

Thompson, E. (2005). "Noise and noise abatement in the modern city." In M. Zardini (Ed.), *Sense of the city: An alternate approach to urbanism*. Montreal: Lars Müller Publishers, 191–199.

Thompson, R. C. (2010). "Am I going to see a ghost tonight?": Gettysburg ghost tours and the performance of belief. *The Journal of American Culture*, *33*(2), 79–91.

Thurschwell, P. (2009). Refusing to give up the ghost: Some thoughts on the afterlife from spirit photography to phantom films. In D. Howes (Ed.), *The sixth sense reader*. London: Bloomsbury, 183–208.

Tierney, T. F. (2013). Positioning locative media: A critical urban intervention. *Leonardo*, *46*(3), 253–257.

Tourisme Montreal (2003). *Montreal tourism development plan 2003–2010*. Accessed online: http://documents.tourisme-montreal.org/Montreal-Tourism/R-and-D/Product-Development/EN/Montreal-Tourism-Development-Plan-2003-2010.pdf

Tourisme Montreal. (2014). *Developpement du tourisme culturel a Montreal: Strategies et actions 2014–2017*. Retrieved from http://ville.montreal.qc.ca/culture/sites/ville.montreal.qc.ca.culture/files/plan_tourisme_culturel_14-17.pdf

Townsend, A. (2006). Locative-media artists in the contested-aware city. *Leonardo*, *39*(4), 345–347.

Trigg, D. (2017). Place and non-place: A phenomenological perspective. In B. B. Janz (Ed.), *Place, space and hermeneutics* (Volume 5). New York: Springer, 127–139.

TripAdvisor (Various Authors). (2018). Cité Mémoire. *TripAdvisor: Things to Do in Montreal*. https://www.tripadvisor.ca/Attraction_Review-g155032-d11980466-Reviews-or10-Cite_Memoire-Montreal_Quebec.html

Truman, S. E., & Springgay, S. (2019). Queer walking tours and the affective contours of place. *Cultural Geographies*, *26*(4), 527–534.

Tuan, Y. F. (2001). *Space and place: The perspective of experience* (8th printing). Minneapolis: University of Minnesota Press.

Tussyadiah, I. P., & Zach, F. J. (2012). The role of geo-based technology in place experiences. *Annals of Tourism Research*, *39*(2), 780–800.

Tuters, M. (2015). Through glass darkly: On Google's gnostic governance. In D. M. Berry et al. (Eds.), *Postdigital aesthetics*, London: Palgrave Macmillan, 245–258.

Tuters, M., & Varnelis, K. (2006). Beyond locative media: Giving shape to the internet of things. *Leonardo*, *39*(4), 357–363.

Urry, J. (1990). *The tourist gaze*. London: Sage.

Urry, J. (2000). City life and the senses. In G. Bridge & S. Watson (Eds.), *A companion to the city*. Oxford: Blackwell, 388–397.

Urry, J. (2001). Transports of delight. *Leisure Studies*, *20*(4), 237–245.

Urry, J. (2011). Does mobility have a future? In M. Grieco, & J. Urry (Eds.), *Mobilities: New perspectives on transport and society*. Burlington, VT: Ashgate, 3–20.

Urry, J., & Larsen, J. (2011). *The tourist gaze 3.0*. London: Sage.

US Department of Housing and Urban Development. (2018). *The 2018 Annual Homeless Assessment Report (AHAR) to Congress*. Retrieved from https://files.hudexchange.info/resources/documents/2018-AHAR-Part-1.pdf

Van Doom, N. (2013). Assembling the affective field: How smartphone technology impacts ethnographic research practice. *Qualitative Inquiry*, *19*(5), 385–396.

van Hoven, B. (2011). Multi-sensory tourism in the Great Bear Rainforest. *Landabréfid*, *25*(1), 31–49.

Vanolo, A. (2018). Cities and the politics of gamification. *Cities*, *74*(1), 320–326.

Verhoeff, N. (2012). *Mobile screens: The visual regime of navigation*. Amsterdam: Amsterdam University Press.

Verhoeff, N., & Cooley, H. R. (2014). The navigational gesture: Traces and tracings at the mobile touchscreen interface. *NECSUS European Journal of Media Studies*, *3*(1), 111–128.

Vermont PBS. (2017). Cité Mémoire: Extended version, with Michel Lemieux [Interview]. *PBS*. Accessed online. *PBS*. Retrieved from https://m.youtube.com/watch?v=CCU_J9wkMGA.

Verrips, J. (2002). "Haptic screens" and our "corporeal eye". *Etnofoor*, *15*(1/2), 21–46.

Ville de Montréal. (n.d.) Cité Mémoire, inspired by the history of Montreal. Montreal's 375th anniversary, *Ville de Montreal*. Retrieved from http://ville.montreal.qc.ca/375/en/legs/cite-memoire.

Waitt, G., & Duffy, M. (2010). Listening and tourism studies. *Annals of Tourism Research*, 37(2), 457–477.

Wang, D., Park, S., & Fesenmaier, D. R. (2012). The role of smartphones in mediating the touristic experience. *Journal of Travel Research*, *51*(4), 371–387.

Wang, N. (1999). Rethinking authenticity in tourism experience. *Annals of Tourism Research*, 2(26), 349–370.

Welcome to High Street Stories. (n.d.). *High Street Stories*. Retrieved from http://www.highstreetstories.co.nz/splash

Weston, K. (1995). Get thee to a big city: Sexual imaginary and the great gay migration. *GLQ: A Journal of Lesbian and Gay Studies*, 2(1), 253–277.

White, D. F., & Wilbert, C. (2010). Inhabiting technonatural time/spaces. In D. F. White, & C. Wilbert (Eds.), *Technonatures: Environments, technologies, spaces, and places in the Twenty-first Century*. Waterloo: Wilfrid Laurier University Press, 1–32.

Wilken, R. (2019). *Cultural economies of locative media*. Oxford: Oxford University Press.

Wilken, R., & Goggin, G. (2014). Locative media: Definitions, histories, theories. In R. Wilken & G. Goggin (Eds.), *Locative media*. New York: Routledge, 1–19.

Wittel, A. (2000). Ethnography on the move: From field to net to Internet. *FQS Forum: Qualitative Social Research*, *1*(1), Article 21.

Woods, R. (2016). *Painting ruins: Graffiti and street art in post-earthquake Christchurch* [PhD Dissertation]. Canterbury University, Christchurch, May.

Wunderlich, F. M. (2008). Walking and rhythmicity: Sensing urban space. *Journal of Urban Design*, *13*(1): 125–139.

Year Zero One. (2014). About. *Queerstory*. Retrieved December 3, 2021, from http://www.queerstory.ca/about/

Year Zero One. (2016). *Queerstory* [Mobile app]. Retrieved from https://www.queerstory.ca/app/

Zardini, M. (Ed.). (2005). *Sense of the city: An alternate approach to urbanism*. Montreal: Canadian Centre for Architecture.

Zeffiro, A. (2015). Locative praxis: Transborder poetics and activist potentials of experimental locative media. In R. Wilken & G. Goggin (Eds.), *Locative media*. New York: Routledge, 66–80.

Zolf, J. (2020). *Into the light with Cité Mémoire*. Jance Zolf Productions. Retrieved from https://gem.cbc.ca/media/absolutely-canadian/s20e17?cmp=sch-into%20the%20light

Zook, M. A., & Graham, M. (2007). Mapping DigiPlace: Geocoded internet data and the representation of place. *Environment & Planning B: Planning & Design*, *34*(3), 466–482.

Zukin, S. (1989). *Loft living: Culture and capital in urban change*. New Brunswick, NJ: Rutgers University Press.

Zukin, S. (1995). *The cultures of cities*. Oxford: Wiley-Blackwell.

Zukin, S. (2009). *Naked city: The death and life of authentic urban places*. Oxford: Oxford University Press.

Index

Pages in *italics* refer figures and pages in **bold** refer tables.

absence(s) 28, 77–78, 107–108, 122–124, 133; *see also* gaps; haunted
advertising 28, 37, 50, 93, 135, 138–139, 143; *see also* branding, urban branding
aesthetic control *see* regulation of urban sensation
aesthetic ordering, 17, 35–38, 40, 42, 56, 66, 73–74, 101, 109–110, 113, 157, 159; *see also* museum, aesthetics
aesthetic pastiche *see* pastiche
affordances 8, 13, 16–18, 25, 71, 84, 91, 100, 102, 110, 147–148; *see also* medium
alienation: alienating qualities of spectacle 54, 114, 144; viewing distance 4, 21, 36, 40–41, 48–49, 54, 113, 144, 153, 156–157
alignment work 33, 40–42, 69, 76, 130, 160
alleyways 57, 72, 79, 97, 99, 101, 103–104, 107, 137, 150–153
Along the Yarra 68, 79–80, **164**
ambience 12, 59, 153; *see also* atmosphere; mood
animation 1, 28–29, 37–38, 60, 80, 89, 97, 100, 111, 119, 151, 153–154, 158–159, 161; animated effects in locative tourism apps 51–55, 128, 139
anthropology of the senses 2, 5, 12–13, 20–28
anticipation 54, 58
architecture: architecture of memory 106; hostile architecture 53; urban architecture 11, 15–16, 28, 75, 77, 91, 107, 110–111, 113, 120–121, 136, 148, 154
archive *see* city as archive
aroma *see* smell
aromascape *see* sensescapes
artificiality *see* authenticity
atmosphere 26, 57, 60–63, 70, 74–75, 79, 99, 101–104, 126, 128–129, 137, 141–142, 160; atmosphere and gaze 128, 145; *see also* ambience; mood
attunement, sensory 26–27, 61, 89, 107, 159–160
audio 1, 31, 38–39, 56, 64, 71, 103, 125, 127–129, 134, 143, 150; intimacy and audio 127–129, 134, **164**; narration 39, 64, 71; *see also* sound
augmentation *see* augmented reality
augmented reality (AR) 3, 7, 13–18, 25, 31, 33, 35, 38, 42, 44–45, 50–54, 83–84, 97, 107, 113, 124–125, 127–128, 130, 133, 136–137, 141, 145–146, 149, 151, 155–157, **164**
authenticity: inauthenticity and tourism 8, 43, 49, 58, 63, 75, 81–83; and tourism 17, 36, 49, 58, 63, 77, 80–83, 121; *see also* simulation
authorship *see* co-production, narrative, urban inscription, user-generated content

Barber, John 24
Baudelaire, Charles 1
being there, importance of 14, 20, 27–31, 70, 89, 160; *see also* site specificity
Benjamin, Walter 1; *see also flaneur*
blandscapes *see* city as shopping mall
Bodiam Castle 60
Bogside 45–47

Boorstin, Daniel 81
Boulton, Andrew 84
branding: urban branding 3–4, 7, 11–12, 16, 26–28, 33, 35, 37, 40, 43–45, 59, 63, 66, 83, 85–86, 91, 93–96, 105, 114–115, 122, 125, 128, 130, 134–139, 141, 144, 148, 153–154, 156–158, **163**
brand policing *see* branding
Buser, Michael 60
bus tours 70, 74–75

carnival 23, 138, 141–142
Catley, Mark 118
CCTV 22, 146, 148
CD (compact disc) 75–76
change *see* dynamism, urban development
Christchurch 2–3, 28, 30–31, 74, 79, 91, 93–124, 133, 143, 154, **164**; *see also High Street Stories*
Christchurch Cathedral 93, *94*, 96, 105
Cité Mémoire 28, 125–155, **164**
city as archive 36–37, 88, 115, 151
city as art gallery 73, 112–115
city as museum 35–37, 73–74, 111, 113, 157–159, **162**, **164**
city as screen 139–145, 153–154, 158
city as shopping mall 12–14, 31, 43, 59, 63, 135
city of culture 45, 157, **163**
city of planners *see* Concept City
CityViewAR, 97, 124
civilising narratives 80–81, 103, **164**
Classen, Constance 23, 36, 109
CN Tower 51
coach tours *see* bus tours
Coats, Alex 96
code 16, 83
collective experience 126, 150–153
commemoration *see memory*, memorialisation
commodification 44, 48, 83, 115; of the city 22, 52–53, 76–77, 82–83; of street art 114–115
Concept City 5, 28, 50, 148
conflict 44–47, *49*, **163**; conflicting narratives of urban space 3, 15, 33, 44, 66, 68, 76–80, 111–116, 157, 159
connection 16–18, 25, 75, 98, 119–120, 123, 127–128, 144, 147, 153–154, 160; connection and disconnection 14, 16–18, 75, 121, 160
consumption: building the city for consumption 8, 12, 43–45, 58, 70, 76–77, 86, 88, 139, 148; cultural consumption 12, 36, 43, 48, 76–77, 82–83, 86, 136, 138; touristic consumption 2, 8, 12, 43, 59, 81, 138, 140, 160
contamination 22, 49, 57, 65
contingency 20, 29, 31, 111, 153; *see also* precarity
convergence 13, 18, 24, 29, 71, 103, 113, 115; *see also* encounter
Cooley, Heidi Rae 15
co-production: of knowledge 2, 26, 30–31, 160; of the locative tour 4, 16, 26, 28–29, 31, 40, 81, 84, 150–153, 160; of urban places 2, 28, 81, 150–153, 158, 160
corporeal *see* embodiment
correspondence 29, 68, 88, 109
Cosgrove, Denis 9
cosmopolitanism 49, 63–66, 157–158, **163**
counterculture 82–83, 114; commodification of 83, 114
Coyote, Peter 82–83
Crang, Mike 147
Cresswell, Tim 9
cruise ships 93, 95
cultural geography 2, 5, 9–10, 26, 84
curation, curated experiences of the city 24, 38, 44, 59, 75, 80, 97, 105, 116, 132–133, 154

dark tourism 60, 96
data layer *see* layer
Debord, Guy 139
de Certeau, Michel 1, 50, 58, 121; *see also* "Concept City"
decorporeal *see* disembodiment
Degen, Mónica 21, 23, 121
Del Casino, Vincent J. 85
deodorisation 23, 58; *see also* regulation of urban sensation
Derry/Londonderry 27, 31, 35, 45–48, *49*, 135, 157, **163**; *see also Walk the Walls*
designers 28, 38, 60, 71–72, 86, 97–99, 103, 109, 119, 126–129, 137, 139–140, 142, 144, 151, 153
destination space 12–14, 18, 27, 36, 45, 49, 74, 85, 128, 141, 161
Detour 31, 71, 82–83, 88, **164**
Deutsche, Rosalyn 28

de Young Museum 148
Diaconu, Mădălina 23
differentiation in tourism development 1, 44, 58
digital literacy 16
digital spaces 12–17, 25, 36, 42, 68–69, 72–73, 76–77, 87
digital tourism *see* technotourism
disable *see* affordances
discordance: discordant rhythms 33, 62, 69–70, 74–75, 89; sonic discord 64, 75–76; *see also* disjuncture; rhythm
Discover Hong Kong 31, **163**; *City Walks* 62–66, **163**
disembodiment 9, 13
disjuncture 17–18, 33, 41, 45, 62, 68–69, 77, 83, 107, 111, 159–160; askew 41, 45; *see also* discordance
dislocative media *see* disorientation
Disneyfication 7–8, 43, 138
displacement 97–98, 101, 106, 121–122
distance *see* alienation
diversity: in the city 20, 38, 68–69, 83, 138–139, 141–143; diversification of mapping practices 84–87; sensory diversity 21, 23, 38, 59, 62–66,138; *see also* mapping, countermapping; other, encountering the other
dressage 40, 70–71; *see also* rhythmanalysis
Dublin 27, 56, 71–72, 85–86, **162**; *see also Dublin Storymap*; *Dublin Walls*
Dublin Storymap 56, 71–72, 85–86, **162**
Dublin Walls **162**
Duffy, Michelle 59
Dunluce Castle 38
dynamism 1, 7–8, 16, 18, 24, 26, 28, 43, 69, 88, 129, 160–161

earthquake 30–31, 91, 93–124; 2010/2011 Canterbury earthquakes impact and recovery 91, 93–96, 111–123, **164**
Edensor, Tim 12, 70, 100, 141, 156
Edinburgh 27, 35, 39–40, 56–58, 81, **162**; *see also World Heritage City*
Eiffel Tower 51
embodiment 14, 23, 69, 120; embodiment and locative media 14, 18, 20, 24–26, 42, 62, 66, 68, 89, 99, 142, 156, 159–160
emergent technologies 1,7–9, 12–14, 16–18, 20, 23, 26, 36–38, 50, 69, 75–76, 80, 85, 139, 146, 148–149, 152, 158
emotion, emotional connection and place 44, 103, 127–128, 144
emplaced experience 25–26, 62; *see also* site specificity
enable *see* affordances
enchantment 10, 12, 33, 37–38, 42, 44, 51, 98, 132, 137, 150–152; re-enchantment 4, 10–11, 14, 56, 150–153, 160–161
encounter 1–3, 5, 18, 20, 24, 26, 28–30, 33, 35, 49–50, 52, 55–56, 62, 65, 72, 74, 76, 83–89, 94, 96, 100, 105, 111, 114, 117–119, 125–128, 133, 136–137, 147, 149, 151–153, 158–160; visceral encounter 99–100, 103, 135; *see also* other, encountering the other
entanglement 1, 4, 9, 15, 20, 33, 81, 91, 98, 109, 116, 123, 126, 156, 160–161; zones of entanglement 26
ephemeral experiences 31, 59, 89, 91, 103, 129, 143, 150; *see also* Transitional City
erasure 77, 79, 87–88, 105, 109, 120, 122, 131, 138, 151, 154, 158
exclusion 8, 43–44, 84, 123; inclusion and exclusion 8, 44, 85–87
experience economy 4, 12, 20, 36, 44, 59, 65, 127–128, 157
extensions of the senses, locative apps as 2–3, 8, 16, 20, 25, 33, 35, 49–56, 58, 66, 68–69, 76, 130,46, 149, 156–157, 161

Farías, Ignacio 70
Farman, Jason 16, 25, 76, 85
Faulkner, William 61
Ferguson, Shelagh 96
fixity 43; and change 29, 76, 111
Flanagan, Mary 69
flaneur 1, 24, 153
flow 8, 16, 27–28, 31, 57–58, 63, 70–71, 73–74, 89, 110, 152, 157–158; *see also* rhythm
Fomison, Tony 113, *114*
fortress city 22
framing, the city 1–2, 18, 20–21, 33, 35–38, 40–43, 48, 51, 97, 99, 109–111, 120, 128, 136, 138–139, 141, 146, 156–157

French Quarter 59–62
Frith, Jordan 15
future imaginaries *see* imaginaries

gamification 3, 35, 39–40, 54, 56
gaps: encountering gaps and seams in the tour 1, 3, 16, 24, 30, 40–41, 68–69, 89, 130–132, 159; in the streetscape 93–98, 108–109, 113, 122, 133, 143, 154
gardens *see* nature
gay village 87, 134; *see also* queering space
gaze 2–3, 7–9, 12, 21, 33, 35–52, *53*, 58–60, 62–63, 66, 71–73, 85, 101, 106, 109, 113–115, 127–128, 135, 140, 145–146, 148, 152, 156–157; collective gaze 40; directing the gaze 33, 45–47, 73, 84, 140; distracted gaze 71; extended gaze 35, 49–51, *53*, 149; intimacy and the gaze 21, 127–128, 145–146, 153; and rationalist urban planning 22, 50
gentrification 11, 79, 103, 105, 115, 123; street art and gentrification 123; *see also* cultural consumption; revitalisation; urban development
geolocation *see* GPS
Germann Molz, Jennie 58
ghost: architectural ghosts 77, 80, 95, 100, 105, 108–109, 123–124, 133, 143, *144*, 154, 159; digital ghosts 55, 129, 142, *145*; ghost tours 1, 56, 60–62, 157–158, **163**; *see also* haunted; traces
ghostly matters *see* haunted
glass, the aesthetic implications of 55–56, 64, 120–121
glitch 3, 16, 31, 68–69, 75–76, 126, 131, 146; performing the glitch 75–76; *see also* discordance
Golden Gate Park 80, **164**
Goodwin, Mitch 79
Google Earth 85
Google Maps 86
Gordon, Alan 138
GPS (global positioning system) 16, 18; positioning problems with locative apps 51, 69, 76, 85, 108–109; and surveillance 146–147, 149
graffiti 28, 104, 112–116, 121, 149; *see also* street art
Graham, Mark 84
Graham, Stephen 147
Greenspan, Brian 17, 88
Grigar, Dene 17
growth machine, the city as 76–77
guidebook 11, 14, 44–45, 85
guided tour *see* tour guides
Guidekick: Golden Gate Park 80, **164**

Haight-Ashbury district (San Francisco) 71, 82–83
Halsey, Mark 114
Hanna, Stephen P. 85
Hansen, Mark B.N. 146
haptic geography *see* sensescapes
Harrison, George 83
haunted: places 60–62, 78–79, 93, 100, 123, 143; urban imaginaries 123–124, 161
headphones 16, 64, 89, 103
hearing *see* sound
Hemment, Drew 18
Herbig, Art 17
heritage: built heritage 38–39, 77–79, 97, 106, 110, 120–122, 151, 154, 157–158; heritage aesthetics 44, 58, 102, 111–112, 119–120, 122, 133, 138, 148–149; role of heritage organisations 77–80, 102, 111, 119, 157
Heritage Vic (now Vic-Heritage) 74–75, **164**
Hess, Aaron 17
Hetherington, Kevin 88, 151
High Street (Christchurch) 74, 79, 93, 96–124, 129, 133, 154, 160, **164**
High Street Stories 3, 30–31, 79, 91, 96–124, 129, 133, 154, 160, **164**
Hight, Jeremy 17
Historic NOLA 35, 37, 41, 81, **163**
Hjorth, Larissa 15, 102
Holloway, Julian 70
homelessness, within the frame of the tour 41, 88–89
Hong Kong 23, 27, 31, 35, 49, 62–66, **163**; *see also Discover Hong Kong*
Howes, David 12, 55, 99, 140
Hume, David 57
Humphreys, Lee 84
hybrid space *see* simultaneous space
hyperaesthesia 44; *see also* experience economy

icons, urban 46, 51, 82–83, 87, 94, 96
illumination 62, 139–143
imageability 11, 40, 74, 103, 106, 115, 135, 160
images *see* photography

imaginaries: future imaginaries 117–124; tourist imaginary 45, 138; urban imaginary 17, 40, 44, 74, 117–124, 159
immersive experiences 58, 135
improvisation 70, 131–132; *see also* city as archive; city as gallery; city as museum; city as screen
Indigenous histories 79, 116, 122, 128, 138, 151
informational layer *see* layer
infrastructure: architectural 28, 38, 58, 93, 136, 146; technological 15–16, 31, 75, 83–86, 136, 147–148
inscription *see* urban inscription
in situ representations 26, 37, 50, 111, 115
interactive experience 15, 17, 56, 96–97, 137, 139, 143, 149–153
interface 3, 8, 16, 25, 126; *see also* infrastructure, technological
interplay: of digital and geospatial worlds 1, 14, 16–18, 24–25, 29, 68–69, 77, 84, 87, 111, 128, 153; of the senses 26; of urban inscriptions 85, 135
interruption 16, 29–30, 70, 76, 88, 123; *see also* pause
intertextuality 85; *see also* reading the city
intimacy 99, 102, 106, 110, 127, 129–130, 134, 139, 142–146, 152, 157; spectacular intimacy 128–130, 142–143, 152–153
invisible architecture *see infrastructure*, technological
Irish Troubles 44–47, *49*

Jackson Square (New Orleans) 41, 59, 64, 81
Jien, Gillian 123
Jones, Caroline 102

Kenny, Nicolas 23

Lagerkvist, Amanda 62
landmarks 11–12, 50–51, 86–87, 97, 105–107, 113, 141–142, **163–164**; phantom landmarks 106–109
Larochelle, Lucas 86
Larsen, Jonas 27
Law, Lisa 23
layer: informational layer 12, 15–16, 126; layering 10–11, 15–18, 23–24, 31, 41–42, 51, 68–69, 84–85, 87, 98, 101, 103, 116, 125–126, 142, 153, 157–160, **164**; relationship between informational layer and architectural space 16–18, 24–25, 29, 68–69, 77, 84, 87, 111, 128, 153
Leaver, Tama 16
Le Corbusier 21
Lefebvre, Henri 10, 28, 70, 83; *see also* rhythmanalysis
legibility, making the city legible 11–12, 43, 73, 85, 106–107, 122
Lemieux, Michel 126, 128, 138, 140, 151
LGBTQ+ history 86–87, 129, 132; *see also* queering space
Liao, Tony 84
Liberties (Dublin) 86
Licoppe, Christian 40; *see also* alignment work
lighting *see* illumination
liminality *see* simultaneity
liveability 80, 96, 121
Lloyd, Clare 16
locals 3–4, 46, 65, 71–72, 75, 77, 80–81, 86, 88–89, 91, 94–103, 106, 109, 111, 113, 115–116, 118–121, 123, 126, 139–140; local perspectives 46–47, 71–72, 77–78, 80–81, 86, 98–103, 106, 109, 111, 113, 115–116, 118–120, 123
location-aware technologies 1, 13, 18; *see also* GPS; locative media; sentient city
locative media 1–2, 8, 12–18, 20, 24–27, 29, 31,36, 40, 48, 50, 54, 66, 69, 76–77, 88, 91, 98, 107, 111, 119, 139, 149, 153–154, 156, 159; as artistic/critical intervention 13–14, 17–18, 69, 76, 158; and tourism 1–5, 7–8, 13, 18, 20, 24–31, 33, 35–89, 91, 107, 111, 126, 156–161
locative tourism *see* locative media
Logan, John R. 76
London 1, 27, 35–37, 54–56, 98, 148, **162**; *see also Streetmuseum*; *Streetmuseum Londinium*
loss 77–79, 89, 98, 106, 109, 154; *see also* absence(s); mourning
Lynch, Kevin 105–106

MacCannell, Dean 81
Mack, Adam 23
magic *see* enchantment
mapping 69, 83–88; countermapping 83, 86–87; mapping practices in

locative media 14–16, 38, 68–69, 71–72, 76, 86–87, 96–97, 107, 109–110, 127, 135–136, 148, 158, **162**

maps 1, 11, 14, 68–69, 71–72, 79–80, 83–88, 96–97, 105–106, 109, 126; cognitive maps of the city 11–12, 103, 105–107, 109; maps and tourism 44–45, 84–85, 105–106; "maps of meaning" 2, 9–10, 18, 157–158; performing the map 29, 33, 76, 107–110, 160; troubling the neutrality of the map 68–69, 84–85, 159

marginality 23, 86–89; *see also* other, the

markets, urban 56, 62–66, 72–73, 141, **163**

Mason, Andrew 71

McCullough, Malcolm 15, 28, 111

McLuhan, Marshall 16; *see also* "extensions of the senses"

mediation 2, 5, 9–10, 12, 15–16, 20–21, 26, 28, 30–31, 33, 38, 40, 45, 51, 60, 62, 66, 68–69, 82, 93, 116, 127, 141, 153–154, 156–157, 159–161

medium 8, 16, 20, 25, 43, 75, 102, 118

Melbourne 27, 68, 71, 74–75, 77–81, 82, 107, 158, **164**; *see also Along the Yarra*; *Heritage Vic*; *Melbourne's Lost! 100*; *Museum Victoria Tours: Walk Through History*; *Our City*

Melbourne's Lost! 100 77–80, 107, **164**

memory 11, 23, 58, 88, 96, 98–99, 102, 106, 109, 128, 135, 138, 142, 148, 159–160; collective remembrance 97, 99; memorialisation 47, 74–75, 79, 83–84, 89, 96–99, 118, *119*

metropolis and mental life 21, 24, 100

Miller, Graeme 98

mobile devices, use of 8, 25, 27, 55, 75–76; *see also* emergent technologies

mobility 1, 8, 13, 18, 20, 27–28, 39, 49, 53, 56, 69–70, 88, 121, 136, 148, 156; immobility 53, 70, 88; mobile narratives 15–18, 24–25, 39, 71, 109; mobilities turn in tourism research 8, 13, 60, 70, 156; mobility as a public good 13, 22, 53, 56, 69

modernity, and the city 12–13, 20–24, 38, 53, 56, 59, 73, 102, 115, 138

Molotch, Harvey 76

Montreal 2–4, 28, 31, 42, 70, 91, 126–155, 157, **164**; *see also Cité Mémoire*; *Montréal en Histoires*

Montréal en Histoires 3–4, 28, 31, 42, 91, 125–155, 158, **164**

mood 60–61, 128, 130–131, 141, 148, 151, 153; mood management 128, 130–131, 148; *see also* ambience; atmosphere

Moore, Johnny 104–105

more-than-visual experience 2, 25, 33, 61

Morretti, Cristina, 30, 100

mourning 3, 77–79, 81, 89, 91, 98, 109, 122, 154

mp3 23

multi-sited ethnography 27–28; *see also* sensory ethnography

mundane architecture in tourism 70, 128, 140–141, 154, 159; blank walls 113, 127, 133, 136; construction zones 74, 95, 110; parking lots 95, 140–141

mundane encounters in tourism 3, 27, 50, 68, 140; *see also* mundane architecture in tourism

museum 17, 37–38, 54, 80, 96, 110, 138–139, 143, 148, 153, 162, 164; aesthetics 17, 35–38, 54–56, 66, 73–74, 101, 109–110, 113, 157, 159; museums and cultural consumption 35, 79; taking the museum to the streets 1, 3, 35–38, 54–56, 72–74, 88, 110–112, 157; *see also* city as museum

Museum of London 36–38, 54–56, **162**

Museum Victoria Tours": Walk Through History 71, 79, **164**

narrative(s): conflicting and counternarratives 3, 38, 48, 68, 77–79, 83, 86–89, 98, 112, 158, 161; locative and mobile narratives 3, 15–18, 20, 24–26, 39, 57–58, 60, 68–69, 71, 77–89, 98–99, 105–107, 109, 130, 132–133, 140, 143, 151, 159–160; personal narratives 15, 86, 99, 109, 122–123, 126, 142–143, 150–153, 159–160, **164**; unified narratives 11, 38, 43, 46–48, 106, 111, 115, 123, 134–135, 137–138, 140, 153, 157; urban 1, 15, 29, 33, 38, 44, 76–82, 98, 111–112, 123, 128–129, 141; *see also* mapping; theming

nature: and the city 63–65, 80–81, *82*, 93, 116–117, 142–143; mastery of nature 117; as urban inscription 81, *82*, 116–117
navigation 7, 13, 24, 29, 69, 149; and locative media 29–30, 38, *42*, 68–69, 105–109, 127, 131, 149; and surveillance 148–149; in tourism 7, 58–59
negative space 109–110
network *see infrastructure*, technological
new media 2, 5, 8, 14, 42, 146
New Orleans 27, 35, 37, 40–41, 44, 49, 59–62, 64, 81, **163**; *see also Historic NOLA*; *Wicked Walks*
new technology *see* emergent technologies
night, the city at night 4, 29, 42, *59–60*, 62, 75, 91, 103, 125–126, 131, 135, 139–143, *145*, 153
noise abatement 22; *see also* regulation of urban sensation
non-human actors 9, 26–27, 160
non-place 95, 115

obsolescence 21, 31, 76–78, 97, 160; obsolescence and user-generated content 77–78
ocularcentric(ity) 38, 49
ocularcentrism 12, 20, 38, 49
odour *see* smell
Old Montreal 4, 42, 70, 125–154, **164**
Oppegaard, Brett 17
oral history 77, 97–99, 101, 151
orientation 33, 40, 85, 108, 113, 160; disorientation 33, 40, 68, 75–76, 105–109, 126; intentional disorientation and dislocative media 68–69, 109; reorientation 64, 69, 76, 83, 86, 107, 160; *see also* alignment work; landmarks; maps
other, the: encountering the other 3, 24, 54, 68, 70–71, 83–89, 97, 101, 158; othered senses 20, 58–59; *see also* diversity
Our City, 75, **164**

pacing *see* rhythm
Paik, Naim June 140
panorama 3, 35, 49–52, 139, 142, 157
participant sensation *see* sensory ethnography
pastiche 8, 43, 62–63, 66, 134
pause 16, 70, 72, 99, 139, 159; *see also* interruption
pedestrian *see* walking
people problems 52, 158
perception, politics of perception 11–12
performance: and locative applications 14, 16–18, 68–89, 111, 124, 130, 135, 141, 146, 149, 152–153, 159; and sensory ethnography 26, 28–30; tourism as performance 2–4, 7–10, 18, 33, 58, 60, 62, 66, 68–89, 103, 130, 135, 141, 149, 152, 156
Perkins, Chris 85
personalisation 16, 73, 87, 110, 133, 142–144, 154–155, 159; de-personalisation 133, 144; personalisation of urban soundscapes 16, 22–23, 73, 153; *see also* intimacy
photography 39–40, 59, 62, 65–66, 70, 75, 84–85, 95, 114, 156; circulation of photographs 39–40, 66, 156; embedding archival photographs in digital space 40, 77–78, 96–98, 101–103, 125, 127, 151, 157, **162–164**; ghost photography 62; pre-photographic histories 122, 128, 151; tourist photography 39–40, 59, 62, 65–66, 70–71, 75, 84, 106, 114–115, 156, **162**; *see also* imageability
Pike Place Market 56, 72–73, 89
Pilon, Victor 126, 128, 140
Pink, Sarah 15
placemaking 25, 96–124; transitional placemaking 96–99, 111–113, 118, 121, 123–124, **164**; *see also* Transitional City
platform *see infrastructure*, technological
playfulness 14, 16, 125; *see also* gamification
Pokémon GO 54, 107
policing 8, 43, 87
polyrhythmia *see* rhythm
porosity 59, 61, 99–100, 104, 121
post-industrial city 35, 77; *see also* consumption, cultural consumption
postmodernity 14, 62
precarity 2–3, 20, 29, 31, 38, 60, 78, 116, *117*, 122; *see also* contingency
Price, Phil 111, *112*
The Production of Space 10
progress *see* urban development
promotional material *see* advertising

proximity 23–24, 101, 140
psychogeography 1, 60, 69
pub crawl 60–62
public art 56–57, 72–73, 79, 89, 96, 111–117, 121, 125–154, 163; *see also* street art
public-private space 13, 65, 73–74, 88, 99, 105, 114, 126, 139, 148, 157
public space 8, 13, 21, 23, 28, 43, 69, 73–74, 88, 100, 135, 139, 141, 147–149, 157
purification *see* regulation of urban sensation

QR code(s) 51–52, *53*
queering space 86–87, 158
Queering the Map 86
Queerstory 86–87, **163**

rambling 71–72; rambling house 71
rationalist gaze *see* gaze
reading the city 15, 18, 26, 28, 68, 83–84, 86, 88; *see also* legibility; narrative
real-imagined spaces 10, 79
rebuild *see* earthquake, revitalisation, Transitional City
red zone 94, 107
reflexivity 26, 28, 84, 151
regeneration *see* revitalisation
regulation of urban sensation 12, 21–24, 48, 56, 58–59, 79, 100, 102–103, 120–121, 123, 138, 148–149; unruly sensations 22–24, 137
repetition 11, 21–22, 70; *see also* imageability
representation: mobile representations 8, 29, 44, 54, 69; popular representations and tourism 11, 44–45, 85; representational practices 9–10, 15–16, 29, 69, 84–85, 109, 122, 138, 151; representation of space 1, 9–12, 14, 15–16, 25–26, 44, 62, 84–86, 88, 109, 114; *see also* mapping; maps
resilience 116–117
resistance 22, 44, 47, 89, 114, 116, 121, 161; resisting sensory purification 12, 20, 23, 48, 65; tactile 54–56, 121
resonance: emotional 104, 158, 160; sonic 102
revitalisation, urban 11, 35–36, 91, 101–102, 113, 115–116, 121, 123; *see also* gentrification
rhythm 1–3, 28–29, 33, 48, 68–77, 105, 109–110, 156, 159–160; and the locative tour 3, 20, 30, 33, 42, 68, 70–75, 105, 109–111, 130–132, 136, 156, 159–160; polyrhythmia 28–29, 33, 70, 89
rhythmanalysis 26, 28–29, 48
Richardson, Ingrid 25
Roland, Zoe 97–98, 103
routes, tour routes 84
Rowley, Tom 71, 86
ruins 38; sensing the ruin 99–105; urban ruins 91, 93–96, 99–105
rupture *see* disjuncture

Salter, Chris 55
Sample, Mark 14
Sandvik, Kjetil 128
San Francisco 27, 71, 77, 80–83, 88, 148, **164**; *see also Detour*; *Guidekick: Golden Gate Park*
sanitisation *see* regulation of urban sensation
Sargent, Nick 121
scripting, tourist performance 84, 91; *see also* staging
séance lounge 60–61
Seattle 27, 35, 48, 50–52, 56, 72–73, 88–89, **163**; *see also Space Needle*; *STQRY Public Art tour*
sedimentation: of images 39–40, 66, 156; of stories 133
selective preservation of history 11, 77, 123; *see also* heritage
self-guided tour 82, 108, 159; *see also* urban exploration
sense and the city, 20–24, 48–50, 56, 58–59, 79, 102, 120–112, 138; sens*ing* the city, 20–21, 24–30, 100, 157, 160–161
sensescapes 3, 13, 22, 44, 48, 99, 102, 148; designed sensescapes 12, 59, 128; haptic geographies 22, 50, 52–65; smellscape 12, 22, 44, 58, 63–65, 79, 101; soundscape 12, 22–23, 44, 58–59, 64–65, 76, 102–103; tastescape 44, 50, 60–63
sensory anthropology *see* anthropology of the senses
sensory ethnography 2, 4, 21, 25–30, 159; multi-sited sensory ethnography 27–28
sensory experience 9–10, 12, 24–25, 35–36, 44, 48–49, 59, 62, 100–102, 111, 121, 123, 140, 157, 159–160;

multisensory experience 9–10, 36, 44, 49, 58–59, 66, 70, 72–73, 100, 156; in tourism 44, 59, 62–63, 68, 72–73, 98, 100–102, 156–157, 159–160; *see also* extensions of the senses; sensescapes; ways of sensing
sensory history, of the city 21–24, 48
sensory imagination 61–62, 99–102, 105
sensory overload *see* metropolis and mental life
sensory studies 1, 109; *see also* anthropology of the senses; sensory history
sensory turn 99
sentient city 29, 75, 146, 148–149
serendipity 17, 33, 88–89, 127, 159
sex work 101–102, 122
Sheridan, Dougal 112
shopping *see* city as shopping mall
Shrine of Remembrance (Melbourne) 74
sight 10–11, 24, 38, 49–50, 56–58, 60, 72, 88; sight and the city 10–12, 21–22, 50–52, 56, 99, 109, 113, 125, 149; sightlines 11, 22, 50, 75, 77, 111, 113, 115, 156; sightseeing 70; visibility 21–22; *see also* gaze; ocularcentrism
sightseeing 70
signposts 7, 12, 33, 39–40, 42, 70, 74, 106, 127, 156; *see also* landmarks
silence 29, 59, 103
Simmel, Georg 21, 24, 100
simulacra *see* simulation
simulation 36, 49, 51–55, 80–81; simulation of sensation 36, 49, 51–55
simultaneity, experiences of 16–18, 37–38, 40, 48, 60, 62–63, 69, 157, 160
simultaneous space 13, 24–25, 48, 62, 73, 84, 87, 114
site specificity 1, 13–15, 20, 24, 30, 110, 127, 140
Situationist International 1, 60
sixth sense 59–62
skyline, city 51–52, 62, 75, 79, 101, 106, 115, 120, 122, 130, 134, 137–140, 143, 153–154; *see also* panorama
slippage 3, 38, 89, 107–108, 119, 160; *see also* discordance; disjuncture
slow tourism 99
smart city *see* sentient city
smell 12, 22–24, 33, 44, 51, 58, 61–63, 65, 72, 78–79, 99–102, 122, 159; and the city 23, 44, 78–79, 99–102, 122, 124, 157; and tourism 58, 62–63, 65, 72, 79, 100–102, 157
smellscape *see* sensescapes
Smith, Neil 114
smoothing out the urban experience 13, 43, 45, 55–56, 59, 130–132; *see also* texture
Sobchack, Vivian 17
sociality of sensation 21, 160
socionature 80–81
SOL Square (Christchurch) 103–105, 107
sonic disjuncture *see* discordance, sonic discord
sonic geography *see* soundscape
sound 12, 22–23, 38, 54, 58–60, 62, 64, 73, 76, 99, 102–103, 128, 143, **164**; hearing the past 1, 12, 61–62, 99, 102, 146; soundwalks 98; *see also* audio
soundscape *see* sensescapes
Soyini Madison, D 26
Space Needle 35, 48, 50–53, **163**
spectacle: less-than-spectacular tourism 65, 70; Society of the Spectacle 21, 23, 139; urban 1, 3–4, 21, 43–44, 70, 91, 114, 126–130, 134, 138–140
spectacular intimacy *see* intimacy
stage: city as (shifting) stage 1, 3, 7, 18, 29–31, 33, 38, 44, 69–70, 81, 89, 91, 103, 108, 111, 132, 134, 140–144, 156, **164**; staging tourism experiences 18, 44, 54, 81, 103, 108, 113, 127, 132, 134, 140–144, 149, 151, 156
St Audoen's Church 56–57, 72
storytelling *see* narrative
STQRY Public Art tour 56, 72, 89, **163**
street art 28, 96, 111, 113–116, 121, 123, 133, 149; as transitional commodity 115, 123; *see also* graffiti; public art
street vendors 58, 63
Streetmuseum 1, 35–37, 148, **162**
Streetmuseum Londinium 36, 54–56, **162**
Struppek, Mirjam 139
subject-object positioning *see* aesthetic ordering
superpowers, sensory 51–52, 157; *see also* extensions of the senses
surrealism 14
surveillance 8, 43, 146–149
symbol 9, 35, 47, *48*, 89, 105, 117

symbolic economy *see* cultural consumption
synchronization 3, 42, 68, 75, 132–133, 136, 146; *see also* rhythm

tactility *see* touch
taking the museum to the streets *see* city as museum
taste 23–24, 33, 36, 50, 58, 60–62, 72, 99, 102, 157; food tourism 58, 158; tasting the museum 36, 38
tastescape *see* sensescapes
techno-mediated *see* technotourism
techno-mediated body *see* extensions of the senses
techno-mediation *see* mediation
technotourism 9, 16–18, 25, 33, 35–36, 49–51, 55, 60, 62, 64, 66, 69, 75–76, 125–127, 130–133, 145–146, 149, 152, 156, 160
Temple Bar (Dublin) 86
temples 65, 66
temporality 81, 132–133, 143; polytemporality 63; *see also* time travel
texture 13, 21–22, 53, 55, 59–61, 64, 99–100, 105, 120–121, 128, 158
theming, urban 7–8, 43–44, 66, 130, 135, 148, 158; *see also* branding
thickening, of the informational layer 2, 15; *see also* layer
thirdspace 10
3-D 31, 36, 38, 72, 97, 124, 127, 157–158, **162, 164**
time travel 1, 3, 35, 37, 50, 57, 62, 71, 81, 87, 125–126, 151, 157, 161
Toronto 27, 51, 86–87, 158, **163**; *see also Queerstory*; *Toronto in Time*
Toronto in Time 36–37, 87, **163**
touch: fear of touch 22, 53, 65; negotiating touch in the city 22, 49, 52–58, 157; negotiating touch in tourism 36, 38, 52–58, 63, 65, 102, 113; and tactility 12, 22, 24, 33, 36, 38, 49–50, 52–58, 61, 63–64, 102, 113; touch and intimacy 102, 129–130; touch and the smartphone 33, 36, 49, 55–56
tour guides 44, 46–47, 59, 70, 72, 130–132, 136, 143, 146, 152, 159
touring, as practice 2, 7, 10, 13, 17, 28, 30, 36, 44, 55, 57, 69, 72, 81, 103, 132, 159
tourism studies 2, 5, 7–9, 17–18, 25, 58, 81, 156
tourist gaze 2–3, 7–8, 33, 35, 39–40, 43, 49, *53*, 60, 66, 83–84, 106, 114, 135, 140, 156
tourist glance 60
tourist imaginary *see* imaginaries
traces 4, 9, 26, 28–30, 35, *57*, 65, 87, 100–101, 118, 121–123, 151, 160
Transitional City 91, 93, 95–96, 105, 108, 111–112, 115, 118; *see also* placemaking, transitional placemaking
The Tree of Life (Seattle) 89
Troubles *see* Irish Troubles
Tuan, Yi-Fu 99, 117

ubiquitous computing 8, 25, 156; *see also* emergent technologies
un-tour 71
urban development 21–22, 28, 43, 45, 50, 76–78, 80, 111–116, 120–123, 136, 140, 159; contrasting narratives of urban development 76–78, 111–116, 120–123; *see also* Concept City; gentrification; revitalisation
urban exploration 1, 7, 56, 82, 127, 159
urban imaginary *see* imaginaries
urban inscription 14–16, 24–25, 28, 81, *82*, 91, 111–123, 148–149
urban markup *see* urban inscription
Urry, John 7, 12, 21, 39, 106, 156; *see also* tourist gaze
user-generated content 16, 26, 39–40, 75, 77–78, 81, 84, 86, 97, 160

Verhoeff, Nanna 15
Versailles 158
Vertov, Diana 140
Victor Steinbrueck Park (Seattle) 89
viewing distance *see* alienation
virtual objects 36, 54–56, 76, 127
visibility *see* sight
vision *see* sight
visual: augmentation 1, 24, 31, 38, 59, 71, 77, 125, 149; homogeneity 11, 123; *see also* more-than-visual experience; sight
VR (virtual reality) 51

Waitt, Gordon 59
walk-along interviews *see* walking methodologies
walking: locative narrative as "writing while walking" 25; methodologies 29–30, 110; ways of walking 1, 69–72, 99, 148, 150–152, 160

Walkman 23
Walk the Walls 31, 35, 45–49, 135, **163**
waste matter 22, 53; *see also* ruins
waymaking *see* navigation
ways of sensing 12–13, 20, 24, 38, 48–50, 61, 161
Weston, Kath 87
White Cube *see* city as gallery
Wicked Walks 35, 60–62, **163**
wildscape, urban 112, 116, 123
workers 23, 38, 44, 46–47, 59, 70, 72, 103, 105, 110, 122, 130–132, 136, 140, 143, 146, 152, 159
working-class neighbourhood 72, 86
World Heritage City 39–40, **162**

Yarra River (Melbourne) 68, 75, 79–80, **164**
Year Zero One 87
Young, Alison 114

Zardini, Mirko 23
Zook, Matthew 84
Zukin, Sharon 35, 43; *see also* cultural consumption